WAR GARDENS

WAR
GARDENS

A Journey Through Conflict
in Search of Calm

Lalage Snow

Quercus

First published in Great Britain in 2018 by Quercus.

Quercus Editions Ltd
Carmelite House
50 Victoria Embankment
London EC4Y 0DZ

An Hachette UK company

A CIP catalogue record for this book is available
from the British Library

HB ISBN 978 1 78747 068 2
TPB ISBN 978 1 78747 069 9
Ebook ISBN 978 1 78747 070 5

10 9 8 7 6 5 4 3 2 1

All pictures © Lalage Snow

Typeset by CC Book Production

Printed and bound in the UK by Clays Ltd, Elcograf S.p.A

To my parents.
Sorry if all of this gave you sleepless nights.

Small pleasures must correct great tragedies . . .
I tried to hold the courage of my ways
In that which might endure,
Daring to find a world in a lost world,
A little world, a little perfect world . . .
Yet shall the garden with the state of war
Aptly contrast, a miniature endeavour
To hold the graces and the courtesies
Against a horrid wilderness . . .
So does the gardener in little way
Maintain the bastion of his opposition
And by a symbol keep civility . . .

—from 'The Garden' by Vita Sackville-West

Contents

Kabul

2012

'Il faut cultiver notre jardin.'

Voltaire, *Candide*

1

It is the Afghan commander who first shows me Eden. I am an embedded photographer in Helmand province and have been talking to Brigadier General Shirin Shah in Camp Shorobak, the Afghan National Army's base attached to the British Camp Bastion. It is 2010 and we have been discussing the war and the distant prospect of peace over black tea, served with dried fruit and nuts. He asks me where else I have visited in Afghanistan and when I tell him bashfully that I have only ever been to Helmand province, he jumps up and exclaims something which the interpreter translates. 'He says you need to see something other than war. You Britishers love your gardens and so do we. Come.'

Shah leads me out of the office buildings and into a bleached mid-morning. Ignoring the stares of the curious Afghan soldiers outside, I struggle to keep up and half skip alongside him as he takes me past a collection of classrooms, across the parade ground and around the back of a utilitarian – although empty – barracks on the other side of the base. He ushers me through a small metal door in a bare brick wall. I am met with an improbable riot of pink and red geraniums, gaudy orange dahlias, scarlet and yellow roses and, oddly, a single maize frond with acid-green leaves. His stride immediately slows to an amble as he points out the flora and fauna. The interpreter, more used to dealing with the minutiae of equipment needs and battle plans, understandably struggles to translate the species in front of us.

Aesthetically, nothing really matches in Shah's garden, but against the backdrop of a military mega-base whose sole purpose is functionality and the administration of war, the smell of damp earth, sweet grass and flowers are instantly recognisable. The domestication of nature in an environment intent on destroying it is curiously paradoxical, but for the first time in Afghanistan something is familiar and I feel at ease. It makes me think of Eden, Milton's 'delicious paradise', that place of innocence, peace and harmony where everything grew and where there was light and hope – until, of course, the snake turned up and man 'fell'.

Over the ensuing three weeks I join a military operation in Nad-e-Ali, then one of the most violent districts of Helmand province. I am working on a self-funded photographic project with a unit of soldiers from First Battalion, the Royal Regiment of Scotland and a contingent of Afghan soldiers deep in the heart of Taliban country.

The war thunders around us with an angry and chaotic intensity. We are shot at; rocket-propelled grenades are lobbed around like frisbees; two British soldiers in the compound next to ours are killed by an improvised explosive device; an Afghan soldier gropes me when I'm washing my socks in a brief moment of calm; we run out of food; we are shot at again; we are angry, tired, scared and long for something else. An Afghan soldier loses his foot on patrol, one of the British soldiers begins to lose his mind. It is utterly war but its battles take place in the middle of a landscape where, when the fighting quells, all is bucolically and antithetically quiet. There is occasional birdsong, bees and butterflies collect nectar from wild flowers at the edges of wheat fields, and the irrigation and canals ditches are full of frogs and water-rat-like creatures staring out from the undergrowth. Some of the empty compounds we take over contain domestic gardens themselves, with rows of runner beans, cucumbers, tomatoes and vines.

I think back to Shah's garden a few weeks later when I arrive in Kabul for the first time. I had pitched a story about the first female cadets in the Afghan National Army to the *Telegraph Magazine* and when they told me they wanted it for the front cover I was elated. My friend, the then Kabul *Sunday Times* correspondent, Miles Amoore, had offered to put me up for a few weeks. He is away when I arrive but emails instructions and I grab a local taxi from Kabul International Airport, blissfully unaware that without knowing either the city or any Dari (a variant of Farsi and one of the two national languages), this is a sure-fire way to make yourself the target of a kidnapping. Such are the potential pitfalls in being a naive, unattached and unlooked-after freelancer in a war zone. Oblivious and delighted to be there, I take in the city beyond the car window. It is dusty and congested with traffic and pollution, even at seven o'clock in the morning. Open sewers run along unpaved side roads, prolific razor wire glints in the sun, ten-foot-high walls separate private houses from public spaces. Donkey-drawn carts sit behind armoured 4 x 4s at the windows of which women in tatty burkhas tap for alms. Litter scatters the streets.

When I arrive at Miles' house or The Old Flower Street Café as the house was first known, a guard opens the door, ushers me in and carries my bags to a single-storey villa on the other side of a garden.

I'll hold my hand up here. I'm not a real gardener by any stretch of the imagination. But, thanks to a gardening-mad mother and brother, I can at least recognise plants. Here there are roses, red and orange geraniums, nasturtiums, buddleias, Michaelmas daisies, basil bushes, something that looks like yarrow, magnolias, a birch tree, bindweed climbing through the razor wire and a single, tall sunflower nodding and bowing beneath a seam of light. The overall effect is an incongruous contrast to the bedlam of the streets outside. It is a world within a world.

Inside, the house is shabby but cosy. By the front door is a coat rack straining under the weight of an assortment of fur jackets, desert jackets, scarves and every manner of hat imaginable including Kevlar helmets. Body armour plates lean against a shelf of sandals, flip-flops, loafers and sturdy boots.

The living room is large and light and like a house well loved, stuffed to the brim with curios and hallmarks of its occupants; faded rugs on the floor, long oriental cushions around a coffee table and two armchairs (one broken and propped up by an old Persian dictionary). On a book shelf are magazines and newspapers and piles of books about al-Qaeda, the Taliban, Afghanistan, the Great Game, carpets, travel guides to Central Asia and counter-insurgency.

Opposite the living room is a well-stocked kitchen and I make myself a cup of tea. When the kettle boils the power surges, causing the bare light bulb overhead to flicker. On the windowsill I notice a packet of Safeway biscuits, a brand which has long since disappeared from the shelves of London supermarkets. I reach for the largest, albeit chipped, mug available. The words 'Operation

Enduring Freedom', the name of the American military campaign in Afghanistan, encircle an eagle carrying the Stars and Stripes. It hovers over an outline of Afghanistan and the date 09-11-01. The bulb's filament settles when the kettle clicks off and I take the mug back to the living room and settle on one of the low cushions with a book. The sun streams through the leaves of a hanging plant on the veranda just outside the window and it is not long before my eyes droop and I fall into a slumber.

Water wakes me. The guard is watering the garden as I come to and I watch him through the window, gathering my foggy thoughts. I go out to the veranda with my laptop and he busies himself around the garden with dogged determination. Mostly watering, deadheading and weeding.

I think of Shah's paradise garden. These two patches of green represent optimism and growth, and they counter the narrative that Afghanistan is a hostile, barren land soaked with blood and of Afghans as a hopeless people blighted by war.

But it is only later that I come to understand this. Two years later, to be precise, when I begin to photograph Kabul's gardens on assignment. It is then that I start to understand that gardening is like breathing for Afghans; gardens are the calm pauses for breath in an otherwise continuous battle cry. And it will be years before I truly understand just how vital gardens are 'against a horrid wilderness' of war.

It is 2012 and there is still just about enough appetite for stories in Afghanistan to make a decent wage. I am living at Miles' House (now called Lally's House) full time as a freelance photojournalist, film-maker and foreign correspondent.

Since my arrival two summers ago the war, insecurity and the extremities of existing and survival have become routine. A suicide attack on a supermarket here, a siege at the British Council there; an explosion in a central hotel one day, a complex attack on another the next; an embed down south one week, a trip to the malnutrition hospitals in the north three weeks later. That has become my life, and despite the instability and surges of adrenalin, I love it.

Life in Kabul is not a daily struggle. For the expats living here full time, the attacks and security threats might be violent and sporadic but we live surprisingly well. Between assignments there are tennis matches at the International Club, touch rugby at a French *lycée*, dinners in the expat restaurants or at each other's houses, followed by after-parties flowing into the next day. There are film screenings and craft classes, Kabul-opoly (Monopoly) tournaments and Boggle nights, and an endless quest to sweet-talk embassy, United Nations or World Bank contacts into giving us access to cheap alcohol.

I have been discussing the idea of a photo essay with Marc Baumann, an editor at the German newspaper, *Süddeutsche Zietung*. I want to look at the aesthetic contrast between private and public spaces of the city, focusing on gardens, and he is looking for something unusual.

I mentally run through the gardens belonging to friends, all of which are nicer than my own: the garden and balcony conservatory at The Chateau, a guest house occupied and run by British journalists Jerome Starkey and Jonathan Boone, and Australian journalist Jeremy Kelly, which was meticulously tended to by their (often stoned) guard, Tahir; the Flower Street House garden full of apricot trees and dog roses where Scottish journalist Lianne Gutcher lives; the house on Street One, where I had once briefly lived with film-makers Leslie Knott and Lucy Martens, the garden of which was the frequent mise-en-scène for languid al fresco dinner parties which inevitably rolled into raucous chaos and, on one infamous evening, a mud-wrestling match in the rose bushes. Then there are the big bureaus like the BBC, which has a swimming pool (known as 'the emergency water reserve') and plump beds full of ornamental flowers; the immaculate lawn at the *Washington Post*, not to mention the pots of herbs and vegetables, the jewel in the crown on the roof of the *Wall Street Journal* bureau.

We might all be living in the netherworld of a war zone and completely dislocated from 'real life', but we spend more time than usual at home (many of us working from the comfort of our compounds) and our gardens are an escape from the ugly reality outside. In them, we can be ourselves entirely and live out a peaceful fantasy of sorts. In his first summer in Kabul, Jonathan Boone dedicated much time to perfecting a lawn with Duchy of Cornwall grass seeds he brought back from England and fending off hungry ants. Emma Graham-Harrison, another friend, found herself growing different varieties of lettuces and herbs otherwise unavailable to buy. I too had once half attempted a crop of spinach, the easiest of all to grow, but the seedlings wilted during an absence from Kabul in Helmand.

But although all of these are wonderfully visual gardens, they are the story of the expat elite living in a very strange bubble, so are not what Marc or I are looking for.

And then I remember Baghe-e-Babur.

Ẓahīr-ud-Dīn Muḥammad – or Babur, as he was later known – was born in 1483 in Andijan, one of the oldest cities in the Fergana valley in modern Uzbekistan. Tragically his father, Sheikh Mirza, died as a result of falling from a dovecote into a ravine, leaving his eleven year old son the ruler of Fergana (present day eastern Uzbekistan). Most of the territories around him were ruled by cousins and distant relatives who, as descendants of Genghis Khan, were always spoiling for a fight. Babur himself had ambitions to capture Samarkand from his cousins thus expanding his empire, and was twice successful until his own kingdom was stolen by a brother and he lost both lands.

After one last but ill-fated attempt to capture Samarkand again, he was exiled to Tashkent. After three years, and having amassed an army, he tried to recapture Fergana, but lost and had no choice but to give up all hope of regaining his homeland.

Kabul at the time was being ruled by an unpopular usurper, Mukin Begh, and in 1504, Babur marched over the Hindu Kush mountains and captured Kabul, thus establishing a new kingdom and the foundations of what became the Mughal empire. The climate and landscape of the city quickly made it his favourite and, every inch the gardening emperor, Babur went on to build ten gardens there.

In his autobiography, the *Baburnama*, he describes a huge garden full of roses and fountains of wine. It was a place from which he could launch campaigns into India and to where he would return after the killing for some peace, relaxation and presumably a glass or two of wine. (Not so different from our own relationship with gardens – but maybe without the killing.) Babur loved it so much that, although he was living in India when he died in 1544, he requested that his body be laid to rest there.

The gardens fell into disrepair after the collapse of the Mughal empire in the mid-nineteenth century and were badly damaged by an earthquake in 1842. Nineteenth- and twentieth-century Afghan leaders left their mark on the original gardens too by adding European-style fountains and buildings. In the seventies a swimming pool was even installed.

During the civil war of the 1990s, the gardens sat on a front line and was destroyed in the fighting. Trees were uprooted, water channels buried beneath mounds of earth dislodged by artillery shells, and mines instead of roses were planted. It was as a deadly wasteland that the garden remained until the fall of the Taliban in 2001. The Aga Khan, spiritual head of the world's Ismaili Muslims and a friend of the Afghan government decided to do something about it. The restoration of the gardens was to be a part of re-establishing Kabul's cultural identity and the renaissance of a city re-emerging from the ashes of war.

Ten years on, and after over $5 million of investment, the restored gardens cater to the social needs of urban residents who don't have a garden of their own. For the small fee of around twenty pence, Kabulis can walk the length and breadth of Babur's terraces beneath cedar and pomegranate trees. They are a reminder of what Kabul once was: a delightful city of colour, bazaars, tree-lined avenues and grand palaces and mosques.

So I decide to start the photo essay with Babur's gardens, but first I have another assignment to finish.

*

The next day, I am standing on the roof of the Nazary Hotel in Herat, the largest city in the west of Afghanistan and arguably the country's cultural centre. I am working with the *Sunday Times'* Asia correspondent, Nicki Smith on a story about women's rights. When Miles left, Delhi-based Nicki took his beat and continued to use me as a photographer. Not only had I built up a good relationship with the paper through working with Miles, she and I clicked from the first time we met. Furthermore I am a woman and, although the lack of rights for women in Afghanistan is well documented, foreign women are not subjected to the same rules and customs as Afghan women and as a 'third gender' we are allowed to speak to both sexes without much difficulty. Male colleagues, on the other hand, are rarely permitted to speak to Afghan women and girls.

Herat is closer to Iran both geographically and spiritually, despite being only an hour's flight from Kabul. Indeed, it is as much Persian as it is Afghan. It was once the capital of the Timurid empire, before Babur took Kabul for his own Mughal empire. Since then, Herat has flourished throughout history as Afghanistan's cultural heart.

Most of Kabul's monuments and palaces were all but destroyed during the Soviet occupation, the civil war and the wrack and ruin which then ensued under the Taliban. Reconstruction is now booming but sadly with little eye for the aesthetic; cheap concrete and glass is favoured in the new gaudy villas – colloquially known as 'poppy palaces' because it is assumed that they have been built from the proceeds of Afghanistan's still-flourishing opium trade.

Herat's citadel, madrassas, minarets, shrines and mosques, however, were saved from demolition as early as the fifties by UNESCO, and although the city is neither unscarred by conflict nor has it escaped the trend for ultra-contemporary construction projects, ancient and modern buildings sit comfortably together here. So much so that Herat still aspires to be included on UNESCO's list of World Heritage Sites.

But Herat's roots in Islamic, Persian and Afghan culture run deeper than buildings and foundations; it is a city of writers, poets, painters and Sufis, and is at once Oxford, Florence, Paris and Vienna with a little bit of Shiraz thrown in. Indeed, it is a city so steeped in culture it resisted an iron-fisted Taliban rule with an underground literary scene.

The sun is falling low behind the mountains but from my top-of-the-world vantage point I have a panoramic view of history: the citadel built by Alexander the Great, shrines, mausoleums, mosque domes and the ancient minarets which are sending the evening call to prayer into the ether above.

Some seventeen floors beneath me are men. They are praying in the courtyard of the mosque adjacent to the hotel. They can't see me but I can see them clearly. They are kneeling on their prayer mats, heads bowed, hands held together in their laps. The rows of skull caps are dot, dot, dots and when the imam's voice dies down, they move in time with their own incantations.

We had arrived in the early afternoon and driven into the city centre from the airport in a clapped-out Toyota Corolla (the backbone of motoring in Afghanistan). The city felt very different to Kabul where the summer rains were already flooding the streets from bruised skies. Herat felt warm and welcoming, like an old friend.

We made a detour via some of the sites and I had half imagined we were entering a bygone era when the road was less travelled, if at all. We stopped at the Friday Mosque, the city's largest, dating back to earlier than 1200. As obvious non-Muslims we were not allowed inside, but we were content to stroll the perimeter, wondering how many mosaic tiles it took to make the front façade more intense than the sky.

I noticed that the garden was as well-kept as the mosque itself, providing a lush intermission from the glare of the mosque complex's white marble floor. The rose bushes dotting the green borders were startling flecks of rich pink and white beneath which amulet sellers and shoeshine boys lay, waiting for the heat to abate.

We drove on to the Musalla complex, the brainchild of Queen Gawharshad in the early fifteenth century. Although the buildings have suffered from fighting and fire, the remains of the minaret and madrassa are impressive, and we stared up at the mausoleum dome and inscriptions. We had our picture taken: eighteenth-century-style Grand Tourists in twentieth-century-style baggy clothes and lopsided headscarves, the garb we don to blend in, but which we can never quite get right. We grinned, fish delighted to be out of water. And Kabul.

The public garden around the complex there, I noticed, was an immaculately tended patchwork of grass and benches on which young male students lounge with books. There was something incredibly languid about the whole scene. It is not that Kabul doesn't have beautiful green corners; it is simply that it is such a structured, militarised and closed city of checkpoints and weapons, blast walls and razor wire that any municipal beautification is overshadowed and engulfed.

Despite feeling like a different country, Westerners are frequently kidnapped in Herat; we checked into the Nazary Hotel as it is one of the few places deemed 'secure' for visiting foreigners and wealthy local businessmen, who are also liable to be kidnapped.

In the lift to our rooms the *Titanic* theme tune played. (The doomed love story on the sinking ship was immensely popular, despite being illegal under the Taliban, and its popularity persists. It is used to sell everything from cakes and ice creams to haircuts and perfume). My room smelled of stale smoke and tangerines and was stiflingly hot. Unable to open the blast-proof windows I sought out the roof for air and the 360-degree horizon. Invisible from the ground, I remove my headscarf, ruffle my hair free and breathe deeply, content.

The following morning, unable to sleep, I am up there again, watching the sun pulling the day.

Nicki and I are to interview Afghanistan's first female chief prosecutor, Maria Bashir, who is hailed as being instrumental in holding husbands and families of abused women to account.[1] It will be a simple case of getting a few situational portraits of Bashir and obtaining access to some of the women she has helped over the years.

The morning is thin and watery in the city and the traffic has yet to clog its thoroughfares. We arrive early and mill about outside the attorney general's office. I notice the immaculately kept flower beds and lean forward to smell a pink rose but it is odourless.

Eventually we are directed to the building furthest away. Nicki and I take this to be a sign that Bashir is either at risk for the work she does in a patriarchal society or that perhaps she is merely the nominal female figurehead for women's justice to show the international community and thus relegated to a corner.

'Or both,' we say when we see the armed guards outside. Inside the building two plain-clothes men carrying AK47s stand outside her office. Bashir, as a woman fighting on behalf of other women in a country which is consistently billed as 'the worst place in the world for women', needs constant close protection from those she has prosecuted.

She is a small woman who looks younger than her early forties. She wears her thin headscarf loosely and her dark hair is pulled back in a scrunchie. Dressed for business in a three-quarter-length black jacket over trousers, she shakes our hands, invites us to sit and returns to the other side of her desk.

It dwarfs Bashir and she seems to shrink, but when she talks about the need for the constitution to change and describes secretly schooling her daughters under the Taliban, she grows in stature; even more so when she talks about the women who are imprisoned for *zina* – sex outside marriage:

A woman who has had sex outside marriage is automatically guilty of *zina*, a crime punishable by imprisonment. A woman who has been raped is also guilty of *zina* – despite the wrong done *to* her – and is liable to imprisonment for 'lustful' behaviour. If the case doesn't go through the legal system her family are responsible for her fate and, having been shamed and dishonoured by her actions, they often force her to marry her rapist to save face or, worse, as a 'matter of honour', they kill her.

False accusations of *zina* against women who do not do their husbands' bidding are commonplace. It is an archaic, perverse and unfair system in a country where a man's word is worth far more than a woman's. But TIA, as we say with a sigh: 'This Is Afghanistan'.

Nicki and I go to a shelter to meet some of the women Bashir has helped. We are directed down a backstreet of a backstreet of a back alleyway where there is an unmarked yellow door – shelters have to protect their own anonymity in order to protect those seeking refuge in them.

There is no garden behind this high wall, the outside space having been concreted over to make way for cars. Inside we pass a darkened dormitory where a few teenage girls sit on pink bunk beds. The curtains are shut to the outside world and they too hide their faces when they see us. It is a heavy, sad place of abandoned childhoods and whispers.

In a large meeting room upstairs a few of the girls are brought to speak to us. Bowls of nuts and sweets are put on the table and hot steam swirls from glasses of tea. One of the girls is around fifteen. She ran away from her husband and his family after she was made to live in semi-slavery and beaten.

Another describes how she was given as *baad* (a bargaining tool given to another family in order to resolve a dispute) at a young age after her brother had run away with the daughter of another family. In a typically unfair resolution, *she* was the compensation for the brother's immoral behaviour and given as a wife to their son. She went on to bear him three children but, when her body stopped working, he accused her of *zina* and had her arrested. He married someone else two days later while she festered in prison. With her honour in shreds on her release, she found the shelter.

Then we meet Sorayah. Sorayah was working in her father's field when bandits kidnapped her. They took her into the hills and gang-raped her. She was able to run away from them in the middle of the night and get to the police. When she reported the violation, however, she was not only locked up for being immoral (she allowed herself to be raped and therefore was clearly 'asking for it'), but worse still, she was detained by them for days and repeatedly raped by several members of the police, including the commander she had first begged for help. Miraculously she was able to escape again but, having dishonoured her family so gravely, she realised that she would probably be killed by them if she went home. The shelter was the only place she could go.

Sorayah has just turned thirteen.

I ask to photograph her and she consents so long as I don't show her face. As the room is very dark and Nicki is finishing interviewing the head of the shelter, I take her outside to the courtyard. She is wearing a *chadori*, an oversized Iranian-style scarf popular in Herat, which covers the whole body. She stares at the ground in front of her and a gust of wind billows in the folds of the fabric. She looks like a forgotten piece of furniture covered with a dust sheet. I feel angry for her but I have a job to do and file the emotion away.

Nicki and I decide to go to the Herat regional hospital.

With its proximity to Iran, where suicide by burning is a common practice, Herat had become the de facto capital of self-immolation over the years. Cooking oil and matches are available in even the poorest households, and for so many girls they offered an easy way out of a daily hell and an alternative to the shelters. But, sadly, death is rarely instantaneous and, as the practice spread, the burns unit swelled with mummified, bandaged women. A new burns unit was subsequently constructed with US development money, supported by Italian and French aid agencies. Today it is a depressing-looking building and devoid of any green or flowering spaces.

We want to speak to some of the women who have tried to end it all, but when we speak to Dr Ghafar Bawar, a Canadian-educated plastic and reconstructive surgeon and head of the burns unit, he tells us that cases of self-immolation have decreased dramatically.

'This is good news,' we say, and assume that Bashir really must be making serious ground across the province. He shakes his head and describes the perverse horror which is growing in popularity instead.

We are silent while we digest what he has said, and I make my way to the ward like a moth.

I can hear it before I smell it, but not long before. It is a sweet and sour smell of burned meat, and I hold the fabric of my headscarf to my face as a mask and fight a gag reflex.

Inside there are ten or so beds. Over half of them are occupied by silent, docile patients swaddled in bandages. The screaming comes from the corner. Bed 1A.

A baby is having its dressings changed and the pain is too much for its tiny nerve receptors to cope with. It screams and kicks and writhes. The young mother sits at the end of the bed, hugging her knees to her chest and looking on, saying nothing, expressing nothing. I estimate her to be about fourteen. An older woman I assume to be the mother-in-law is on a chair next to the bed, looking at the wall, as still as a stone.

The surface of the child's skin is like dried glue someone has tried to rub away. Thus removed, a shiny, vulnerable dermis like red, raw porcelain glistens. The hair is matted and patchy like mange, and one ear is bandaged under gauze. The child wriggles and wriggles and arches its back, unable to understand anything in the world in that instant other than excruciating, visceral, inescapable pain.

'Infant immolation has become the new thing,' Dr Ghafar had explained in his office. He outlined how, feeling trapped and abused by their new family, young mothers were taking to hurting the only thing they were used for – the children they produce.

Having lived in the country for two years I well understand the grim lot for women there; the patriarchy, familial structures, complex tribal dynamics and the brutal cycle of abuse which are all magnified by a crippling poverty. But I never imagined I would have to understand this.

Reyhana, the skinless child before me on the bed, was born a hermaphrodite. Disability and abnormality is little accepted in Afghanistan. Her/his mother was accused of deliberately making a weak child and probably beaten or shunned. She and her mother-in-law brought Reyhana into the hospital three days ago after the mother dunked the child in scalding water.

'She tried to tell us Reyhana did it,' Ghafar had told us, exasperated. 'She tried to tell us Reyhana deliberately stepped into a bowl of boiling liquid. Reyhana who is still too young to walk.'

Looking down at the little mite I want to cry but I try to fight the urge and filter the scene through my camera. The act of photo-graphing is calming but I have to breathe deeply to steady my hands. I concentrate on composition over reality but the viewfinder soon mists up from my tears and I have to stop to wipe it clean. That Rey-hana is an innocent and helpless is one thing; that her/his mother is also just an innocent child driven by primal desperation to commit an unnatural act is an unfathomable injustice and way beyond my comprehension.

Reyhana's distress and the mother's silence is too much so I leave the ward.

The other bandaged patients are like mummies and they look at me with curious but benign contempt.

'Are you all right?' asks Nicki, who is waiting outside.

'Yes,' I say, voice breaking. I press the flats of my palms against my eyes to cool them. I sit on a chair, lean forward and catch my breath on that sickly smell of ferrous coagulation. As the wails of a burning child fill the corridor, I think of Medea, the 'child slayer'.

We fly back to Kabul the next day and I try to leave the story behind. When the taxi pulls over at my house and I step through the compound door and into the familiar garden, I feel as if it is the threshold of a personal meridian line away from the reality outside into a secret, twilight world of my own, but I shudder at the memory of Bed 1A. Our guard has been watering, and as I cross the garden to the house it smells fresh and clean. I am oh so happy to be home and I concentrate on the post-assignment routine and just getting back to normal.

I unpack. My clothes smell rotten so I leave them in a plastic bag and set about sorting out my equipment, systematically charging batteries, cleaning lenses and organising memory cards. Then I splash cold water on my face and go out to the veranda with a cup of tea and my laptop to begin editing. *The Sunday Times* does not need the pictures for a few days but I really don't want images lingering on a to-do-list. I want to finish this assignment quickly and begin with the gardeners of Kabul.

I scan through them as quickly as I can. I try to be objective, but the pictures are ungodly and inhuman and I begin to fidget.

Two Blackhawks fly overhead and the imam in the mosque at the end of the road begins to cough into his tannoy, his daily preparation for the evening call to prayer.

It is only when I'm looking at the pictures of fragile little Sorayah and the skinless Reyhana, trying my hardest to be clinical and distant, that a wave of searing sorrow and anger rises and I fear things are becoming undone.

I step down from the veranda and pace on the grass. It feels cool beneath my bare feet. I inhale deeply, hoping to recognise an earthy smell to remind me of home, but there is no smell at all and I suddenly feel very homesick. I look up at the needle-tipped stars muddling the sky and another memory bubbles to the surface like sulphur: the satyr of Sangin.

Eighteen months ago I had 'embedded' with the newly deployed US marines in Sangin, a violent epicentre of the opium trade in Helmand. A little boy had stepped on an IED intended for the American soldiers. He is just a half boy by the time the marine surgeons lift him onto the table. His legs are nothing more than strips of skin, flayed flesh and sinew, and tourniquets stick uselessly out of his exposed intestine. His torso is so drained of blood it resembles alabaster. He looks, I think coldly, like a maimed satyr, and he is filed away in my memory as such. I filter the scene and create emotional distance with my camera. As he breathes his last on a cold metal operating table the US marine surgeons treating him sigh heavily. They shake their heads at the pity of it all before administering the body as a corpse.

Then I step outside and, with shaking hands, light a cigarette beneath a thankless sky.

As a war photographer, foreign correspondent, reporter – whatever I may be – there are many things you train yourself to accept: people die, limbs are lost, there are bangs and booms and other horrible noises, you are sometimes scared. Ghastly scenes realised in films become a reality, there is poverty, there is sickness, there is inequality, more people die. You accept it all as truth and try to report the facts without judgement. Then you log it away in a cupboard at the back of your mind in a file marked 'to forget'. Only you can't.

And you keep doing this because somewhere deep inside you there is a grain of hope that rightness will eventually be restored and there will be balance again in nature. You learn to deploy coping mechanisms, to move on, and you try to look for brightness and to stay light.

Sitting with my now cold cup of tea a million miles from home I feel an inconsolable sorrow and I begin to doubt. Neither the natural order of the garden around me nor the beauty of the flowers can console me right now; the entrance to that mental paradise is firmly locked.

Above me, the insects and moths hurl themselves at the night lights. I am alone and suddenly very, very far away in that twilight of a foreign land. And at that moment I fear I am beginning to unravel.

2

The blade cuts smoothly and noiselessly. The red flesh sizzles when it hits the heat and the skins begin to blacken with the garlic and onions. I poke the mixture with a wooden spoon and, referring back to the recipe for 'charred tomato salsa', I realise I have already gone wrong. By the time my housemates, Harry and Camille, arrive home from their offices the room is filled with burning smoke. I have hurled the offending recipe book across the room and am urgently searching the internet for 'what to do with burned tomatoes' on my laptop, which is precariously balanced on a tin of chickpeas. Nearly everything is back to 'normal', and my most disturbing recent memories are locked away. Camille and Harry ask about the trip to Herat and I tell them all the good bits. I don't tell them about Reyhana.

The following afternoon, having called Jolyon Leslie, who having worked on the original reconstruction of Babur's gardens has agreed to give me some context as well an interview about his own garden, I am donning a clean set of 'work clothes' again: baggy faded blue linen trousers, an extra-large shirt from a Zara sale which reaches the acceptable 'just below mid-thigh' and a thin cotton headscarf. It is not that Kabul demands scruff, it is just that while many expats have their own drivers or use one of the private car companies which cater solely to foreigners to ferry them around a very localised area, I tend to walk.

Firstly, I like walking. Secondly, our neighbourhood, Qala-e-Fatullah, is a middle-class area comprised of a cross section of moderately wealthy Afghans. The foreigners living here have a smaller budget than the embassies and large multinational or high-profile institutions two kilometres up the road in the more heavily militarised areas of Wazir Akbar Khan and Sherpur. When describing it to friends at home, I refer to it as the Battersea of Kabul. With no obvious military or diplomatic targets Qala-e-Fatullah is a relatively safe area, but not without trouble; there have been targeted burglaries and kidnappings but largely conducted by opportunistic bandits.

My decision to continue walking the streets is also a calculated one; if would-be kidnappers are watching the movements of foreigners, which they undoubtedly are, those who are driven around in fancy cars clearly work for organisations with money and are therefore more valuable as a hostage. To be dressed as a scruff and walk the streets is, in my mind and the minds of most of my friends who also walk, proof that, unlike the foreigners driven around in armoured 4 x 4s, we are not afraid of the environment. It is also a way of showing solidarity with the Afghans who don't have the luxury of choice.

When I check the clock on my phone I realise I am late. I run across the grass, out into the street and up to the main road where I leap over the open sewer and scuttle towards Street Two. The street numbers aren't marked so I count the corners as I go.

The few people out and about are unhurried and amble through the city without a care in the world, carrying piles of flatbread or bags of pomegranates home from the market. The skies are filled with kites and flocks of pigeons; *kaftar bazi* (pigeon fighting) is a national sport.[2] Through cracks in doors and gates left ajar, there is hushed, ordinary life. Women wash dishes and clothes, children play tag, mothers chastise them and grandmothers cook. The layered, stolen glimpses of life are fleeting, but when Kabul is like this, the war feels far away. It feels like the magical first day of the summer holidays and is part of the magnetism which keeps pulling so many back here.

On reaching an unpaved and rocky dirt track, I make for the 'blue door opposite the café' and ring the doorbell. An immaculately dressed young man in a freshly pressed *shalwar kameez* opens it furtively. I ask if this is 'Jolyon's House' and, when the door opens wide, I step into the garden.

Blooming flower beds surround an immaculate lawn. A pergola covered in vines and roses creates a sheltered pathway on one side and on the other a dense, leafy area for shade-loving plants. Pumpkins and squashes sit on a metal frame surrounded by daisies; bright red geraniums are stacked in terracotta pots. A rake, pitchfork and spade lean against them. A couple of buddleia with swollen heads flirt with white butterflies and an ancient bicycle leans against the back wall. It is just the right balance of controlled order versus disarray that appeals to me and, for a split second, I am transported to the South of France.

A softly spoken, clean-shaven man in a navy blue linen shirt and chinos steps down from a raised veranda at the back of the garden to greet me warmly. In flawless Dari he asks the door-opener to bring two cane armchairs onto the grass, along with an assortment of green tea, nuts and dried fruit.

Originally from South Africa and the son of a viticulturist, he admits he never imagined that he would end up leading the redesign and reconstruction of some of the most important Mughal gardens in the world built by the *first* Mughal emperor.

I throw him a few questions about the history of gardens in Afghanistan to get some context, but he talks so fluidly that I can barely get the information down in my notebook. His knowledge is limitless. But then, he has lived in the country on and off since the 1980s, working on United Nations reconstruction projects before working with the Aga Khan Trust for Culture in the early 2000s.

He tells me that the Afghan elite of the 1920s were very self-conscious about, and proud of, their gardens. They were heavily influenced by the modernisation of the country by the then king, Amanullah Khan and his wife Sorayah. Amanullah was very Westward looking and overturned traditions such as strict dress codes for women. He is also credited with creating a cosmopolitan education system, advancing trade links with Europe and was a great advocate for equal rights. Gardens for the elite of the twenties and thirties were formal demonstrations of wealth and status rather than practical sources of food and shelter, which was still the overriding purpose of 'land' for the poor.

The idea of gardening for pleasure rather than necessity continued through the twentieth century, as did the push-pull game between modernisers and traditionalists. The sixties and seventies were a time when women cut about in miniskirts and heels, foreigners were welcome and life was a little bit more relaxed – for the educated classes of Kabul, at least. The other side of the country still lived modestly, and along tribal and ethnic lines.

When war with the Soviets erupted in 1979, despite efforts to combine modernising Afghanistan, the country teetered on the edge of the dark ages. But Leslie explains that it was the Western-backed mujahidin who were the real enemies of gardening during the civil war which followed the Soviet departure ten years later in 1989. 'They cut down everything, destroyed what they could. They tore up Babur's gardens, the trees and bushes, filled in the canals and for no reason other than hooliganism as far as I can tell.'

Under the Taliban, Afghanistan remained dependent on international assistance, and Leslie was allowed to stay and continue working on reconstruction projects. 'Most of the Taliban came from rural areas and were complete softies when it came to flowers,' he says. 'I remember waiting for a flight from Kabul when they were in power. They had their own private garden at the airport and were far more interested in polishing the rose leaves than checking I had the right papers to be there and travel around.'

It is a curious image: the turbaned baddies – the men so reviled and feared by the West today fighting against our own soldiers in the dusty wildernesses – bent double over a rose bush, keenly watering and polishing leaves in their spare time.

Since the mass return of refugees and exiles to Kabul after the fall of the Taliban, land prices have soared. Despite continued insecurity, new building projects have been springing up all over the city, including those garish 'poppy palaces' and high-rise apartment blocks, neither of which are Afghan in design nor suitable for a country also wracked by earthquakes.

Private gardens began springing up too. Ancestral lands which had been laid to waste by movable front lines were suddenly reclaimed and cultivated so diversely that they were productive all year round – a necessity when supplies were so low. I would come to recognise this need to garden productively in other war zones around the world and come to understand it as one of the key motivators for war gardeners. 'But,' Leslie says, 'the first thing most people did was plant a tree – for shade, kindling and fruit, obviously, but more than that. It is about putting down roots. It's part of the Afghan psychology.'

'Which is why the reconstruction of Baghe-e-Babur was so important?' I ask.

He nods. 'It is a matter of national pride.'

I think about what we would do in this situation in England, Great Britain, the United Kingdom, whatever we call ourselves now: what would happen if everything we held important had been destroyed?

Our cathedral spires, thatched cottages and medieval castles, our Gothic houses and stately homes, the London parks where kings and courts had hunted, our Roman walls and Stone Age monoliths so dear to us. They are stamps of history which make up who we are as a nation; they are part of our cultural DNA. How would *we* react psychologically if we saw it all destroyed in front of us today?

I have seen pictures of Kabul taken throughout the mid-twentieth century and it is a beautiful and beguiling place. The air looks clear and crisp, the public parks are seemingly in permanent bloom, modern cars beetle through wide, generous and tree-lined streets. It is clean, the market stalls are abundant with plump fruits, people even bathe in the Kabul River – something unthinkable of today's water festering with rubbish and sewage.

I have also seen pictures and footage taken in Kabul over a period of twenty years from the Soviet invasion through to the fall of the Taliban in 2001. The city quickly descended into a desperate place of wattle buildings crumbling back into the mud from which they are constructed. Tanks and downed Russian helicopters litter the roads instead of cars. In photographs taken during the civil war things worsen: the city is replaced by a terrible wasteland; anything left standing is pockmarked and broken, and the few faces scattering the scenes are either war-hungry partisans or war-weary bystanders – no in-between apart from the children who look bereft of childhood. Nothing good exists in those pictures.

'The gardens were not only an important part of the culture of Afghanistan for the world's stage,' Jolyon continues. 'They were about giving Afghans – both those returning and those who stayed and all of whom were pretty broken – a sense of pride, a sense of their own identity, a sense of their own shared history and its importance.'

Very few photographs or accurate visual records of the original gardens survived so when reconstruction on the gardens started, it was a matter of detective work for those concerned. 'We didn't have a clue,' Jolyon chuckles.

Ingeniously, they used antique prints and ancient miniature paintings which depicted scenes set in the gardens. The team looked at other Mughal and Timurid gardens in Samarkand and Herat that they knew Babur had admired. Babur, although no stranger to violence, was also a poet and a historian who documented the flora and fauna of the lands he conquered. They used drawings made by Charles Masson, a British East India Company explorer who had travelled and sketched extensively in Afghanistan. They combed through old texts, including Babur's autobiography, the *Baburnama*, which describes a central axis, pools of water and waterfalls, marble-lined channels and a monumental gateway. It wasn't an easy task, by any stretch of the imagination and, often, the different sources contradicted each other. They found early accounts of people climbing the walls to get at the walnuts, for example, while another source referenced quinces.

'We were as painstakingly accurate as we could be but, with so much guesswork, we took a lot of joy in thinking about the seasons. We played around with colour too, which was great fun on such a blank canvas. We wanted there to be flowers in bloom for as much of the year as possible. We also had to be clairvoyants and think very hard about where shade would be created, how it would grow over the years and where families would want to picnic.'

But the first thing they had to do was de-mine the area and then excavate. Remarkably, these excavations revealed a buried structure from Indo-Greek and Kushano-Sasanian periods which dates the site of the garden to as far back as around AD 230.

'Then we had to replace the topsoil, re-terrace it, dig channels, excavate the buildings and rebuild the walls. The real challenge was the quality of the soil. The sewage system here is so poor that the earth is thin and unproductive.' And all this against a backdrop of the beginnings of one of the longest wars the twenty-first century has seen.

But while he talks it strikes me that, although the reconstruction team were effectively tidying up after two decades of chaos, the conflict erupting around them and all the trappings which skip alongside war were merely an annoyance rather than an existential threat. The restoration almost belittles the war. It says, 'OK, you guys carry on fighting, we've got more important things to sort out.' If war is anxious, uncertain and terrifying, gardens are the antithesis. They are solid worlds of hope and life, and their gardeners work at a cognitive distance from violence.

'There is something very special about the climate here. Things just grow,' Jolyon continues. His own house, he explains, is rented and he only moved in a year ago when the lease on his previous house expired. When it came to the garden, he tried to plant indigenously. 'Roses are native to Central Asia and grow like weeds here but a lot of them now have been over-bred, over-cultivated and are too ornamental.' He went to the countryside around Istalif, a village just north of Kabul (also loved by Babur who waxes lyrical about the wild tulips and clear springs in the *Baburnama*) to find wilder dog roses. He added to this the buddleia, hollyhocks, pomegranate, fig and Judas tree along with a Russian olive: a species of elaeagnus native to both Central Asia and southern Russia which thrives in poor soil. He says with a wry smile, 'It drives the Afghans mad that it is still referred to as Russian and not yet Afghan.'

The sun is beginning to drop and Leslie's garden is drenched with amber; it looks even more like the garden of a European holiday house on the Mediterranean and I ask to photograph it for the magazine.

While I'm snapping away in my own little world – or rather, Jolyon Leslie's world – of life, colour, growth and order – he calls Engineer Latif, the chief horticulturalist at Babur's gardens, and arranges for me to meet him the next day. I am slightly overwhelmed by the unsolicited gesture. But, as I am to discover, gardeners are enormously inclusive and proactive, operating an almost tribal network of contacts, cohorts and cultivators.

Mud and wattle buildings cling perilously to the hills. A child with a stick thwacks a donkey lumbering beneath water jugs on the steep slope. Two other boys run helter-skelter to the main road holding smoking cans suspended on a piece of wire. One of them wears oversized flip-flops, both their faces are smudged and their clothes ripped; the *spandi* boys. Spand is a mustard seed widely available in markets in Kabul. The smoke it creates when burned is believed to ward off evil and misfortune. Originally used by spiritual leaders in funeral rituals, today spand peddlers are children sent out to earn a wage in support of their families. Outside my taxi window the *spandi* boys skip between near-stationary cars in traffic jams waving the burning seeds and their gag-inducing stench at open windows and air-conditioning vents. They tap at the windows and hold out their hands, hopeful for a few scrunched up afghani notes, the equivalent of a few pennies. Being paid as much to get rid of them as for the power of the magical smoke, they are a permanent fixture of any journey around the city.

Sitting in the middle of the chaotic lanes of traffic are dirty-blue smears: war widows. Women left destitute after the death of their husbands and unable to work are left with no other choice but to beg. Beneath burkhas, most of them don't even have enough energy to lift a hand but just sit hunched over, hopeless, helpless.

An American military convoy appears in the rear-view mirror of my taxi (the journey to the other side of the city is too far to walk) and their sirens force other vehicles to pull over and make way.

A man sitting on a donkey-drawn cart hurtles in the opposite direction, ignoring the tannoy's shout to 'Stop!' He jolts and jigs unsteadily but remains determined in his path. A policeman steps out to obstruct his way until the convoy passes. As the traffic returns to a crawl a fight breaks out between a driver and a man on a motorbike a few cars ahead.

We cut over a trickle of the Kabul River and cling to the road running adjacent to it. The stench of rotting rubbish and waste is worse than the spand smoke, so I hold the end of my headscarf against my face to breathe. A few figures – opium addicts – emerge from the Stygian filth of the riverbanks. They pick their way over the jagged rocks and silt. Addled by narcotics, they live in a halfway world, somewhere between this life and the next.

Although this sensory overload is part of a standard journey across the capital – unremarkable to the habitués – it is hot and draining, and by the time we arrive at Babur's gardens in the south-west of the city, I am bedraggled, sweaty and my head aches.

At the entrance of the garden wall is a fixed metal barrier fence intended to herd queues to the security check; the garden is a soft target for would-be suicide bombers. Once through, visitors are ushered past an enormous wooden gate.

The guards fastidiously check my camera, manhandling it and asking me to turn it on and off. It is an irritant I have become accustomed to.

Two days before the attacks on the World Trade Center and the Pentagon, Ahmad Shah Massoud, leader of the Northern Alliance[3] and enemy of the Taliban, was assassinated by two Tunisians posing as journalists, both of whom also died. Their bombs were concealed in cameras and a battery pack. His murder remains unsolved but it is thought that either al-Qaeda or the Taliban were responsible. Massoud was fighting a war against the Taliban who in turn were protecting al-Qaeda. Either way, the incident has left Afghan security officials with a deep mistrust of cameras, their batteries and, of course, foreign photographers.

Just as I am about to lose my temper with the overzealous guards who are now inexplicably but systematically going through my wallet and flicking through my notebook upside down, an elegant, aquiline man wearing a pale grey suit and crisp white shirt appears. The guards almost stand to attention when they see him, cease their inspections and wave me through with renewed respect.

Engineer Latif Khoistani, I soon realise, is that kind of man. As we walk into the huge caravanserai – a restored, brick courtyard complex originally used as a place of rest for weary travellers but now used as administrative offices and gift shops – members of staff and colleagues are deferential and wave at him. He waves back with a polite acknowledgement.

We step through another enormous wooden door some three sto-reys high and find ourselves at the foot of eleven hectares – around twenty football fields – of Mughal garden. The noise outside is imme-diately muffled as is my headache and annoyance. Emerald-grassed orchard terraces flank a central water channel which extends up to the furthest wall, behind which lies the Queens' Palace – another building complex restored by the Aga Khan and now used as an exhibition centre, Latif tells me. He points at a smaller, white marble building, 'And over there you have Shah Jahan's mosque and behind it, Babur's tomb.' The chimneys and alcoves of the mosque remind me of a much smaller version of the Taj Mahal, also built by Shah Jahan, and I tell him as much. But, as it is the gardens I am interested in, he offers to show me around each of the fifteen terraces.

'It's a traditional paradise garden; a reflection of the gardens of heaven and designed to be both beautiful, productive and sweet smelling. But it is also a history garden,' Latif says as we walk. 'Visi-tors love to get lost in the story of Babur, the buildings, the gardens and the peaceful environment, away from the centre of the city and all the chaos.'

It is mid-afternoon but the sun has already tried its best to bleach the world. Bright swatches and slashes of pink and yellow flowers fight the obfuscation and, underfoot, the grasses squelch soft and wet; they are being soaked with fresh water from a hose. The waterer has rolled up his traditional *shalwar kameez* trouser legs over his knees and is also profiting from the cool water in the heat. The spray from the hose refracts it into a rainbow, which moves with the hose. I wonder, idly, if there is Mughal gold at its feet.

We cut across the path and onto a terrace swollen with soft pink and white cosmos.

'When we originally laid the plants down, we wanted as many varieties as possible to grow here, and now have around 5,000 to 5,500,' Latif estimates. Species of trees include pistachio, walnut, almond, apricot, pomegranate, mulberry, black cherry, chinar, quince and the Judas tree – Babur's favourite.

It was Latif himself who was responsible for sourcing the plants from all over Afghanistan, and who set off on a motorbike to engage with those gardeners and horticulturalists who had outlived the war, far and wide.

With arid deserts, high mountain altitudes, densely packed forests and sub-continental humidity countrywide, Afghanistan is as topographically diverse as it gets. It was trial and error with the microclimate created by the garden walls, and the plants had to be moved often. Now the gardens employ thirteen gardeners to care for them year round, and another eleven are taken on as temporary staff over the spring and summer months when work intensifies. It is summer which always makes Latif anxious, 'Sometimes I can't sleep for worry about how to keep the trees and grass alive in the heat.'

We amble down to the greenhouses which are bursting with colour and life. Here, young pink bougainvillea and oleandas sit shoulder to shoulder with dark burgundy coleus and begonias. Bright green pelgonias jostle in front of creeping mosses, ivy and an aloe, all of which are sporadically punctuated with scarlet chilli peppers. They are all waiting behind the scenes for their chance to shine. A gardener waters them from a small jug which he fills from a tankard of collected rainwater at the entrance. There is an intensity to his concentration as he carefully lifts the leaves of each plant, ensuring the water flows from the nozzle with precision. It is as if he is feeding a docile child.

We climb up to the top terrace and look down at the perfect symmetry of the water channels. Beyond the garden wall we can see Kabul. The emerald life and freshness in the by now softening sun looks incongruous against the city of tan and beige: a green ink spot in an urban jungle, a sweet smile in the scarred, gnarled face seen from the back of the car window.

A layer of purple smog hovers over the city. It is this which is a constant problem for Latif: dust and pollution, sadly inescapable. The other major problem he and the gardens face is the lack of effective planning control. With land prices at an all-time high, the city's skyline is fast changing and ultra-modern high-rise buildings are beginning to stab into the dust clouds. Of course, with the expanding population come cars, which will add to the pollution. Latif looks visibly and physically upset when he notices more black spots on the leaves of a tree beside the wall.

While he examines the blight and makes notes in a small pocket book, I observe the visitors ambling along the orchard terraces and a small group of picnickers on a lower terrace. As it is a midweek day there are fewer people than usual, but since Babur's gardens were opened to the public in 2008, they have seen over one million visitors – an average of one hundred to a massive ten thousand a day on national holidays. Latif, finished with his notes, explains. 'Many people are returning from abroad, maybe from Europe and the United States, where they were exposed to the idea of private gardens and picnics in public parks, but there are few safe places to walk in Kabul.'

Behind a wall on the edge of the garden is the male-only swimming pool. Shrieks of delight accompany excited splashes. High above us, a dance of kites begins. I scan the buildings behind the gardens and see a group of children on the roofs: the kite runners. Tissue paper and glass-coated strings cut through the afternoon with rush and a flash. It is so hard to be young in Afghanistan that to see carefree children on the edge of a paradise garden – albeit engaged in a kite-battle – is rare.

I spot a young man and woman beneath a tree holding hands, oblivious to the world around them. In a conservative country, where the genders are so divided and public physical displays of affection between men and women tantamount to pornography, where love is arranged through families and not the heart, I am surprised. They remind me of a copy of a miniature painting I have of Shah Jahan in a garden with his courtesans. I smile and imagine they are lovers braving the storm of true love against the odds, and that this is their furtive tryst.

Seeing my gaze Latif says, 'This is a garden for the Afghan people; it is Afghanistan's garden!'

I ask Latif what his favourite tree is and he shakes his head. 'I have a friend in India who is always teasing me. He says I treat the trees like my own children and that now I have over 3,000 of them. I couldn't possibly favour one over the other.'

I press him, 'Surely everyone can choose one . . . I mean, I like oak trees,' I enthuse.

'OK,' he finally says after a pensive silence, 'the plane tree. It is tall. Its shadow lasts all day and it lives long. You can't get more noble than that.'

We have stopped at the marble enclave of Babur's tomb (painstakingly restored by Indian craftsmen). I ask Latif to translate the inscription and he says with a gentle smile, 'If there is a paradise on earth, this is it, this is it, this is it.'

We step back onto the orchard terrace and, as if on cue, the sunlight filters through the fruit tree leaves and hits the cosmos, poppy and nasturtium petals with grace. The darting flash of insect wings glitter like fish in water. I think to myself that this garden overlooking the harsh city, this *must* be as close as possible to paradise. My spirit feels lighter and the heaviness of the Herat trip ebbs.

My phone beeps. It is Nicki. 'How's the gardening? I've just found something extraordinary for you.'

3

The ruins seem to rise slowly out of a thick layer of city smog and dust three kilometres ahead. The wide, asphalted and modern motorway is arrow-straight and sits at odds with the mud-wattle, higgledy-piggledy buildings flanking it.

The taxi pulls over next to a crumbling stone wall and a sign tells me that the National Museum of Afghanistan is just over the road, but it is the iron and steel skeleton bare to the elements next to it that we are destined for. Its smashed-up, hollow window frames smudged black with burned-out sadness; a massive crumbling neoclassical façade and columns improbably supporting the remains of a jagged roof. Beyond it are the sure, immovable mountains.

A small, sandbagged Afghan army checkpoint covered in camouflage netting and messy concertinas of razor wire sits at the foot of the palace. A tatty Afghan flag, undisturbed by any breeze, hangs limp. We walk across a vacant area of scrub beneath it. Another sign reassures us that the area has been cleared of landmines – ubiquitous annotations of the violence of former front lines.

A group of teenage street children are kicking a football to each other and on seeing me, a foreigner, quickly abandon their game to crowd around asking for *baksheesh;* money. Without the charm or 'cuteness' of prepubescence, they are wild and unruly. One tries to grab onto my trouser pockets and shouts. Another is missing the lower part of his arm – presumably lost before the de-mining initiative. His amputated stump is crudely – although not recently – scarred, and for no reason other than to shock, he hits me with it and laughs when I flinch. The subversion of normalcy is disconcerting but Zia, my friend and fixer, looms his full six-foot-something over them, growling.

Life is so fragile here. These are children of the dust, who will live loitering in a half-life where the future is short and brutal, where limbs are snatched by mines planted long before they were even born.

Zia ushers me ahead, still looming over the teenagers like a bear and I climb up to the crumbling ruins.

The Afghan soldiers yawn out of their camouflaged shadows. While Zia explains why we are here through a chicken wire gate fence, I stand back and take in the palace – my favourite place in the whole city.

The ground floor is a loggia of some forty heavy arches built out of pale stone and arranged in a horseshoe shape. The upper floors are comprised of two galleries of Corinthian columns precariously holding up the fragile ceiling or soaring into a roofless sky.

Built in the 1920s by the reformer King Amanullah, Darulaman Palace was originally intended to house the parliament and secretariat and sat in the middle of a luxurious parkland of exotic trees Amanullah had brought home from state visits to Europe. In the intervening years it has suffered the slings and arrows of Afghanistan's outrageous misfortune. Corroded, burned and looted, the palace is a physical metaphor for the country and home only to stray dogs, scorpions, snakes and an Afghan army lookout.

But it is not that history we have come to see. It is the improbable garden in the ruined palace courtyard. It is a wild and scruffy patch-work of marigolds and maize fronds, beans and begonias crammed in together as unlikely flower bed fellows. And this is what Nicki had stumbled across a few days previously.

A man comes to greet us. 'Salaam wailekum', he says, and I see that he has few teeth. His face is as gnarled as a walnut, and when he strokes his wispy white beard, listening to Zia introducing us both, the veins running over the back of his hands are like wood grain. Despite the warmth of the afternoon, he is wearing at least four layers; his blue shirt and olive-green V-neck jumper are tucked into his brown *shalwar kameez* trousers. Over the bright green nylon jacket that had once been part of a boiler suit and which I take to be his 'official' work uniform, he wears an oversized pinstripe waistcoat with large and useful pockets I imagine to be full of string and secateurs.

The sunlight is making me squint and a bead of sweat trickles down my back beneath my heavy camera rucksack. My headscarf has trapped hot air in its folds and I suddenly feel a little faint. I fan my face with my hand and the old man takes his cue and leads us to the shade at the back of the courtyard where we sit on the stone steps beneath the arches.

'His name is Mohammed Kabir,' Zia says as I pull out my notebook.

Defeated by the heat, I ask a lazy non-question. 'Tell me about your garden.'

He peers at me. 'Well what do you want to know? It's here for you to see.'

'Let's start at the beginning.'

Kabir tells his story in a voice which, although thinned by age, is even and unwavering.

He was born in Charikar, a small town around sixty-five kilometres north of Kabul and the capital of Parwan province. It is nestled in a green valley at the foothills of the Hindu Kush and has been host to many a bloody battle over the years. Today it bustles with life and commerce and just gets on with things. When I last drove through, its main drag of leafy trees and shops selling everything from kitchen goods to tinned foods to plastic toys and buckets, half reminded me of a seaside town in southern Europe – minus the American military checkpoint and the sea.

'I am 105 years old,' Kabir says. I look at him dubiously and ask Zia to clarify this. It might seem pedantic, but ironing out personal details is key to deciphering an often confused narrative. In a country where around seventy per cent of the population is illiterate, where birth certificates were, until recently, an afterthought, where years roll into each other only to be defined by who was in power, where fact and fiction are at best contradictory but mostly just blurred, it is not uncommon for an interviewee to give a date of birth and describe a childhood clearly set years before this – and stubbornly argue if you point this out to be technically impossible.

There is a short exchange between the two men and I doodle a snail in my notebook next to his age.

'I think he is telling the truth,' Zia turns to me in mumbled *sotto voce*. 'He didn't change his story once.'

'I am a gardener for Kabul municipality and look after the army's garden here,' Kabir begins and goes on to explain that the soldiers based here subsist off a small kitchen garden where a few edible crops are grown: beans, potatoes and okra. It makes sense; the Afghan army has always preferred a (recently slaughtered) lamb stew over the processed, dehydrated rations issued to foreign soldiers. Colonel Shirin Shah, the gardening base commander I met in Helmand two years ago, pops into my head and I realise that, as this is a nation of farmers and gardeners, it is in no way surprising that the army lives off the land.

'But what about the flowers?' I point at the messy square of colour in the middle of the courtyard.

'Well,' he says, 'I just decided to bring some seeds from my home and plant them in the courtyard. The soldiers helped me to dig and water. I am an old man,' he reminds me.

I ask him why he would make a garden in the ruins of a forgotten palace where only the military and the ghosts will see it. He looks at me as if I've asked him to count up to three.

'Everyone needs a garden. This is our soil. When you work with it, things grow. It's nature, life. I am a poor man, sometimes my family and I only eat once a day, but I can live without food; I couldn't live without seeing green leaves and flowers. They come from heaven. Each one,' he insists 'is a symbol of paradise. I have a flower in my garden at home and have counted seventy colours in its petals; tell me that it doesn't come from heaven!' he exclaims.

He pauses to look at his oasis shimmering beneath ribbons of heat and I follow his gaze, thinking of Babur's earthly heaven and of Eden and the tree of life and everything that followed. As if reading my mind, he says softly, 'I feel like I'm in paradise when I garden.'

Water, he explains, is his biggest problem. I nod; not only are the ruins situated on a mound, they are at the foothills of barren mountains. But it is not this which is the root of his problems. It is Washington.

'Washington has built a military base near here and they have stolen our water.' Kabir becomes animated and I try not to smile. It is true that there is a NATO base a kilometre or so away from the palace – there are many dotted around the city, most of which have disrupted city life one way or another. As support for international troop presence wanes, the bases have increasingly become the scapegoat for a multitude of municipal problems.

In a culture driven by rumour, conjecture (and an unerring belief that Afghanistan is actually the centre of the world), conspiracies concerning the true motive for outsiders being in the country abound. The CIA is considered to be actively funding the Taliban along with Pakistan and Iran (perhaps not so surprising a theory given the CIA's support of the mujahidin against the Soviets); the British are in Helmand to avenge their defeat in the Battle of Maiwand in the second Anglo-Afghan war; Western governments are directly invested in the continuation of opium production; the war is just a huge cover-up while Afghanistan's mineral wealth is exploited by the international community; if America itself is not responsible for 9/11, then it is either the Israeli or Pakistani intelligence services. Or Iran. Although some theories have their feet in fact, most are wildly inaccurate.

That outsiders are to blame for the depletion of water levels in Kabul city is an axiom for Kabir. And to him 'Washington' is as good a collective noun for all foreigners as it gets. It is also a reflection of how poorly the international community understands Afghan public opinion. But fortunately for him, the Afghan soldiers at the palace have a well from which they help him draw water.

I ask him what else he loves about his garden and he hugs his knees like a schoolboy, smiling proudly.

Zia translates: 'It makes him very sad to see this palace in ruins but since he came back to work here, he's tried to make it look like it used to.'

'What does he mean "like it used to"?' I ask. The palace has been in ruins for years.

After a few minutes of discussion Zia says, 'When the gardens were first started.'

I don't understand the reference and start flicking back through my notebook, looking for this vital bit of information I appear to have missed.

Finding none, I ask for clarification.

The story is remarkable. Kabir first started working in the newly built European palace as a gardener when he was a teenager alongside his father and uncle.

'When the gardens were built, they looked like this. It was different then.' He picks up a stick and begins to sketch an outline map in the dirt. 'They were all the way over there, and there and behind us there' – he points to the furthest points we can see – 'so you had different areas for the trees, different areas for flowers, different areas for shade and water. There was a pathway here' – he draws a straight line – 'which separated the flower beds, and there were different types of apples and apricots here and here. The king had been travelling and brought back different species from Germany, France, Italy, England – all over. We needed to use donkeys, horses and even elephants to move the big things around,' he says.

I am a little sceptical at the mention of elephants – they are not indigenous to Afghanistan – and it sounds like a tale of fancy. However if it is true, Kabir is a living, breathing window into a version of Afghanistan few would believe ever existed.

'It was a very modern garden for the time. But it was a different era then,' he sighs a little forlornly.

In a career spanning over half a century, Kabir continued to work as government employee in various guises. His preferred job was in the palace gardens. With a wistful gaze he describes his favourite memory, 'The king's mother was very kind to me. She used to come and sit in the shade beneath the apricot trees with us and chat and smile.'

I find this dubious and imagine the story to be the imaginings of an old man. With my journalistic hat on I want to press him for more details, to pick holes and find flaws in his story. But I stop. For him, it is a real memory and it makes him happy. Happier than remembering a brutal time of war which seems never to end, so who am I to take that away? Instead I ask him to describe the weather and what was in bloom during the afternoon in the garden with the king's mother.

'Oh, sunny. It was always sunny then,' he says simply, 'everything bloomed.'

The sun, trapped in the courtyard of the palace, has created an inferno and I am wilting again. But when we stand in the courtyard garden I feel cool and protected from the heat. It is in no way reminiscent of the formal gardens the palace would have been used to – in the middle of the ruins it looks rather like an unkempt toupee, but as he points out the areas of zinnia, miscanthus, maize, cosmos and coleus, I see that he has tried to maintain structure. He moves between each plant like a teacher in a playground, chastising and praising each in turn.

'Since starting this garden I feel I am getting younger. Every tree, every plant, every flower gives me energy.'

I ask him what he will do if and when the palace is restored.

He shrugs. 'My garden will be destroyed. But still,' he goes on, 'I feel younger and more powerful here. People say I look younger too.' And he shows us his beard, which he is convinced is darkening the more he gardens.

Before we leave I ask the soldiers if I can wander around the ruins. I turn back into the palace and make for the cool, dark interior. It is so vast I feel like I'm Alice in Wonderland – albeit a very ruined Wonderland.

The ceiling has collapsed on one side and shafts of sharp sunlight score the shadows on another. In front of me are the remains of a grand spiral staircase, the banister of which has long since been looted. I climb up to the second floor where there is more light – and a lot more rubble. A collapsed floor gapes like an open wound of steel and stone. It is as still as a grave, but soft toots from traffic and the faint tinkle of bicycle bells reminds me that the city is still breathing.

Scrawled parachutes, helicopters and tanks with captions in French and English describe the recent history of Canadian, British and American special forces whose date-stamped litany of graffiti is a signature to the official end of the Taliban's regime.

This close, the ruins are somehow even more forlorn, and I am reminded of Stalin's maxim 'a million deaths are a statistic, one is a tragedy'. So it is with buildings. From a distance, ruined buildings are in a way more digestible but the absence of any attempt to clear the rubble renders the palace frozen in time. Nobility and grandeur lingers here, and it is easy to imagine the elegant men and women in Edwardian dress perambulating along the galleries, perhaps protecting themselves from the sun with silk umbrellas.

I take another flight of precipitous stairs to the top floor where the wind and dust are masters of the world. It is silent there and ethereal. I scramble over to what was once a dining room and survey Kabul through the remains of a window. The long, straight highway bustles on, mutely carving the open horizon, ferrying toy cars and antlike people.

I scramble over to the other side of the long gallery overlooking the courtyard and rest on a balustrade. From that great height the garden below is the size of a postage stamp but an emerald in a vast canvas of tan and devastation. The acoustics of the courtyard mean that I can hear echoes of Kabir, Zia and the soldiers, still pottering in the garden. They are laughing easily. The garden really does make people happy, even when everything else is unravelling.

'Lali-Lali?' Zia has seen me up near the clouds and his voice echoes. 'Shall we go go?'

Reluctantly I drag myself away from the ruins and back to earth. I ask the soldiers what they make of the garden. One of them is picking the petals off the bright orange head of a marigold like a love sick poet and explains that in the evenings they sit and drink tea here. 'It's good to have greenery around. Green is happiness, green is peace. Who doesn't like that?'

The water is perfectly blue – a crystal of tourmaline shining out from a dull rock. At its shore frolic young Afghans. They wait impatiently and loudly for their turn in the back of one of three speedboats which make a loop around the lake at top speed. Couples and young families clamber into blue pedalos for a more sedate experience. On the sandy strip of beach, wiry horses are raced within an inch of their lives by young men eager to show off a native equine prowess. Larger groups and families recline on semi-private, raised platforms with urns of green tea and mounds of kebab and *naan* from one of the many *chai khonas* (tea houses) or eateries catering to day-trippers.

I am in a taxi driving along the edge of Qargha Lake. Built on the outskirts of Kabul in the 1930s the reservoir was converted to recreational use in the 1950s.

The car continues on a road heading away from the resorts and, turning off up a steep dirt track, it stops at a blast wall chicane. I pay the driver and weave through the concrete maze to an enormous steel door which clicks open immediately. A few uniformed guards point me towards the basement of the house, but before I reach the door a smartly dressed man with salt-and-pepper hair and a neatly trimmed moustache steps out to greet me.

'Dr Zabi Mojadidi,' he says kindly. 'Come. Where shall we sit?'

'Outside,' I suggest, 'in the garden.'

He leads me outside to a paved patio. It is the first of a number of terraces and covered in potted cacti and geraniums. The second is a lawn flanked by colourful flower beds and the third, a vegetable patch.

We sit beneath a parasol at a table fashioned out of a tree trunk in another patio in the middle of the grassy terrace. He points at some boulders next to us. 'These were unearthed when we were building the house. The workmen were going to smash them up to make gravel, but I like them just as they are.'

He rubs the edge of the table and reiterates his love of recycling nature. 'Sadly we had to dig up quite a few old trees for the building work so I tried to replace what I'd disposed of. They were going to throw this one away, but why trash something if you can make something out of it?'

He managed to save the oldest tree of all – a walnut which he guesses is around 150 years old. 'It used to fruit abundantly, but this year I don't know, we've hardly had any walnuts – maybe fifty or so. I need to research what might be troubling it.'

The vegetable patches are bigger than I had first thought, more kitchen garden than cottage garden and abundant with cauliflowers, basil, spinach and rhubarb which are all plump, succulent and healthy. He and his wife brought many of the seeds from America.

In the early nineties, Mojadidi left for Virginia (he had been a scholarship student at Virginia Tech in the sixties and seventies) and remained there for eleven years. He returned to Afghanistan in 2004 to work as an engineer with a privately owned company, and in 2009 he was persuaded by old cohorts and allies to take on the mantle of governor of Kabul.

'I thought it would be a good opportunity to help rebuild the city, but I soon realised that the role was merely symbolic and I couldn't do what I wanted without abusing the system. So I quit.'

He continued to work as a structural engineer however, and tells me that the house and this garden is the product of his own hard work and determination not to walk the well-trodden path of corruption and abuse of power.

Using a traditional Afghan design, updated to suit modern living, he built his new home and then set to work on the garden.

It is by far the brightest and most manicured garden I have seen so far. With its patio for barbequing, outside lights, parasol for shade, it is also the most American. But there are water channels, and I ask Mojadidi if he was influenced in some way by the Mughal tradition.

'Maybe subconsciously,' he says. 'But I love the sound of water and when we have guests we sit and listen to it. It's pleasing for the ear. It *is* an Afghan garden, through and through.'

Babur's gardens were divided along fault lines of shade, fruit, beauty and water – an earthly paradise. Mojadidi's garden contains all of those elements – they are just laid out in a slightly different way and with a different colour palette.

I ask him if he was here during a recent Taliban attack on a hotel near the lake and he nods.

'Were you afraid?'

'No. I've got good security up here,' – he points out the sentry posts – 'and the lake is an extra buffer. That's why I'm out here – not just the better air.'

As a former governor of Kabul, a political activist who is outspoken against different political parties and the ISI (the Pakistani intelligence service), *and* as the son of a former president, Mojadidi has every reason to need extra security. He is followed by his enemies when he leaves his house, and is often threatened.

'They did the same with my father when he criticised the Soviets. He was incarcerated for five years. People don't like it when you speak out.'

I ask which is his favourite area of the garden.

'This one,' he says pulling his right knee across his left and smiling, 'It's right in the middle of everything. I love sitting here when the moon rises. My wife always jokes that I love the moon and the garden more than I love her. It is not true. It is the moon that reminds me of her when she is away.'

Gaza

May 2013

"'It's in the garden no one can go into,' she said to herself. "It's the garden without a door.'"

Frances Hodgson Burnett, *The Secret Garden*

1

The sun is a scorching hot white and I squint in its glare but a swathe of bougainvillea startles bright pink over the stone walls lining the road to the beach. I wind down the window and stick my head out, eager to see the sea. The air feels lightly salty and smells tangy with algae, and when I see the water it is all greens and cerulean, flat and gleaming glassy smooth beneath a young sky of pale blue and white. It is going to be a gorgeous spring in the Mediterranean.

Only a few days before arriving here, I had made a tiresome journey from Jordan, taking a taxi from Queen Alia International Airport to the Allenby Bridge, one of the main ports of entry to Israel and the only one possible if flying from an Arab country, which I had been. (Many Arab countries do not recognise Israel, and there are no flights from there). The border guards were stringent. Why did I have so many Afghan stamps? What had I been doing in Dubai? What was I doing in Abu Dhabi? In Istanbul? And Delhi? What am I doing in Israel? 'Holiday.' I had lied, backing it up with a truth: 'I've come to look at your flora and fauna.' To have mentioned Gaza or Palestine would have led to further delay and scrutiny. After an hour and a half they let me go. Paul, the former company commander of the soldiers I had photographed in Afghanistan three years ago and now on a new posting with the Palestinian Security Forces, was waiting for me. We drove out through the contour lines of an ancient seabed towards Jerusalem, that wonderful, horrible, beautiful, ugly, sublime, toxic and holier than holy, paradoxical city.

But that was four days ago. A few hours ago, I had made the journey across another, harsher border through a complex network of metal corridors and heavy turnstile gates under the watchful eyes of security cameras which tracked my every move in an empty border terminal. As the final steel gate had rumbled shut I had walked another kilometre or so along a caged walkway beneath a corrugated iron roof. Pale and bald fields, fringed by dusty dunes, lay either side. A lone bird circled overhead, wings ticking the sky as it scoured the ground for seeds.

Passing an abandoned wheelchair I stepped out into the light at the other end and into the largest open-air prison in the world – forty kilometres long and eleven wide. Gaza.

After Hamas was voted into power in 2005, Israel, having already pulled out its soldiers and settlers from the former small fishing village of Gaza for fear of what the new government would do – perhaps rightly so since unlike its counterpart Fatah, Hamas refuses to acknowledge the existence of the Jewish state – has imposed several severe travel restrictions. Since 2007 it has had complete control over who enters and exits Gaza, hoping to contain Hamas within the security walls, and since then it has effectively been cut off from the world.

The population has continued to grow exponentially. Gaza is today one of the most overcrowded places on the planet. 1.8 million people live within 365 square kilometres. On average, that's almost 5,000 people per square kilometre. In the United Kingdom, there are around 420 people per square kilometre. Unsurprisingly, pollution, lack of water and electricity restrictions have lead some United Nations reports to estimate that by 2020, Gaza will be unliveable.

With little to sustain itself, Gaza is heavily reliant on an arterial network of tunnels at the southern border with Egypt, through which are smuggled goods ranging from food to nappies to cars to weapons. Palestinian militants have been fighting back against the blockade with Qassam (rockets) aimed at Israeli towns along the border ever since.

In the meantime, a little under two million people live shoulder to shoulder, trying to get by as normally as possible in an open-air cage.

A horse-drawn cart rumbles next to a clapped-out banger. A smartly dressed man in a suit carrying a briefcase crosses in front of us, absorbed in thought. Two young men in baggy jeans and enormous sunglasses pose outside an electronics shop, latest iPhone models in hand. Ravens perch on piles of rubbish. Women in long dark *abayas* lug bags of shopping between children skipping like butterflies along the pavement playing tag, their laughter infectious, coming in spurts as we pass them. Rugs hang over balconies and electric wires score the sky. A martyr poster hanging from a street lamp flaps. The photograph is of a young man in his early twenties killed in the last war, my taxi driver explains in broken English.

That was the last time I was here too. It was winter then and Gaza was burning beneath Operation Cast Lead, an Israeli incursion into Gaza which aimed to counter Hamas rockets. A fractious ceasefire had been agreed when the world's media was allowed in.

I had not been to Afghanistan by then and, naively, I had no conception of the extent of war and its aftermath. I was remarkably unprepared but I learned quickly.

Every single person I encountered then had lived through tragedy. A man working as a porter at the border lost his home, his wife and two children in an airstrike. A little girl had lain beneath rubble for four days next to the body of her father she had witnessed executed in front of her. There was a bald patch in her hair where the doctors had sewn up a gunshot wound she had survived. I found two boys playing in the shell of a building covered in English graffiti saying 'Arabs must die', and 'Make war not peace'. They described IDF soldiers dressed as Hamas soldiers looking for other enemy fighters. Finding none, the soldiers had filled orange-flavour drink bottles with their own urine and left them in a fridge.

In the north the rural, agricultural areas of olive groves and fields had been churned up by military vehicles and shelling. Most of the buildings still standing were deserted, but in the shell of one home I saw an old man sitting at a makeshift table drinking tea amidst the rubble in a still light. It was unclear where the house had ended and the garden began. He had lost his sons and wife and was disinclined to leave their home.

Shelling continued and hospitals filled up. By the end of the war an estimated fourteen hundred were killed, over a thousand of whom were civilians.

I left Gaza shattered and carrying an overwhelming sense of guilt that I *could* leave so easily and return to another life in London with all its luxuries and hedonism. At a friend's engagement party shortly afterwards I had an overwhelming desire to punch holes in walls. Instead I filed it all away.

But that was four years ago. The photograph of the martyr on the lamp post above me has faded, along with my own anger, and since then I have been curious to know how Gazans live in a tiny patch of land where war seems to come and go as regularly as the seasons. And as the population only ever expands, how do they survive, while being strangled.

The smell of sweet dough from a bakery lingers at the junction and wafts into the car. Hazem, my fixer, tells the driver where to turn at a shady street.

We arrive at a stone-walled house of pale yellow. Another bright bougainvillea hangs into the street. The road is barely paved, but judging by the size of the houses it is a moderately affluent area.

Hazem rings a bell and we hear shuffled steps approaching. An elderly man peers around the side of the door and Hazem introduces us. 'This is your first gardener.'

Pots of cacti line the inside wall of a courtyard and I fiddle idly with a papery bougainvillea petal while Hazem explains what I am doing.

The man's eyes narrow, 'Why should I speak to you?' he says. 'You journalists only come here when there's trouble, you promise to change our future and then you leave and nothing ever changes for us.'

When he discovers my nationality he huffs. 'All these problems are thanks to you British anyway.'

'I don't want to talk about the war,' I say. 'I want to talk about your garden, your cacti.' I point at the spiky mounds on the steps.

Hazem continues to talk to him in Arabic and at length the man nods and takes us upstairs.

'I don't have a proper garden. But I do like growing things.' He opens the door onto the flat roof and there, at our feet and of every size and shape imaginable, are some 500 cacti.

'I have been growing them for twelve years,' he says as he walks a narrow path between the pots. 'The first one was a present from a friend. I was fiddling with one of its needles and realised that unlike people, they don't always hurt you. I can run my hand over the prickles and, like a good friend, it doesn't cause pain.' He picks up a small plant to demonstrate.

'Why cacti?' I ask. To me they are just hardy desert plants, as ubiquitous in this part of the world as a hedgerow is in England.

Their attraction, he explains, is that they don't need much water; in summer he only waters them once a week, 'which is good because the water quality is so poor that if they needed any more it would be a problem.'

Before growing cacti and before the blockade he ran a successful bakery business which he had built from nothing. It was destroyed when five members of staff were killed in a rocket attack. The cacti, he says, are his way of repeating the process of building something from scratch.

They are easy to grow too. He takes cuttings from a mother plant and puts them in a pot of soil and waits. 'With no roots of their own, they begin to suffer and search for water. In this search, they begin to grow their own roots and when they do, I start caring for them.'

He sounds like a proud father and, his temper softened, bids us to sit and calls his wife to bring tea.

At the start of Operation Cast Lead, he tells me, forgetting his initial refusal to talk about the war, he was sitting on the steps between pots of cacti grafting and changing their soil. 'The planes passed overhead and I knew something was wrong. When I heard the news of war I ran straight to the supermarket to buy food.'

The tea his wife brings us is strong and teeth-shatteringly sweet, but restorative in the heat of the day now amplified by the tarpaulin above us.

He sighs and pours a second round. 'People in Gaza, we are just trying to live like everyone else in the world. We are good and love life but the occupation is a huge problem. War is so normal for us now. We don't feel free and life is hard but all we want is peace. This,' he points at the pots, 'this is the only freedom I have.'

I ask him which his favourite plant is and he points to the largest one; a 'golden barrel or,' he chuckles, 'mother in law's cushion.' He had it brought in from Egypt through the tunnels in Raffah for $400. 'I can't reproduce from it but its flower is very special.'

He picks up a cactus with a wilted bloom. 'The flower has a short life, maybe just a few days, less if there is no water. And they only come one by one. Last night I could see that this one was about to flower so I came out here at midnight to catch it. By dawn it had died.' He brushes the dried petals away.

I privately suspect that the short-lived, unpredictable life span of the cactus flower is what draws him so obsessively to them as a species. It is a perfect metaphor for the fragile and temporary peace. But I say nothing.

He takes me through to another area of the roof where he has built a greenhouse with sheets of plastic. The shelves inside are loaded with more spiky plants and, selecting one coated in a fine cobweb-like mesh, he strokes it. 'This one is the Old Man. Where else could you find anything as beautiful as this? Soon there will be no more water in Gaza, but my cacti will live on.'

As we prepare to leave I realise I have not asked his full name, but he shakes his head. 'No, I'm not telling you. It's not important. You can just call me Sabaar.'

Hazem, my fixer, translates with a smile. It is the Arabic word for cactus. Prickly. Robust. A survivor.

We drive north out of the cluttered and vertical city towards Beit Lahiya, where the landscape changes.

Four years ago it had been a horrible mass of rubble and discord; the buildings stood limply in cindered soil beneath a pallid January sky, but today, hope seems to thrive in the pastoral vista.

Abu Faisal greets us at the end of a grassy farm track. He is smartly dressed in a blue shirt, beige windcheater and navy slacks, and is eager to show us to his garden. He is a lab technician at the Islamic University in Gaza City, but as the son of a farmer he is very involved with the machinations of the land, and flowers are his passion. His skills in botany and horticulture are entirely self-taught. 'It's not so different to farming, but you can experiment a little and you work out the temperament of each plant.'

We sit on a stone bench next to a wall and are surrounded by pale roses. It is a lush garden of dark greens and pale, pastel blooms. Toys are scattered here and there and he calls his children to tidy them away. But before we discuss his passion, he describes in almost flawless English how the blockade has affected his family's land. Not only have they not been able to export crops, they have not been able to import decent fertiliser or plastic sheeting to protect the young plants. It is a frustration I am to hear time and time again.

'But when I'm gardening I forget everything and all the problems we have,' he says. 'You are alone with your thoughts and it can be very peaceful.'

He walks me around the paved paths littered with buddleia and hydrangea. Thirsty white butterflies dart from flower to flower, and fern rockeries of shining granite stones emerge from beneath dark tree roots. The dusk brings a woody dampness and everything is smudged with a glaucous blue. I half imagine the rock enclaves are a home for hiding imps.

At the end of the garden, he points to an avocado tree he successfully grafted, and the three types of vines he grows for making vinegar and providing shade. There are abundant blue acacias which also give shade, encourage wildlife, can be used as fuel and fodder for animals and produce nitrogen which in turn feeds other flowers.

He cultivated the roses from cuttings in his own nursery, and he takes much delight in them. 'I've been experimenting with botany and ways of making Beit Lahiya more green, focusing on endangered trees.' His dedication to green-ification is admirable given the proximity to the Israeli border, the inevitability of another war and by default, the destruction of his garden.

He shows me to his densely planted orchard just behind the house. 'It's not good for the trees to be so close together, but we are running out of land.' He grazes his hand over a graft. The scion branch poking out of the frayed tape is anaemic and desiccated. He laughs, 'I was too rushed when I tried to bind it. It is like the Jews and the Arabs. You can't just stick us together without really working at it.'

I ask him about phosphorus. Used by armies to hide troop movement beneath its smoke, white phosphorus is highly flammable, burning everything it touches – buildings, trees, soil – and it eats through skin and muscle. Phosphorus wounds are the stuff of nightmares and its use as an incendiary weapon against combatants is prohibited. It was, however, extensively and indiscriminately fired over densely populated areas of Gaza by the IDF where its troops were not present.

Abu Faisal shakes his head in sad bewilderment. 'The wind carried the smoke silently in clouds and destroyed the crops. It smelled of acid and tasted of iron, and when you breathed, it burned.'

The after-effects, he says, were worse for him than the land – even today he has nightmares about that war and the Israeli special forces dressed as Hamas fighters searching the houses. 'The garden is another way of trying to forget the memories from then,' he says solemnly.

It is a calm, quiet garden; far from the madding overcrowding of the city and without obvious barriers, it feels far from reality. What do other people say when they visit? He chuckles, 'When I describe my plants having their own character to my friends, they laugh at me. The best compliment came from an Israeli soldier. He congratulated me on my roses. I was flattered but I did not feel comfortable, especially as he was trespassing on my land.'

We have come to a tall cypress tree and Abu Faisal pauses next to it. 'It was a present from my best friend. He was a true gardener but was killed while driving an ambulance in the war. It's the only thing left of him.'

'I'm so sorry,' I say, and I try to find the words to comfort him. But I feel a little stupid and in the end I don't say anything at all. He places his hand on the trunk of the tree, pats it and smiles fondly, remembering his friend.

Our shadows are drawing long gills in the ground so we prepare to leave, but Abu Faisal wants to introduce me to his neighbour.

We walk out of his garden and up the track through a patch of scrubland and onto a sandy path leading towards the dunes on the border. There are tufts of beach grass dotting the horizon, and the combination of the silence and the colour and warmth of the early evening sun make it feel like an Arabian arcadia of sorts. My flip-flops kick up the fine sand behind me, which is deep and still holds the warmth of the day.

A few hundred metres ahead are rows and rows of strawberry plants and moon-headed onion flowers nodding in a thin breeze. There is someone tending to some of the ground-level plants, unaware of our arrival, lost in the rhythm of thinning out dead leaves and moving on to the next.

When the man stands to stride through the avenues of strawberries he is clutching a handful of berries. At a tap outside a shed he washes them and looks at my camera a little warily, but he takes us up to the flat roof of the shed and scatters the ruby-red fruits on a table, inviting us to sit.

The view stretches out over a choppy sea of dunes beneath a dignified sky where the first evening star shrugs through the dimming light. We are on the edge of another world. Beyond the dunes, watchtower glass glints out of the haunted horizon of the border wall.

The man, Jihadth, catches me staring at the border and says somewhat gruffly, 'We call the hills around us' – he waves at the dunes – 'the shooting area. It is where the IDF train so we live with the sound of gunfire all the time. Sometimes the horizon is just a line of tanks firing, but at least the water pump drowns out the sound.' He stamps his booted foot on the roof of the shed. 'My son-in-law was shot in the back by a stray bullet a few years ago. One minute we were just drinking tea in the shade and telling each other jokes, and the next minute, boom, he's on the ground screaming.'

As if on cue, a supersonic boom of artillery thuds in the distance over the noise of the water pump, making me jump.

It doesn't bother Jihadth, and he continues without missing a beat. 'I enjoy the work. When it is harvest time, we sleep outside with the crops. Nothing can beat that.' Even during cross-border attacks, Jihadth refuses to leave, preferring instead to sit it out, loyal to his land, determined to defend what is his.

I reach for a juicy strawberry. They taste like summer, but to him they are a bitter reminder of the blockade. The strawberry, cherry tomato and carnation flower business in Gaza used to employ around 8,000 families and export to Spain and Holland.

Since Hamas came to power and the subsequent closure by Israel of the Karni crossing, Gaza's main cargo crossing, his fruits have become an unsustainable crop. He trades locally in the city but is almost always undercut by cheaper imported strawberries coming through the tunnels from Egypt.

Two Apache helicopters buzz overhead like wasps. It is getting late and I am worried about losing the light entirely and being unable to photograph. I ask if he can show me his non-commercial garden.

We clamber down the wooden ladder and he leads me to an over-grown, fenced-off scrap of trees and shrubs growing out of the fine sand on the edge of a maize field. There are a few citrus trees, a couple of youthful-looking olives, a sprig of which he gives me, acacias and a fig, urgently trying to ripen. Thorn against thorn, a pink rose scrawls over an enormous cactus.

A woman with a kind, open face appears from behind the shed: his wife. She is wearing a red scarf over her head, knotted under her chin like the Queen, and carries a basket which she drops beneath a vine to begin picking a few bunches of grapes. 'For vinegar,' Abu Faisal explains.

Jihadth points to an oversized, overgrown shrub at the entrance of the garden, three metres high. It is a cumbersome, lurid green and not anything I recognise. 'My boy,' he says sadly.

In 2005, after a semblance of a peace deal was brokered by Palestinian and Israeli Prime Ministers Mahmoud Abbas and Ariel Sharon, Israel withdrew all of its settlers and soldiers from Gaza. Jihadth's son took a plant from a settler's abandoned garden as a souvenir of victory.

Later his son went on to join Hamas and was fighting for them in 2011 when he was killed.

Jihadth is silhouetted and I am certain he is close to tears. I understand now that this tree is why he will never leave his land.

We stand there in the embers of the day, the sun quickly dropping. There is no shelling now, no stutter and rattle of distant firing or buzzing aircraft. Instead, the simple hollow stillness of grief interrupted only by the slow rustle of the shrubs' leaves which seem to be saying something unintelligible, inaudible.

A dark indigo begins to fall.

2

I am restless and stand at the window waiting. In the first light of day the spattered spray from the waves lapping outside my window looks like rising smoke. It is still mostly dark but as the sun kindles, gradually, the spray-smoke diminishes and a pallor rises of a new day beneath the retreating night.

Downstairs on the hotel veranda I find life in a thick, black coffee. I watch the waves again. Their spume blurs the water, and when I half close my eyes it foams into a scattering of white meadowsweet and cow parsley. I down the dregs from my cup and head outside.

The landscape of old Gaza was very different to the twenty-first century's metropolis. Nineteenth-century prints depict romanticised Roman or Phoenician ruins toppled at the feet of Western explorers, or crenellated fortresses, rolling clouds and Arabs swathed in silk, or Bedouin tents at the foot of date palms and minarets. Even travel photographs from the 1970s show just a small bundle of single-storey houses on an asphalted road before undulating dunes and palms.

Today almost everything natural has been usurped for modernity: dunes for asphalt, fields for cement, fruit groves for cars, trees for high-rises. Like some of the gardens I encountered here, every square inch has been put to use. With little land to accommodate an expanding population, Gaza has no choice but to build up and over instead of out.

The apartment block at which we stop is just a kilometre from the border and well out of the city centre proper. The whole building looks neglected; there are missing windows on stairwells and absent doors on landings. But it is home to Huda, a proud woman.

It is also home to her husband, six sons and their wives, and each of them has between six to nine children. Not surprising, given that almost half of Gaza's 1.8 million inhabitants are under the age of fourteen. She counts them on her hands and I'm reminded of the little old lady who lived in a shoe with so many children she didn't know what to do. I too make a few calculations and work out that Huda's household is somewhere in the region of fifty-six members strong. Ten or so of her grandchildren crowd around us outside. They wear shabby seventh-hand cast-off clothes and only a few have shoes. Nonetheless, they are excitable and rowdy and curious as to what their grandmother is doing talking to a foreigner with a camera.

I have partnered with PARC Agricultural Development Association, a Palestinian NGO working in Gaza. I had contacted them before arriving and they not only gave me the accreditation I needed for Hamas border paperwork, they also offered to help by introducing me to some of the people to whom they are teaching kitchen garden techniques. Huda is one of them.

She is dressed head to toe in bright green with a light blue head-scarf that she keeps readjusting around her face, anxious to look presentable. Her garden is fenced off by corrugated iron sheets and chicken wire dug into the pale soil. Inside, the area is no more than ten metres square and home to citrus trees, a fig and chickens.

The area was also hit by phosphorus and she explains that this is the first year since the war two years ago that the trees and plants have started to produce. 'We couldn't care for the plants properly and we lost a lot of them.' Even her livestock starved to death. 'There was no water, and animal food is expensive, you know.' She twiddles the end of her headscarf.

The effects of the wars have left their mark on the household. She describes the children having nightmares and diarrhoea in their sleep and talks about the deep depression they feel all the time and the medication she herself is taking. 'We all jump whenever a door slams.'

After Afghanistan, this is something I understand. Even back in London, my own stomach plummets when I hear a car backfire or a clatter from a construction site, and Bonfire Night has become habitually hellish. At home I am quick to bristle over trivial things and am surrounded by malaise. At night I either battle with a debilitating insomnia or horrible, nonsensical dreams. But unlike Huda and her family this was a path I consciously *chose*, and as such, have only myself to blame. I am just a war tourist and can leave at any time. Huda and her family are not so lucky.

We hear artillery firing in the near distance and I look at Huda who has jumped but is busily distracting herself by pulling some bindweed from the fence and muttering.

She picks a bright green lime and holds it against her dress, grinning and making it disappear within the folds of fabric. When she starts walking through the trees I follow, identifying clementine, fig, orange, olive and pomegranate. She stops to mutter again when she sees leaves spotted with blight or weeds cluttering up the ground.

Along the back wall there are vines creeping through the wire fence and an allotment area, home to herbs, aubergines and peppers. A honeysuckle climbs over the corrugated iron. Its fragrance is exacerbated by the morning heat which already burns my toes. There is a chicken coop in the far corner and she summons a grandchild to collect the eggs.

At sixty-three she is part of a generation born at the same time as the state of Israel was created and the cooling embers of one conflict began to ignite another. But when she talks about her childhood it is with fond memories of being outdoors. She never went to school; she worked on the ancestral land.

Today there are few employment opportunities for her sons, and with the depressed economy, prices have become exorbitant. But unlike the little old woman who lived in the shoe, Huda knows exactly what to do with the children: feed them. And it is her garden that enables her to do so.

Not only can she feed the three generations of her family with fresh produce, she can also preserve and pickle the surplus as well as making olive oil. In an ideal world she would sell this too. As an illiterate woman now empowered as the breadwinning matriarch, she is proud of this achievement.

Huda's garden reminds her of the good old days of her youth. She shows me a blanket which she will sleep under in the garden as and when the mood takes her. 'I like to be here all the time.' Nearby, a muezzin calls for the faithful through an acoustically challenged tannoy. She excuses herself to pray on a mat rolled up in her blanket and spreads it out beneath a lemon tree.

Not wanting to intrude on her moment with God, I remove myself to the other side of the garden to make notes. A thunder of artillery fire in the distance startles me but goes unnoticed by Huda as she prays, and in her green dress she almost disappears into the foliage of the citrus trees, her slice of the way things were.

This is, I realise, more important to her than the food the garden yields, and perhaps is what she wants above all else: to retreat to the past where things were more simple, removed from the uncertainty and violence of the present. But maybe, I think, that is what we all crave: a return to the innocence of Eden before we fell from grace.

When we leave, it is to a chorus of twenty or so *maʾa salaamas* (goodbyes) from Huda's grandchildren, with Huda behind them smiling and waving, still clutching the lime.

We drive to Beit Hanoun, a city on both the northern and eastern border. Old Ottoman empire papers make reference to Beit Hanoun's wheat harvests, barley and summer crops, and in the nineteenth century the Palestine Exploration Fund[4] described gardens surrounding the village and a fresh well. It is now a city of some 20,000 Palestinians and, judging by the construction sites on the edge of the city, it is still growing.

We pull into a wide street of modest village houses away from the urban sprawl and up to a white two-storey building. Its façade is dotted with spots of grey cement slapped on hurriedly: Polyfilla for bullet holes. It is surrounded by pink geraniums and roses, and against the bleached and dusty road, it is the only patch of colour in the street.

Badria is sitting in the shade of a vine-covered patio running alongside the house at a plastic garden table with several other women. As soon as they see me, they scatter into neighbouring homes like marbles.

Badria is a farmer's wife and she and her neighbours have been tying up bunches of thyme to sell or make into *zaatar*, a delicious toasted sesame seed and thyme condiment. The air is deliciously fragrant with the lemony sweetness of the bruised leaves.

She has two gardens, she tells me. One is this patio on which are potted plants and flowers, and the other is her enormous allotment stretching behind the house to her husband's fields. Beneath the impossible sun it looks scrappy and bald in patches. The pale earth is blinding and the grasses beneath our feet scratch and scrunch. It is not a beautiful garden. Practical, yes, but certainly not beautiful. But then, what is a 'beautiful garden'?

Spotting some fully grown onions she kneels down to unearth them and points at the lemongrass, telling me to smell. Beyond her are the thyme fields and a few nectarine and lime trees. Previously, she grew pomelo and aubergine and had a greenhouse for seed propagation, but it was destroyed in the recent war when this whole area was torn apart by tanks.

Having harvested what she needs she dusts her brown velvet *abaya* and suggests we retire to the shade. Her husband brings us a Coke bottle filled with pre-boiled water (fresh running water having all but dried up thanks to Israeli sanctions) and she slices an onion as we talk. Like Huda's, Badria's vegetable garden means that despite limited means, they can still eat. 'It takes a lot of looking after, especially since the phosphorus, but how else can we survive?'

'But this garden,' she points to her pots, 'is just for enjoyment.'

The flowers, she explains, do what they like; they are her joy and company. There is a vine, which appears to be supporting the wire fence, and a pot of orange chrysanthemums at its root. A large daisy bush sits in a corner and a smart red carnation presides over everything. A mature rose is next to the vine. 'This morning some children came and stole some of the flowers,' she says sadly, but it is such a monochrome town that I am not surprised.

Her flower garden, I soon realise, is her 'room'. 'I try not to stay inside in the darkness unless there is danger. It is very gloomy and makes me worry about my children.'

With four children, Badria has much to worry about. 'We're in a state of relative calm at the moment, but war casts a long shadow,' she explains. In the last conflict one of her daughters was wounded by shell shrapnel. In the previous one, another daughter lost all her hair from fright and a third developed severe psychological problems and fitting. Her youngest son still has screaming nightmares. 'Suffering is just something you have to accept.'

We can hear the IDF training on the border and I am glad when she talks more loudly, using her voice to drown out the noise. Her hands shake but she continues to slice and wipes away a tear, blaming the onions and smiling up at me, but nevertheless embarrassed.

In addition to acting as a sanctuary, Badria's garden is also her sentry post. 'From the moment they are at school or out of the house I'm scared for my children. I look for them in the street from here until they're home and I can protect them. Even now, they are at school but I still worry. What if there is another war and I can't save them? At least if I'm out in the garden all the time I can watch for them,' she says laying down her knife and standing to lean on the fence, scanning the pallid dust. 'One day, I hope we will be living alongside Jews and we are all safe. To be safe is to be alive.'

She picks a small pink rose from the bush and gives it to me. Its petals are velvet soft and smell like smoky, sweet tea. Thanking her, I press it in the back pages of my Moleskine notebook. Four years later, I will find it again with the olive sprigs Jihadth had given me. Perfectly flat and an autumn pink, I frame them all between two sheets of glass which I hang on a wall.

The next day, the NGO drives me south to Khan Younis, the second-largest city in Gaza. It is about six and a half kilometres inland and so densely populated an area that the refugee camp of the same name became a target during the war of 2009 and suffered massive barrages of heavy artillery.

The farmland around the city stretches out to the border, three kilometres away, and although still technically part of Gaza, it belongs to Israel's unilaterally imposed and poorly delineated buffer zone known as the ARA: the Access Restricted Area. The zone comprises an estimated seventeen per cent of the entire territory and around a third of potential agricultural land. But being so close to the border, any farming permitted happens under the watchful eye of the border patrols at designated hours of the day.

We arrive at a brightly painted yellow and orange house. A path runs up to it and a gloriously golden field of wheat, benefitting from year-round sun, stretches all the way out to the border wall on my left. A rusting length of barbed wire hangs between wooden fence poles beneath which a few fragile poppies quiver in the faintest of breezes.

Hassan abu Daggar emerges from the house in a shiny tracksuit, flip-flops and thick spectacles. He is in a state of high excitement when we arrive and eager to speak to the NGO official.

The Israeli army, he tells them, crossed into the buffer zone at dawn that morning and started shooting at his house. 'Has another war started?' he keeps asking, hurrying us out of sight to the back of the house.

Two benches crudely fashioned out of wooden planks sit in the middle of a neat green lawn and pretty flower beds burst with holly-hocks, dog roses, geraniums and aromatic herbs. 'The kitchen garden,' Hassan says. 'Or at least it will be one day. For now, it is the safest place, out of sight.'

In the far corner there are a few chairs on a paved area beneath a peach tree. His five children are sitting close together and very silently on the concrete steps next to us. I smile at them but they look straight through me as if I am a ghost.

Notwithstanding the morning's shooting, Hassan lives in a state of perpetual concern. Three months ago a teenage boy was killed by what the IDF later claimed to be a stray bullet. He was playing football near the border. A year or so before that, another farmer strayed too close and was shot in the mouth by a sniper.

Hassan is not a wealthy landowner. The yield he produces from rented land is just enough to feed his family; their existence is hand-to-mouth, but he is following in the footsteps of his forefathers as a man of the earth.

The area is close to the border and vulnerable to a land incursion. It is also close to the smuggling tunnels of Raffah. 'They think we have tunnels here too and fire F16 rockets every now and then to scare us. It's no way to live, but what else are we supposed to do? Where are we meant to go?'

There was a moment after the last war when he thought that the conflict would be resolved but the result was just confusion. Unsurprisingly, living in the firing line has taken its toll on Hassan's family. 'Now, one of my sons is incontinent and one has lost the ability to speak. They can't be on their own. Ever.' I look at them and smile, hoping to elicit a smile back but their faces are blank. Sad children.

'My wife is a bag of nerves too. Any gunfire sets them all off. Last night was bad. When they start crying I don't know what to do to make it better. I feel so helpless.' It is clear Hassan is close to cracking. He is talking so hurriedly the translator has to get him to pause.

He takes a deep breath.

'That is why I made this green garden. We didn't have anything before – we didn't need it but it is the only place out of sight, and the only place where we feel protected and safe. It's a somewhere for them to relax.'

With such a young population, there is a real need for places where children can be children. In the West, the childhood 'monster' is a fairly innocent trope to counter disobedience which relies solely on the imagination. The 'monster' is the most frightening thing hiding in a cupboard, under a bed, down dark alleyways or at the bottom of a swimming pool and to be feared and revered. For Gazan children, the 'monster' is real and omnipresent, and Hassan is fulfilling the need for an 'anti-monster' with his garden. Unable to protect their reality of an omniscient militarised monster, he has created a safe world hidden from it where they are free to be children, 'a little perfect world.'

When I arrive back at my hotel just outside Gaza city that evening I'm in dire need of a leg stretch, and with a few hours left of sunlight I decide to walk into town with a vague notion of stopping at the Al Deira, a popular – and expensive – hotel overlooking the beach, for a bite to eat. I do not really know the way, but it is only about three or four kilometres and I have cash in my pocket for a taxi if I get lost. I follow the seashore south.

Quickly distracted, I stop at a spice shop along the main road and pick up some fresh *zaatar*, *sumac* and dried rosebuds that make a delicious tisane. At a convenience store a group of children follow me. The eldest is around twelve and swings his only leg between his crutches. Another boy is missing an eye. The other three are wild and manic and demand cigarettes. Youth is short in Gaza.

I continue through Al Shatti, a permanent refugee camp built for the Palestinians fleeing the 1948 war. The brick and cement conglomeration of tower blocks is today home to more than 85,000 refugees. It is around seventy times more populated than the centre of London, I am told later. There is little drinking water, a feeble power supply and a dearth of jobs.

I walk down to the sand, passing a massive sewage drain leading directly into the water through piles of litter and toxic waste. Further on, there are small groups of women and children sitting on the shore enjoying the evening sun and the sound of the water, successfully ignoring the rubbish.

I pass a silver-haired man with weathered mahogany skin and a young boy of around seven entwined like seaweed and looking out to the liminal horizon. They are sitting in a raised, recessed area delineated by a row of tyres overgrown with ice plants flowering pink around what appears to be a bamboo beach café. Wanting to ask about the succulents someone has so deliberately planted in rubber, I approach them.

The silver-haired man calls for the owner of the café who speaks English and is happy to act as an interpreter between the man, who is his friend, and myself. The café owner has a cousin in Birmingham and needs to practise his English.

The man's name is Awad abu Awad. His pale green eyes are lambent and made larger by the pin-pricks of his pupils, contracted from the gleam of the sea. 'A garden?' he says. 'No, I don't have a garden. There is no space in Gaza for a garden to feel free. Even the water is not ours.'

Awad is a fisherman and the café is favoured by fishermen returning to land after long days on the water. But while land close to the borders is a buffer zone, so too is the sea. It has been weeks since Abu Awad has fished.

Fishermen like him have access to less than a third of the fishing areas allocated under the Oslo accords. That's six out of a potential twenty nautical miles from the coast.

The loss of potential earnings is huge. At six nautical miles out Awad, with limited line and net length, struggles to catch many fish. 'The water close to the shore is polluted. It's untreated waste and contaminates the sea. Anything you catch here will poison you. You need to have bigger nets and better equipment which I can't afford.'

And if he accidentally strays beyond the boundary, navy ships shoot. 'My boy was asleep in the boat with me the other day,' – he squeezes his son – 'and he woke up to the sound of shelling and gunfire. It was terrifying.'

The few fish that he does catch he sells and makes around $100 a month, although prices are decreasing daily thanks to cheaper alternatives from Egypt.

He blames Hamas for the troubles. 'They are worse than Israel. All they want to do is strangle us.' Like Hassan abu Daggar, like everyone, he is in prison and he never stops holding on to his son or looking at the sea as he talks like a mer-king.

But he laughs when I mention having spent time in Afghanistan. 'Wow! Now *they* have got problems.'

He returns his gaze to the green seam of water in the distance. 'I have just one dream – to be able to build a house for my family to live in comfortably and for my children to have a happy and a safe life. But until that time, this patch of greenery is where I come to breathe.'

He pauses and adds something which makes the café owner laugh. 'He says he has one more dream: to travel to the West Bank. He heard it was the most beautiful place in the world. He is right.'

I never make it to the Al Deira Hotel restaurant but stay instead in the café with its owner, Abu Awad and his son perched on a tyre watching the ocean ebb and flow with the moon's rhythm – an untameable body of water, unable to be owned or controlled.

Is the land similarly un-ownable? The war might be the commonality here for Jews and Arabs but land is the universal protagonist. Land means so much to so many and in so many guises, and it is mapped both physically and in our mind's eye. We love it, want it, feel it, feel born of it, tied to it, part of it and ask to be buried *in* it.

We can temporarily possess land, occupy it, tame it, burn it, cement it, but can we ever really *own* it? The countries in which we live are black-ink outlines upon maps and their borders, checkpoints and barbed wire barriers are conjurings of social and political imaginations. But the issue of owning it is so fraught that the ground beneath us – the soil, clay, chalk, lime, mineral particles, geosmin, the leaves rotted with time – is explosively potent – the Jews and Arabs hate each other *because* of it. Wars *are* land.

But perhaps gardening and trying to control the land is the closest we can come to making a piece of the earth – at least for a while – our own. It is, after all, the last thing we will ever know.

But we can never own the sea. And Abu Awad, the mer-king next to me, knows it in his core.

3

The sea is lapping gently outside. Overly hot and sleepless, I listen to it pulling at the shore with the to and fro of a heartbeat. I go to the window and pull back the cheap nylon curtains to let in some air. The sun has yet to come up but the darkness is beginning to melt into the flat grey water. Unlike yesterday, there is a thick mist obscuring the horizon, a fuzzy wall hiding the rest of the world. I stare at it, trying to stare through it, but can see nothing but obfuscation. On the shore, a few small rowing boats prepare to push out blindly into the wall.

A thud in the distance is followed by the faint stutter of artillery. The boats on the water don't alter their course but pull themselves into the sea mist until they are entirely enveloped and only the sulphurous light of the battleships remain.

I fall into a warped dream memory of Sangin, southern Helmand. I am with American marines and we are in a walled garden of red roses, pelargoniums, begonias and runner beans. There are butterflies and honey bees drinking from a sunflower and a bird larks shrilly from an apple tree. But the battle taking place a kilometre or so outside the compound walls is louder than the bird and we hear the thud of artillery and the stuttering clatter of rifles.

We hear over the intercepted radio frequencies that 'the garden compound' is surrounded. The enemy is preparing to attack. 'Leave no survivors,' the interpreter translates. We are trapped. I look at the faces of the soldiers, expecting to see deadpan calm, but see instead a sweating fear. In time with the shells landing outside and in time with the waves lapping at the shore the collective heartbeat of the soldiers in that wilted walled garden is deafening. I look around at the garden but it has inexplicably faded. My camera strap tightens around my neck and I feel like I am falling. I awake gasping for air.

A few hours later I meet Ghada in the hotel. She is a friend of an old friend who put us in touch. She is vivacious, has a dry wit, a sense of the silly, an infectious laugh and I like her before our coffees have even arrived.

It is Friday, the start of the weekend in most Islamic countries, and Ghada, who is a teacher, suggests spending the day together. I have an appointment with a roof-top gardener but she says she has nothing else to do and is happy to interpret. 'Besides,' she says as we climb into a taxi, 'I'm nosy! I want to meet the gardeners of Gaza!'

The sea mist has dissipated and the residue of moisture radiates a diamond-bright light. The sharp clarity of the world from the car window is familiar. The streets are empty today but through open doors in gates I catch glimpses of family life: old men sitting on chairs fiddling with prayer beads; grandchildren playing or helping the women of the household with chores; a bonnet of a car is raised and the engine being hammered; a young girl reaching to a vine overhead. Small groups begin to emerge from their homes, errands in mind, and as we pass a market, a cacophonous rabble haggles over piles of fruit and vegetables.

These glimpsed vignettes remind me of Kabul. It is just five months since I left Afghanistan but in the intervening months in London I felt dead, alone and perversely homesick for the raw never land of Central Asia. And although Gaza is more secular then Kabul, less obviously militarised and more crowded, the two cities occupy a liminal, isolated space cut off from the rest of the world and are thus linked through their rawness and strive to exist despite war.

The taxi drops us at the end of a narrow street in the middle of the Daraj district, one of the most densely populated quarters of Gaza. The street is made darker than most by the sheer height of the buildings. There are few people around, only a little girl in a blue tracksuit and an old man sitting silently, lost in thought. Above him are some faded posters, faces undulating across the corrugated iron fences, mourning the loss of those killed in the conflict.

In a workshop making *zibdiye*, the heavy clay bowls used with wooden pestles few Gazan kitchens are without, we ask if anyone knows Abu Ahmed.

Of course they do; it's a tight-knit neighbourhood. They direct us to a building a few metres away.

Inside the heavy steel and iron door it is dark and dingy. It smells grimy but we start climbing the deep-set concrete stairs to the sixth floor and knock at a plywood door, slightly breathless from the sudden exertion.

A young girl of around sixteen or seventeen wearing a grey hijab and a black *abaya* answers. She takes us inside and up a further two flights of stairs inside the apartment and onto a flat roof. We have a 360-degree view of the urban landscape of Gaza: a mouth of jagged concrete teeth, knocked about in a bare-knuckle fight, steel construction beams, satellite dishes, cement frames. Everything clings vertically to the natural contour lines of the ground, a middle distance rising and falling like the dunes which had come before them. I am struck by how small Gaza is, how easily I can see the security walls and a glimmer of southern Israel beyond. A tantalising view of freedom.

In stark contrast to the urban setting, the roof is lush and green and almost entirely given over to large blue plastic trays raised on wooden slats and bricks. Rocket, tomatoes, onions, cabbage and lettuces grow out of them and a thin meshed netting provides shade. Beneath a thicker tarpaulin at the edge of the roof are lines of plastic drains cut open with holes at regular intervals. More lettuces and onions grow through them.

A man leans over one of the trays, engrossed by two small test tubes of coloured liquid and clearly perplexed he notes something down on a piece of paper before tucking a red pencil behind his ear and apologises for not having met us at the door.

Abu Ahmed comes from a long line of farmers who worked on land now part of Israel. With no other choice but to adapt, he is now a hydroponic gardener using hydro-culture to garden without soil. Plants grow on gravel or on rocks with only their roots exposed to a mineral nutrient solution made up of fish waste. It is gardening at its most elemental and deconstructed, but an ingenious solution in a land so bereft of space.

His blind sister was the initial beneficiary of a UNFAO (United Nations Food and Agricultural Organisation) programme to enable landless Gazans to farm. She was given a few large pots and stones to begin with. Without work, Abu Ahmed took it upon himself to expand the project with her once he understood the rudimentary principles of hydroponic gardening.

The only thing hindering this type of gardening is the need for electricity for the water pump and a constant supply of decent water, neither of which are reliable in Gaza. There are power outages for hours every day but, worse than that, the coastal aquifer, having been over-pumped to accommodate the expanding population, is deteriorating. Over 60 per cent of Gazans do not have access to a continuous supply of water, and it is estimated that by 2020 there won't be any at all.

Abu Ahmed tries not to let these things affect him and is satisfied that at least what he grows is free from pesticides and poison. At such a height, the wind can damage the leaves, 'but on the other hand,' he says with a shrug, 'this is such a good place to come and breathe fresh air. It's the calmest place in Gaza.'

He shows us the different plant varieties he is growing, and the more I look, the stranger it seems. With so many drains and pipes and gigantic tanks given over to gardening, it is as if the natural world has started to reclaim the industrial one. It is both modern and futuristic, yet with the backdrop of the drab, grey high-rises, semi-apocalyptic. He shows us the abundant lettuces and herbs and a lemon tree he is trying out. 'It's still early days but I'm hoping to bring the citrus trees back to Gaza. It's an amazing thing to look at a seed and think that it has the potential to feed us.'

He takes out his acidity regulating kit at one of the blue trays and them moves droplets between test tubes, simultaneously noting down the results.

'God says it is good to be surrounded by greenery. It takes twenty minutes by car to find something green in Gaza but here, I have it all.'

I ask him if his garden was affected by the conflict. 'War is war,' he shrugs. 'It is psychological, it is religious, it is fear. But we are still standing.' He describes having to bury the headless body of his brother; he had been decapitated by shrapnel from an explosion near Beit Lahiya where they had been visiting friends.

If he is affected by the memory, he certainly doesn't show it and continues pipetting, annotating and chatting simultaneously.

But like Huda, Badria and Hassan, Abu Ahmed feels helpless faced with the need to protect his children against 'the monster'. 'How do you provide for your family during war?' he says. 'There is no water, no gas, no electricity, no food in the shops. In the last war people were eating anything they could. Rats, mice, everything. At least we have food up here.'

The girl who opened the door to us, Esra, appears from behind a row of overgrown drainage pipes. Beneath her *abaya* I can see she is wearing skinny jeans and sparkly black sandals. There is a silver and pink 'Hello Kitty' necklace peeking out from under her hijab and brightly coloured tin bangles jangle from her wrists. She asks if we would like to see her flowers.

Part of the floor beneath is a vast concrete room of about twenty square metres. It is only half built and has no windows. Instead a tarpaulin blocks out the elements, which renders everything a lurid green. There is a large table, a handful of metal chairs and two sofas with foam spilling out at their seams. On one side the tarpaulin has been replaced by a neat wooden picket fence beneath which are mismatching window boxes and flowerpots. Some have been doodle-painted with flowers and leaves. There are geraniums, spider plants, chrysanthemums, a dahlia and even a cabbage.

The walls are covered in pastel chalk drawings: a boat with enormous sails, a horse, an outline of Al-Aqsa (the Islamic shrine on the Temple Mount in Jerusalem's Old City from which the prophet Mohammed is said to have descended into heaven), and a map of the Holy Land with 'Freedom to Palestine' written over it in pink. The whole thing is surrounded by love hearts and her name several times over.

This is clearly Esra's 'room'.

'I prefer it on the rooftop upstairs,' she says, Ghada translating simultaneously, 'I take my friends there too. They love it. At night you can see the moon so clearly. It is nice to eat up there. I like spending time with my dad too. He is a wise man and knows everything about gardening. I want to learn as much as possible from him. Older people can teach you a lot about life. But when it gets too hot, I like to sit here with my flowers and study. Flowers are hope and life. Life and death live so closely together here that you come to realise that very small things can bring you great moments of happiness. Everything stops during war. You realise that every dream you have belongs to someone else – the Israelis.'

She gets up to move a geranium pot three inches to the left. There is a baby pigeon sitting on the edge of a window box and, having been discovered, it coos crossly and flaps it wings in protest. But it doesn't fly away, instead sinking back into its plumage.

'You see,' she says, 'there is life up here.'

In abundance, I think to myself, in absolute abundance.

Esra sees us out of the apartment and down to the street. When Ghada and I each decide to buy a *zibdiye*, the craftsmen wave away any suggestion of payment. I still don't know if it is because of the respect they have for Abu Ahmed's family or because Ghada charmed them or because they were just feeling generous.

'Hungry?' Ghada asks. She takes me to Atfaluna.

From the outside it looks like one of those restaurants aspiring to Dubai's international standards but lacking resources and skilled chefs, one which almost always ends up being an expensive and indigestible experience.

Silly me. Atfaluna is staffed entirely by the deaf and run as an NGO of sorts. I still order modestly, ignorant of the prices in Arabic script, but Ghada overrules me and orders almost everything.

We feast on a selection of fish, hummus, sizzled aubergines, grilled artichoke hearts, stuffed peppers, pickled cheeses, slices of beef, chicken à la something delicious and braised lamb kebabs.

We begin talking about some of the gardeners I have met during my travels in this area. 'The only thing that is bothering me,' I say, 'is that apart from the cactus guy, they are all farmers to whom flower gardening is second nature. I wonder if there are any people who garden *only* because it's something beautiful to do, and not because they already can.'

Ghada ponders and then says that yes, she thinks there are. One of her pupils has an uncle with a garden and once we have digested lunch we head to Jabaliya in a taxi. It is halfway between Gaza City and Beits Lahiya and Hanoun, and suffered similar destruction over the years. Perhaps worse, as its refugee camp was considered to be a Hamas stronghold and pounded.

In the intervening years much of Jabaliya has been rebuilt and I am confused, therefore, as to where we are when we arrive at a nondescript fence of upended wooden boards around two metres high. Two of them read 'The Palestinian Political Prisoners and ex-Prisoners Association 1996'. Another is from a UN agency. The signs, I quickly realise, are incidental. They are just pasteboards upcycled into an enclosure wall.

The door swings open on a wire hinge before we have even enquired if we are in the right place. Naif Dubaidi is small and bright and impish in clean navy trousers and a whiter than white T-shirt, around three sizes too big for him, with sleeves hanging well below his elbows.

'Are you the people from the television?' he asks eagerly.

Ghada corrects him and he invites us in.

His garden is a climbing frame. Scaffolding poles have been fixed into a frame for young plants to climb and creep their way up. Baskets and pots hang from the horizontals above us: geraniums, ferns, cacti. The orange dust of the flower beds below has had to make way for immaculate grass pathways intersecting the garden. Onions with their allium-like flower balls are tall and indifferent to the bees on the bright orange snapdragon angling for their attention. A mature red rose climbs through a palm tree, an elaeagnus slashes the shadow yellow beneath a shelf of yet more pelargoniums. The grass path becomes a playful pattern of three squares. At the back, there are raised squares and beds, ready to be planted. On another shelf are Naif's tools and a couple of bicycles.

It is a riot of acid spring green and bright punctuations of colour befitting a young spring garden and, at around five metres square, it is also a large garden. The fact that it is walled and hidden from the road reminds me of an Afghan compound and I feel strangely at home here.

Under a vine, Naif has laid out a dusty bottle of Coca-Cola, an expensive luxury I feel guilty he bought. He shoos away any concern; like his father, he is a shopkeeper and soft drinks are not hard to come by.

Through his shop he has been able to gauge Gaza's situation. 'Life since the occupation has been turned upside down. Over the years there has been less and less money available for people and I have fewer and fewer customers. It is sad to watch – especially the young. I just think for them it's like a life sentence four times over. My generation saw life before the blockade.'

He explains that the garden he had before this one was full of rare flowers he had collected over thirty-five years and trees twice as large. 'It was magic. People came from all around to see it.' He and his family had been taking refuge a few kilometres away during the 2009 war. When it was over they returned to find that a single shell had rendered it a cratered sandbank packed against the side of the house.

He was undeterred and coped by recreating his own version of heaven on earth. He systematically set out to 're-root' and to dig.

'There's no suffering here today. When I'm working on the plants, I think the best of life again. I have energy, hopes and dreams. I always wanted to have a huge garden when I was younger but this is all I can afford now. If it was bigger, I'd plant things you'd never seen before and I'd have a pond full of fish, trees full of birds and maybe some horses. I couldn't live without a green space.'

He closes the gate behind us, holding a hoe in one hand, and we hear him sigh happily before whistling softly as he scrapes away at the earth, at peace in his heaven.

Ghada suggests we go back to Gaza City via the graveyard.

I am a little unsure why but already know better than to doubt her. The car pulls up at a long avenue lined with cypress trees which looks more like it's leading us to a plush villa in Tuscany than a cemetery in the middle of Gaza.

It leads us to a limestone archway and a shoulder-height wall over which vermillion roses ramble. On the other side of the wall are the dead: thousands of white headstones in neat, regimented rows. Each grave is surrounded by planted flowers: geraniums, rosemary and daisies in a neatly clipped lawn. There are olive trees and buddleias dotting the grass, and butterflies flit through the afternoon sun.

The Commonwealth Gaza War Cemetery was completed in 1920 and is home to the graves of over 3,200 British and Commonwealth servicemen who lost their lives in Gaza in 1917 when the British were fighting their way into Palestine against the Ottoman Turks still in control of most of the Middle East. They hit a wall of enemy machine guns and shells and suffered an estimated 6,000 casualties in three days. Around 800 headstones lack identification and are marked simply with 'Soldier of the Great War. Known unto God.'

For forty-five years the graves have been tended to by Ibrahim Jeradda, aged seventy-six. He took on the mantle of responsibility from his father when he turned eighteen, and as his own son has recently taken the reins, Jeradda has officially retired. Unofficially he doesn't quite trust in his son (now in his fifties) to do the job properly, and watches over the cemetery gardens through beady, eagle eyes.

With his walking stick and long brown *jubba thobe* – a floor-length traditional man's shirt – covered with a brown knitted cardigan, he looks every inch a custodian. We three make a ludicrous trio as we walk through the avenues of headstones. Hard of hearing, he shouts his answers to Ghada who has to shout back at him and then, forgetting to adjust the volume, shouts the answers at me, making me jump every so often in surprise.

The cemetery is home to Christians and Jews, each headstone marked with a cross or star accordingly, which Jeradda shouts at and points out with his walking stick. Ghada and I chuckle behind him.

We walk among the first few rows of graves and he lists the different flowers adorning them: marigolds, red geraniums, cornflowers, Michaelmas daisies and carnations. 'I feel what these plants feel,' he says, his voice softening a little, 'I have to make sure they are fresh and happy at each grave. If they are wilting and sad, so am I.'

In his office (a small shed) he pulls out a medal box. It takes me a while to work out what I'm supposed to be looking at, but then he waves the framed certificate and I read the Duke of Kent's signature.

It is an MBE. He was awarded the honour in 'grateful recognition of outstanding contribution to the Commonwealth War Graves Commission'.

He pins it to his cardigan and we walk back to the graves and sit on a low carved stone seat in the slanting sunbeams of the afternoon.

The cemetery became a battleground in 2009 and 280 graves were damaged. The Israeli military blamed explosions from a Palestinian ammunition cache they had hit, the Palestinians blamed the Israeli troops for deliberately destroying the cemetery. The War Graves Commission weren't allowed into Gaza to survey the damage so it was left to Jeradda and his team to assess. 'It is our duty to care for both the living and the dead. There are no borders here. This is Palestine. The souls are now in paradise and that's all that's important. They are at peace now and nothing can hurt them.'

After the war came the clean-up. 'We replanted and grassed, bit by bit, and restored or replaced the headstones, piece by piece. War is war,' he says philosophically. 'It is always a big story. People have been fighting since time began.'

But there is another more urgent challenge Jeradda and his band of gardeners face, he says, as a mournful muezzin begins a call to prayer. Water. He has a sprinkler irrigation system but the water quality is poor. If it's not saline, it contains too much chlorine. Very rarely is it fresh. And like Abu Ahmed, his irrigation system struggles with the power cuts.

'But this is my garden,' he says, 'I make sure it is always looked after, come what may.'

He walks us around to his nursery, a floral delight blooming with small plants and shrubs waiting to take the place of those that die thanks to poor water.

It is not a historical garden like the Emperor Babur's in Kabul, but there is something about its formality and the on-going restoration that is familiar. There is a similarity between Jeradda's personal pride and that of Engineer Khoistani's, the chief horticulturalist in Kabul.

The cemetery is a monument to the fallen, but with the overwhelming lack of public parks in Gaza, people seek ing a calm place to picnic find their way there often. In order to avoid being overrun, or worse, allowing in bored vandals, he closes on Fridays, granting special privileges to a small number of his 130 grand- or great-grandchildren to visit 'on rotation'. A group of them is sitting quietly beneath a tree on the other side of the garden and he squints at them, saying, 'Yes, those are mine,' and leaves us.

Ghada takes a phone call and I walk between the graves.

To read the headstones is deeply moving. A carved Star of David catches my eye. Rifleman Magasiner, 11th Battalion London Regiment, died 9 November 1917 aged twenty-one. Next to him is Rifleman Glithero from the same battalion, same date of death but a year younger. There is a cross beneath his name, and a lump rises in my throat when I read the sparse epitaph: 'Not forgotten by his mother and father.' Then there is Private A.T. Avison, Machine Gun Corps, died 15 November 1917, aged thirty-three, buried with a cross amidst carnations. Second Lieutenant R. Allison, Denbigh Yeomanry, 16 June 1917, aged twenty-five. A small pink snapdragon is at his headstone. Second Lieutenant Joseph, Northamptonshire Regiment, died 19 April 1917, aged twenty-one. Tiny sea snails crawl over his

Star of David, perhaps out of the sea grass at the foot of the headstone. Private Alexander, 10th Battalion the London Regiment, died 15 August, 1917. His twenty-year life is marked with daisies. The names continue, and on every row are new dates, new ages, and new abrupt endings to short lives. A list of names in another foreign corner of a field that is, for them, forever England. Far, far from home.

That evening, Ghada and I meet up with one of her friends and we walk along the marina packed with people enjoying the warm evening and getting on with living. The beaches are full of people too, and touts patrol with plastic swimming rings and armbands. Defying the faint whiff of sewage sulphur, a group of women escape the heat in the shallow water, fully clothed, their robes swirling next to plastic wrappers. A boy throws handfuls of water up to the sky, large droplets catching its fading light and carrying it back to the ocean.

We sit on a bench and eat corn on the cob from a street vendor and agree not to talk about Israel, the blockade, Hamas or even gardens. Instead we laugh at a group of children cartwheeling in front of us, gossip about our crappy love lives and our plans to lose weight while openly lusting after the pink candyfloss touted a few metres away.

It is a happy evening by the sea.

'We have been locked up like prisoners. We cannot fish, we cannot farm, there are no jobs, there is no water, there is no food,' says Eymad Gazal as we walk through his garden.

'But if *they* die, *we* die,' he says, checking the underside of a lemon tree's leaves for black spot. At first I think he's talking about the

Israelis, but then I realise he means bees.

Today is my last day in Gaza and I am working with Hazem the fixer again.

Like his father, who taught him the basics, Eymad is a beekeeper, but on his own admission, 'it is hard to keep bees in Gaza.'

It is a large orchard garden of citrus trees and palm fronds. It is not particularly beautiful; functional high-rise apartment blocks loom over it and the noise from a nearby construction site is intrusive. Pots of flowering geraniums and roses sit on a balustraded veranda of his relatively opulent house.

'Orange groves and lemon trees have grown here for centuries, but now many have slowly withered and died,' he explains. 'Many were pulled up or burned in 2005 when the Israelis were forced to leave the Gaza Strip. The trees that remain are vulnerable to drought and the construction of new buildings – 'concrete trees' he calls them, pointing at the looming apartment buildings.

He keeps most of his hives in the ARA, the Access Restricted Area which runs the length of the border. 'It is the only place that will not be built over.' Of course the restricted access has its drawbacks. 'When the Israeli army comes over the border, it becomes a complete no-go area and I cannot check on them. But they carry on trying to make honey regardless; they fly into Israel or Egypt to collect nectar. Bees do not see borders.'

He wants to show me the hives he keeps close by. We walk out to the dirt track outside his house and he grabs some smocks from the back of his car, handing me one. It feels peculiar wearing a second layer of clothing, not to mention hot beneath the baking sun sailing across the sky and a rising humidity. Beads of sweat start to trickle down my back. I struggle with the gloves – they are too big for me to be able to hold the camera properly. The apiarist's facemask feels unnatural too, like being in an old diving suit, but I tell myself to stop being so precious.

We are now standing in a grove of orange, lemon, date and pear trees. It is pastoral and peaceful and the sound of construction a few hundred metres away has vanished. Eymad planted them for the bees now residing in the half-dozen hives dotted in the grove. Lines from The Lake Isle of Innisfree, my favourite W.B. Yeats poem, pop into my head: 'Nine bean-rows will I have there, a hive for the honey-bee / and live alone in the bee-loud glade. / And I shall have some peace there, for peace comes dropping slow.'

Unfussed by the buzzing and swarming around him in his glade, he puts on his smock and mask but leaves the gloves off.

'Won't you get stung?' I shout.

'I do not feel it any more,' he shouts back nonchalantly, and reaches for the tin smoker.

When Eymad starts smoking the bees they cloud angrily around both of us. It's uncomfortable and unnerving. My instinctive reaction is to start flapping and run away, but I breathe deeply and trust that the protective clothing is thick. I try to take some photographs but the bees have covered my camera like spilled oil. The images are slightly wonky and overexposed. He lifts out the trays of sweet comb and shows me the thousands of hexagonal homes. The honey glistens in the sunlight and my tummy rumbles.

Back on his veranda Eymad makes me taste various batches.

Shamefully, my palate is too immature to detect the nuances of each type, but my greed is voracious and I feel rather like Winnie the Pooh.

Although it was his father who originally taught him, Eymad has received specialist training from Israeli apiarists and has been able to travel around the region learning more advanced techniques. 'Everyone knows how important bees are to our ecosystem, and the beekeepers over there want to keep their bees happy and free from blight so for this alone Israel and Gaza work together.' His special dispensation allows him to maintain his hives to a decent standard. 'Officially, that is where I get my queens from.'

'And unofficially?' I ask.

He chuckles. 'I once bought a beautiful queen from a Turkish beekeeper I met in Israel. I wrapped her up in a tissue and smuggled her back into Gaza in my suit handkerchief pocket.'

Eymad's bees might not see borders or war but they certainly endure the suffering. His own stock has diminished from 800 colonies to 400, and each of them produces only a third of what they used to. He hazards a guess that pesticides are to blame, 'or maybe they are empathising with us,' he jokes. With cheaper Egyptian imports, he has also had to drop his honey prices, which means that his turnover has shrunk by three quarters: from $40,000 a year to just $10,000.

But Eymad, like Abu Ahmed, does it for love. 'Life in Gaza *is* very difficult and our future is unclear. Eventually there will be no fresh water and we will be living in a concrete jungle or be eradicated entirely by Israel. But when I am with my bees in my garden I feel more hopeful – I breathe the fresh air and feel healthy.'

He takes a spoonful of honey, having given me my third, saying, 'the sting of life in Gaza disappears with bees.'

That night I sit in the hotel restaurant watching the sun sink into the wine-dark sea. Salt sprays the air and my notebook is damp. As I write, the ink smears beneath my hand, already made uneven by Badria's rose, pressed in between the back pages. A succulent ice plant creeps to the water from the beach, its yellow flowers scattering a luminous phosphorescence on the sand. Storm clouds swarm on the horizon and, as the light dims, their liverish underbellies break with fissures of electricity.

'We are expecting another war,' Ghada had told me when we heard distant artillery fire snapping outside the cemetery. 'The political situation is complicated and there is more activity outside than normal so it is not *if*, it is *when*. All we can do is prepare.'

It takes a year for her predictions to be realised. On 8 July 2014, after a miniature game of cat and mouse between Israel and Hamas, a seven-week war explodes. Sixty-six Israeli soldiers and seven civilians are killed in Israel. Over 2,100 Palestinians are killed in Gaza, two thirds of whom are civilians. Gaza – and its gardens – is destroyed once again.

But I am not to know that as I make the long walk through the caged walkway and back to Israel.

Israel Kibbutzim

May 2013

'Two things cannot be in one place.
Where you tend a rose, my lad, a thistle cannot grow.'

Frances Hodgson Burnett, *The Secret Garden*

1

My passport stamps look suspicious to the border guards so I am made to wait.

I watch them doing nothing apart from watching me and how I react to their suspicion. It is a psychological game and there is no point questioning it or them.

When a few Gazans with medical dispensation arrive the guards jump into action, barking orders and manhandling a confused elderly lady in a wheelchair.

It is degrading to watch and I turn away.

My suitcase and camera bag is up next for inspection. Every item of dirty laundry is examined, every bottle of shampoo, conditioner, tube of toothpaste, the honey Eymad had given me and even some preserved aubergines from Ghada's mother are scrutinised. I protest when they try to confiscate the food and a senior guard intervenes. I'm allowed to keep the honey but the aubergines are binned.

The guards move on to their next victim, a mother carrying a small wailing baby. I look up at a security camera and a metal door buzzes open. My bags are searched, my papers inspected and I am made to wait again.

A second door opens and I am free to enter Israel.

It is immediately and undeniably modern and clean, and the contrast with Gaza just behind me is stark. The asphalted car park is pristine, there is a coffee vending machine, there are few buildings. Dazed, I am unsure whether I have just dreamed Gaza. But I find my hire car, drop my bags in the boot, sit at the steering wheel and change SIM cards – unlike most neighbouring countries, neither Gaze nor Israel have networks which recognise each other.

I look at the map on my iPhone and orientate the day ahead.

During the war in 2009, frustrated by being unable to get into Gaza until a ceasefire, I had spent a lot of time in the kibbutzim and moshavim on the border interviewing people as the sky smouldered.

Kibbutzim (kibbutz in the singular) are communal settlements in Israel usually based on agriculture. Moshavim (moshav in the singular) are slightly larger and more of a cooperative settlement of individual farms.

The first kibbutzim were founded in the early twentieth century by young socialist Zionists fleeing the pogroms of Eastern Europe. Their dream was not just to settle land but to build a totally new society, and one which was inclusive to both Jews and Arabs.

In the early days, living was rough. The mountains of Judea were rocky and inhospitable. Galilee in the north was boggy and the desert of the Negev in the south was arid. Malaria, typhus and cholera were prolific, but the early pioneers were determined to realise their dream, and by the 1930s and '40s numbers of kibbutzim were flourishing and their populations expanded exponentially where they were able to absorb the flood of refugees fleeing persecution in Europe and neighbouring Arab countries.

As unrest between the Jews and Arabs began to rise, kibbutzim became more militarised, and an important part in the development of the Israeli state.

The kibbutzim are founded on the same principles of communal living and working and equal share of all things community related; members of the kibbutz are required to give themselves and everything they have to the good of the collective.

The collapse of Communism resulted in the temporary weakening of socialist beliefs around the world – including in the kibbutzim. Their rural patterns of settlement also sat at odds with the increasing popularity of urban settlements rapidly expanding in the West Bank, and the 1980s saw a huge decline in membership. The general and, some would argue, global plummet in 'self-sacrifice' has further contributed to the decline of the original dream of the early agrarian Zionists. Today's kibbutzim are different places entirely.

In 2009 I found them to be peculiar cul-de-sacs of bungalows and chalet-style houses. There were manicured communal areas, playgrounds and community centres. But each house had a garden, and the memory of them stuck with me ever since. The kibbutzim close to Gaza are the intended target of Hamas rockets and I want to find the gardeners here who live in the shadow of war.

In the Erez crossing car park I stare down at a small digital map. I pick a kibbutz three kilometres away and, lighting a cigarette, pull onto the smooth tarmac motorway.

The road into Zikim is flanked by ripening fields of wheat and barley, stretching down to a sliver of sand I had glimpsed from Abu Ahmed's hydroponic roof. A tractor rolls through a light dust in the distance and, further beyond, the industrial factory chimneys of Ashkelon ribbon the midday heat grey.

Zikim takes its name from the Hebrew *zik* meaning 'point of light in the wilderness'. A wilderness it must have been when a group of Romanians settled it in 1949. Emigrants from the United Kingdom soon followed, and I was later to learn that Bob Hoskins had lived there in the late 1960s as a volunteer.

The yellow steel entrance gate to the kibbutz, usually manned by Israeli soldiers, is deserted and wide open so I drive straight in and park in the shade of a tall fir tree. I grab my notebook and camera and begin the search for the gardens on foot. It is a short search, for at the end of a cul-de-sac I come across a house with a large patio, over which are hanging pots of zealous pink geraniums, cacti, a very young olive tree and a pelargonium with lemon-scented leaves. The gardeners, Avraham Atzili and his wife, Etti, are sitting on the veranda reading newspapers.

It is a little unusual to enter a kibbutz without being formally invited by one of its members so they are surprised to see me. But they put down their papers and, while Etti puts the kettle on, Avraham shows me some of the new ferns he has been planting on a shaded shelf.

They have lived there, he tells me, for fifty-eight years. 'In 1955 we started with just a wooden hut. There were no restrooms or anything like that.' Both born in Israel, they were members of socialist youth movements and joined the kibbutz shortly afterwards as part of the development of the state of Israel.

'It was like living in the middle of the desert back then. There was nothing here.' He was serving as a Nahal soldier. Nahal soldiers were the paramilitary wing of the Israeli Defence Forces encouraged to help establish – and defend – agricultural settlements. 'I was digging trenches, not flower beds,' he says. 'Security was always a problem.'

Etti joins us with a pot of strong black coffee and a plate of biscuits. 'And now?' I ask.

'The Quassam from Gaza are the problem,' he says. Rockets. 'Most of the time they go straight over us or are shot down by the Dome.' The Iron Dome is a highly sophisticated weapon-defence system shielding Israel from aerial attacks. 'In the last war, we stopped counting after a hundred rockets.'

'It is scary,' Etti says, 'but you get used to it and you know to go to the shelter.' She points at a square of concrete tacked onto the edge of their house I assumed was an extension. 'Everyone ran away to other parts of the country in the last war, but fleeing is not the answer.'

'Before the blockade,' Avraham says, 'there were fewer rockets and things were a lot easier. There was a free flow over the border; Gazans would come up here to work and everyone was friendly with each other. What can you say about it now though? We always feel unsafe, as if we are in a constant state of war, and I imagine it is the same for them too.'

'I can't imagine how it will ever stop.' Etti shakes her head.

'The garden brings you to a place of peace. It makes you think about peace, tranquillity and makes you feel calm,' Avraham says.

Etti nods. 'When I get up in the morning, I am glad to see the green leaves, the flowers and the sea. Welcoming the day like that lifts you. I sometimes tell the flowers that I love them, but behind his back,' she stage-whispers, pushing the biscuits towards me. 'Have you seen many gardeners here?' she asks.

We are around three kilometres from Abu Faisal and his pastel roses, and Jihadth with his son's tree are no more than four kilometres away so, technically, yes, I have seen many gardeners here, but I don't want to tell them I was in Gaza. There might not be a war on but relations between the two sides are stretched. Instead I tell them they are the first gardeners I've spoken to here, 'in Zikim'.

'You should meet Jaqui,' Avraham says suddenly. 'His garden is wonderful. Come! He'll be eating. I shall take you to lunch.' He creaks up from his chair and takes me to the community centre and up to a communal dining hall.

There are a dozen or so long tables stretching across the room at which are sitting the kibbutznik enjoying lunch. The arrival of a stranger to their community raises a few eyebrows, but as one of the oldest members, I suspect Avraham can do what he likes. 'There he is.' He spots his friend, waves and then directs me to the canteen where there are pans of boiled vegetables, chips, chicken and pasta. I am ravenous and, loading my plate, follow him to the end of a table where his friend is nursing a coffee.

They speak to each other for a while in Hebrew.

Jaqui nods, drains his coffee and says something to me. I understand not a word and shake my head. 'English?'

It is his turn to shake his head. '*Deutsche?*' he asks. '*Ruski?*'

I shake my head again but say hopefully, '*Français?*'

114

'*Mais oui!*' he says incredulously, '*Je suis français! Et vous? Vous êtes française?*'

I tell him that I am English and that although I am rusty, I was nearly fluent in French a long, long time ago.

'*Bon,*' he says, 'Come and find me when you are finished.' He nods to the rest of the room and leaves.

Half an hour later Avraham directs me through the kibbutz to Jaqui's house. 'You won't miss it,' he says. 'Just look for the clocks.'

I arrive at a painting hanging on the exterior wall of a bomb shelter. It is a simple beach scene: sky, sand and a willowy figure in the sea, but the tableau is complicated by a piece of driftwood which has been stuck to the wall. A clock melts off the painting to join it, Dali-style. Another hangs like laundry over the driftwood.

Jaqui is waiting for me. 'I have to go and run some errands but I will show you the rockets first.'

And there, beneath the melting clocks are two mangled contortions of metal shell casings with a few plants growing out of them.

'We had five or so Qassam land recently, and they make good flowerpots, don't you think?' He is right, they do make good flowerpots, and we head inside through his eclectic garden of sculptures, paintings, flora and fauna.

Introducing me to his wife, Marlene, he leaves. She makes fresh coffee and asks about the gardens of Kabul. 'People are people, no matter where. They will always make gardens. It is human nature,' she shrugs.

They have lived in the kibbutz for thirty-six years, moving from Paris to adopt a purer version of socialism.

She explains that when they first arrived there were just a few buildings and the dining hall. The countryside looked as it does now, although the skyline of Ashkelon was smaller. And there were certainly no issues with Gaza.

'I used to work with twelve Palestinians in the dairy farm. They needed the work and we needed help. We were all friends and would go shopping and hang out in the Gaza markets at weekends where there was always fresh fruit and fish. But the first intifada[5] changed all that. The whole region exploded again.'

Having lived with the sound and the fury since then, they are now used to the rocket threat. If anything, fear of Qassam makes them more resolved to stay put. As does Zionism.

'The hardliners, Hamas, they say "Go home, go back to where you came from." But what does that even mean? Jaqui's grandfather was killed in Auschwitz, his mother was hidden away in a French convent as a little girl. We've always been a people who have had to move around. It doesn't make any sense when they say, "Go home". We *are* home.'

When Jaqui returns we talk more generally about kibbutz life. Zikim still operates in the traditional way; the work is rotated yearly and, regardless of whether you are in the fields, the mattress factory, the kitchen or the school, everyone receives equal pay and has an equal say in community matters. Having injured his back, Jaqui now drives people to and from Ashkelon when needed and Marlene occasionally works in the dining room, although she is now retired. She helps new French immigrants understand life in Israel.

Of the two of them, Jaqui is the gardener and he proudly shows me the designated garden areas. The first is a pastel flower bed of pinks and lilacs. It is comprised of roses, pansies, snapdragon and lavender, and there is a small olive tree at one end. It is the most recognisably European of all the areas in both colour and content, and very like it belongs to a French farmhouse.

I ask about their water supply. Jaqui says simply 'rain', and shows me the tanks which collect water from the gutters. 'It's enough to last for the whole summer if you are careful. As the water is untreated it is also better for the plants.'

In another bed there are exotic bird of paradise flowers, a frangipani with solid leaves, a pinwheel, various brassicas and mustard-yellow yarrow flowers. Jaqui's statues and sculptures reach out from behind tree trunks or skip beneath succulents, and a headless bust of a woman watches over a group of pansies.

Nearer the house Jaqui has planted rosemary, mint, thyme and a cactus, which Marlene says is just like any Israeli: prickly on the outside but quite lovely when you get past that. A bunch of wild garlic hangs by the front door; so very French, I think to myself again.

Marlene herself is a fan of Japanese gardens and her contribution to the garden is a pebble path. 'I find the movement of stones has a flow. There's a kind of Zen calmness that comes with them.'

But the garden she loves above all else is the sea, which is why they chose to live in Zikim. 'I stand at the window at six every morning and just watch it, listening to the birds. There is so much life here.'

Feeling confident enough to admit to having just left Gaza I tell them about Abu Awad a few kilometres away, looking out over a lifeless sea – a fisherman who can't fish. 'But that's crazy,' she says, shaking her head so hard her curls bounce, 'his children will all starve to death and all because Israel is afraid?' Then she sighs. 'I long for a time when there are no borders.'

I ask Jaqui why he started gardening. He was brought up in Paris where there are few green areas. 'Just a few trees and formal gardens, but I used to read about flowers in books as a boy, flowers like poppies and cyclamen. I could never visualise them. Then we came here and the whole place was full of flowers and growth. Israelis love their flowers – a lot of them here are protected species and we would travel one hundred kilometers across Israel just to see a rare plant bloom. Gardening now is a very therapeutic way of moving the body. Some people relax with alcohol or television. For me, it is gardening.'

He wants to show me an old Palestinian house overlooking Zikim and we scramble up the side of a dusty hill over friable dry rocks. It is a beautiful stone building with a skinny-columned portico from where we can see the flat blue horizon marking the edge of the world. Inside the house the walls are painted with fading wide red and white stripes and the ceiling is frescoed with geometric patterns and *trompe l'oeil*. Green and blue wooden doors lead into similarly derelict rooms. In one there is a desk covered in papers and, oddly, a single dusty brown lace-up brogue shoe. In another room the windows are open to the elements and there is a broken sofa, an upended chair and piles of fading books in Hebrew.

It was built during the First World War by a wealthy Arab family, the Alamis. They believed that Arabs and Jews could easily coexist. Abandoned and situated at a height which affords only a silent wind to blow a passage through the abandoned debris of a more hopeful

Jolyon Leslie in his garden, Kabul 2012. 'There is something very special about the climate here. Things just grow.'

Badria with onions on the edge of her allotment garden in Beit Hanoun, Gaza, April 2013. 'I try not to stay inside in the darkness unless there is danger. It is very gloomy and makes me worry about my children.'

Ibrahim Jeradda MBE, custodian of the Commonwealth Gaza War Cemetery, April 2013. 'It is our duty to care for both the living and the dead. There are no borders here. This is Palestine. The souls are now in Paradise and that's all that's important.'

Huda with a lime in her garden in Gaza City, April 2013. 'I like to be here all the time.'

Teenager Esra Ahmad in her father's hydroponic rooftop garden, Gaza city, April 2013. 'I feel free up here.'

Naif Dubaily, a shop keeper, standing in his beloved garden, April 2013 – the first thing he rebuilt after his house and land were destroyed in Operation Cast Lead, 2009.

Jaqui's clock installation in his garden in Zikim Kibbutz, Israel, April 2013. 'I like to surprise people.'

Mikhail on her porch in Sderodt, Israel, April 2013. 'I live in a part of the world where, let's face it, people could do with a lot of good hash and it's cheaper to garden. And legal.'

A sculpture garden of grief, Israel, 2013.

Schlomo and his nasturtiums, Nir Am Kibbutz, 2013. 'My plants are lucky, they don't have to deal with sadness like me, only the dust encroaching from the desert.'

Esti, Kfar Azar Kibbutz, 2013. 'If women were in charge there wouldn't be any war.'

Gulam Hazrat in the garden at FOB Lashkar Gah, September 2013. 'If the Taliban come back they will cut off my head for working here.'

Daram on the military cot bed with his granddaughter in his hospital garden, Lashkar Gah, Helmand, April 2014. 'I encourage my patients to sit and read here while they are waiting or recovering from a treatment. It is a restorative, fresh place.'

Mirwais Khan in his orchard, Nad-e-Ali, Helmand, April 2014. 'They [the British and American military] did not have permission but they entered our homes, they killed, they cut up our land and destroyed our peace.'

Mullah Issa in his mosque. 'I don't have a garden but the Koran says, if you want to see god, give a gift of a rose to a neighbour.' Shin Kalay, Nad-e-Ali, Helmand, April 2014.

Kelly Wilson, chief horticulturalist at Arlington Cemetery, Washington DC. 'In 2011 [during Obama's troop surge] we had a problem working out where to put the earth dug out for the coffins.'

past, it reminds me of the crumbling grandeur of Darulaman Palace in Kabul.

When the kibbutz was founded in the forties, the building was given over as a nursery for babies, a children's kitchen, a library and a school for Holocaust survivors who had arrived in Israel as orphans. Avraham, Jacqui tells me, was their teacher. I imagine twenty or so little starved and haunted faces taking comfort in the safety of their new home and the kindness of a younger Avraham.

Outside, Jaqui points to the wire and plastic flowers leading up to the corner of an exterior wall where there is another *trompe l'oeil*. This one is a more modern, photorealistic one of a hole smashed into the stone wall. Through the painted hole is depicted a limestone stairway climbing up through a dense, damp forest lined with ferns and evergreens and leading up to a jungle. Of all the things I expected to see in the side of an abandoned Arab house, this is not one of them. It is so real I can almost smell the mineral earth and the tropical humidity.

'I wanted to provoke people,' Jaqui says, proud of his work, 'to make people see. There is a garden inside everything if you look hard enough.'

Sderot is the largest and closest town to Gaza. At only a kilometre or so from the border it is bang in the centre of the cross hairs of Hamas' sights and as such has become an easy target since the second intifada in 2000. It absorbed some 10,000 rockets in a decade, sometimes as many as four a day. It is known as the bomb shelter capital of the world – there is one on almost every street corner, and the Israeli government has installed a seven- to ten-second alarm system to warn its citizens of an impending rocket attack.

The constant danger takes its toll on the population. An estimated seventy-five per cent of children aged between four and eighteen suffer from sleeping disorders and acute anxiety. At the end of 2007 around a thousand people were receiving psychiatric treatment at the community mental health centre.

Rockets aside, it is a quiet, suburban place full of students and creative types attending the town's numerous schools and colleges. Wide-open playing fields sit at the end of suburban neighbourhoods of bungalows, numerous sculptures dot the roundabouts leading to shopping precincts and many of the shelters have been brightly painted. It also has a media centre catering to visiting journalists, but by the time I find it, it is late and they are about to close.

But when I explain the search for gardens to a girl in her thirties, she scribbles a number down for me. 'Try Mikhail.'

I dial the number.

'Sure! Come on over!' says a thick Chicagoan accent, and she gives me a set of complicated yet, as it happens, accurate instructions.

Her home is immediately identifiable from the road. A white picket fence surrounds a vegetable patch on one side. A raised bed of ornamental cacti lines the facing wall. She is weeding and I cough politely.

'Welcome, welcome. Come in.' She turns towards me, moving her long salt-and-pepper hair out of her eyes with the back of her hand, holding a trowel with the other. She is wearing a knee-length skirt, a black T-shirt and pink rubber crocs. 'Sorry, I'm all shabby. You know how it is,' she says as she leads me around the back of the house to the entrance. A mature vine clings to a mulberry tree chased by Star of David bunting.

She points out an Uzbek banana tree which – to my untrained eyes – looks very like a regular banana tree, and the vegetables she grows to sustain herself throughout the year.

'Beets, mangetout, fava beans, black-eyed peas, carrots, and parsnips. I think I'm the only person in the country with parsnips! Rocket, radicchio, peppers, tomatoes, potatoes, spinach, chard, pumpkin, corn – you name it.' I notice the apricot tree, okra, a sunflower 'to attract the birds', and purple flowers of wild garlic. 'I've allocated a space for annual flowers too. If I can't eat everything I grow, I give it away to neighbours.'

She apologises for how messy it is, but to me it looks like nothing except a wonderfully stocked kitchen garden.

In another flower bed against the back wall she lists an aromatherapist's dream. Lemongrass, fennel, hibiscus, oregano, mint, sage, dill, thyme and lavender, and I realise it's the first time I have seen lavender outside Jerusalem. 'I make tea with some of these aromatics. Thirsty?'

She rummages in her kitchen, muttering the names of the different leaves she has dried for infusions while I explain war gardens, Afghanistan and Gaza.

'I get it,' she says, 'every garden is a kind of therapy for people, right? And God knows we need that in this world. Try this. Hibiscus and . . .' She smells it. 'I think it's mint but I labelled it thyme so . . .' Her casual familiarity and vagueness is incredibly warm. That I'm a complete stranger sitting on a sofa in her house with a notebook matters not the least to her. Her tea does matter.

I wonder if people in England would be quite so welcoming to strangers from a foreign land. But then, Mikhail is an intellectual hippy who, judging by her rugs, cushions, wall hangings and pictures, has taken the road less travelled more than once.

She is working as an English language teacher while studying for a bachelor's in cultural studies at a university in Sderot. Her real passion, however, is garden therapy.

'I had a friend who was teaching psychology at a university and she asked me, what do you do with Freud in the garden? Jung in the garden? Nietzsche in the garden? I knew a bit about philosophy and so I helped her develop a whole project about gardening therapy. Gardening is one of the most effective ways of re-earthing yourself, being calm and not a fanatic. I live in a part of the world where, let's face it, people could do with a lot of good hash or a garden, and it's cheaper to garden. And legal,' she laughs. 'I mean even growing parsley in a window box can be therapeutic.'

She was born in Israel and went with her family to Chicago where her father was a zookeeper ('it was a brilliant place to be able to go after school every day') and returned in her late teens to her homeland. At first she lived in Bersh'eeva, the capital of the Negev. 'But my garden there was starting to get way too much shade from the new buildings around it, and I wanted to live in a smaller town so I moved here.'

It was around the time when Sderot was absorbing about three or four rockets a day so I am surprised. But she says proudly, 'I wasn't going to let Hamas stop me, and I figured that they'll soon get bigger bombs, target bigger cities or there will be a diplomatic breakthrough. There are certainly fewer rockets these days, so I was right.'

There was no garden when she moved in and she spent a long time pulling up the paving slabs and rubble and creating the garden now surrounding her house.

In the interests of being green, she harvests rainwater, but she dreams of having an irrigation system which will make additional use of grey water.

She is almost self-sufficient, but has to buy the staples like rice and flour. However I wouldn't put it past her to have a patch of wheat one day when she says 'I grew a sesame the other week, just as an experiment. It's a pretty plant!'

Mikhail is generous with her knowledge. 'People stop by the garden and ask me how I grow this and that, and some families got together to ask me to teach their children. And it's nice to hear them learning and realising that their waste can turn into compost rather than trash.'

Inevitably, we move on to politics, and Gaza which she used to visit a lot in the eighties. 'There was a great beach, great little restaurants, great markets and the Gazans were welcoming. We were all aware that it was an occupied territory and that it wouldn't last but our relations were much easier. There wasn't all this hatred and resentment. I don't think anyone could have predicted where we are now back then.

'Gaza used to be a small village.' She lights a cigarette and mumbles through the filter until it is lit. 'It's huge now. No one can deny it's worse on the other side. They live like miserable wretches and their government doesn't help them. They are used as human shields and there is a lot of pity for them as their government doesn't bother to protect them from those monsters. If *our* kids are having problems,

I can only imagine how frightened the Gazan mothers must be for theirs. Everyone wants to have an OK life. We are going through some tough times here and trying as hard as we can to keep normal.'

I tell her about Badria, living just a few kilometres from where we are sitting. I tell her about her children and her fears for them. I tell her about Esra who does her homework surrounded by pastel drawings of flowers and a picture of Jerusalem. But Mikhail is slow to empathise.

'You know,' she begins after mulling for a few moments, 'when they pulled us out of Gaza, we left them a gift of greenhouses. A gift. The workers wanted to take them with them but some wealthy American philanthropists bought them for the Gazans for millions of dollars. The whole place was looted and stripped within a week. Can you imagine how demoralising that felt for the people who built them? To see their work destroyed. And for what?'

I bite my tongue. The greenhouse problem was well documented when it happened in 2005. Pro-Israeli media showed images of Palestinian men carting off irrigation pipes, plastic sheeting and water pumps from the commercial greenhouses Israeli settler farmers had left behind. Pro-Palestinian media showed departing Israeli settlers vandalising the greenhouses, some setting fire to them, rendering them useless.

After $25 million of investment, the greenhouses were revived and the first crops of peppers, strawberries, tomatoes and herbs – estimated to be worth $20 million – was ready. Eight tons of peppers were prepared for export through the Karni crossing, Gaza's cargo terminal for Palestinian merchants. For the greenhouse project to maintain itself, twenty-five truckloads of produce needed to pass through Karni daily. But the crossing was run by the Israelis and the opening times were, at best, erratic; most of the time, no more than three trucks would be processed. The subsequent fast demise of the project, not to mention the exorbitant waste, was demoralising. The greenhouse project closed and it has been a contentious issue ever since.

We move on to the war. 'I used to go out to that hill where all the TV people went. There were loads of people watching the war going on from there and it was sad, you know. But we were all so conflicted as we also thought, well it's nice to see them getting bombed for once. Cast Lead was just a retaliation to the thousands of bombs falling on Sderot, so we finally went over and bombed a few houses. Big deal. People were like "Yeah. Fuck them. See how they like it."'

Her words grate but I try to put myself in her shoes. What would I really think if, say, this situation was happening at home? Our political opinions may differ but so do our contexts. She has lived through decades of change and conflict. I am an outsider in all of this.

A stray cat jumps into the garden and she gets up to feed and pet it. Her cigarette smoulders red-tipped in the ashtray.

'God, what a life. What a stupid disaster.' She sighs, suddenly deflated. 'We should all be having more fun. Them *and* us. How long are we going to have to live like this? Another generation? Living in uncertainty?' These are not rhetorical questions. She is leaning forward, asking me and waiting for an answer I cannot give.

The evening sun fills the air with a low, warm light and, turning to the garden, her face softens. 'But meanwhile, as Voltaire says, "we have to cultivate our garden."'

I smile. The adage from *Candide* is scrawled at the front of my notebook and I show her. '*Il faut cultiver notre jardin.*'

We have been talking for hours and it is late. When she finds out that I am about to drive back to Jerusalem only to return again tomorrow, she insists I stay in her spare room and is adamant when I protest. 'Your project is pretty neat and you seem like a nice girl. If you're heading out to the kibbutzim every day just stay here. I'd like the company anyways.'

It is a generous offer and, although we don't agree politically, I like Mikhail. Besides which, with dwindling time and finances, the less time and money spent driving and the more time spent with the kibbutzim gardeners, the better.

The room is modest but comfortable, and lined, floor to ceiling, with gardening books. It has been an intense day and I am exhausted. From Gaza straight into a kibbutz, and now here I am lying in bed surrounded by hefty tomes of horticulture, permaculture, cacti and a few, familiar faded Penguin paperbacks. I fall asleep on page one of *Far from the Madding Crowd*.

2

A broadcaster is reading the news in Hebrew on the radio, a kettle whistles ready and I can smell my favourite smell of all: toast.

'Home-made, of course!' Mikhail tells me proudly. She is preparing for her midterms and needs to go to the library so I offer to drop her off at the university campus.

On the road south the agricultural lands expand but I catch glimpses of the Gaza Strip. From the comfort and safety of a hire car the jagged border looks out of place – a parallel world superimposed by a clever computer program.

On my left are acres and acres of flat green fields, orchards and permanent polytunnels of strawberries, lemons, vegetables, mangoes, bananas, tomatoes, grapes, melons, pears, oranges, tomatoes and cucumbers, all destined for the world's supermarkets. Not for nothing is Israel considered to be a world leader in agricultural technologies.

When I arrive at Nirim kibbutz I realise it is more or less parallel to the Access Restricted Area of Khan Younis and Hassan abu Daggar whose garden keeps his mute-from-shock children out of the gun sights of trigger-happy soldiers. It is so close that if I had a pair of binoculars I am sure I would be able to see him.

I turn back to the kibbutz community. Nirim is much smaller and more modest than the more northerly kibbutzim, but it is deathly quiet and I cannot find a soul to speak to. There are no cars in the drives and I realise that most of its residents are probably occupied with work in the fields.

But around the end of a paved path I bump into an elderly man snailing along in a mobility cart, out of the back of which are poking a few garden utensils. He asks if he can help, first in Hebrew and then in broken English.

His name is Aglily and, as it happens, he worked in the cemetery garden full time before retiring. He misses it. 'I may be old but I still want to work.' I think of Ibrahim striding between the war graves with his MBE glinting sharply. Aglily parks his cart and eases himself off the seat. He has lived in the kibbutz for sixty years, forty as graveyard gatekeeper and guardian, he tells me.

His garden is dense with forest ferns and splashed red with geraniums. A pink rose climbs over an ivy-clad date palm. Smaller pink geraniums in terracotta pots line a paved path leading up to a covered patio in front of his house.

There I notice relics from the past. Hundreds and hundreds of old tools and kitchen implements: sickles, scythes, forks, spades and paraffin lamps. There are sieves and scales and pots and pans and a pewter tray, inscribed with 'give us this day our daily bread'. There are scissors and menorahs, saws and axes, metal platters and massive saucepans.

They are the well worn, well used, broken and mended rudimentary tools of the kibbutz used by the arrivals from Romania, Russia,

Poland and Germany who were escaping persecution and desperate to find and build new lives in new homes in their own land, safe in the knowledge that, finally, their people could live peacefully. They are the tools with which Aglily created his house, his garden with its paths and deep-rooted tree and, quite possibly, the original kibbutz. They are the tools which built modern Israel.

He blows the desert dust from a few leaves. 'It brings me great happiness to work with nature. Greenery always makes people feel at ease and at peace.'

It is a short interview; in fact, it is barely that. Aglily is a sweet, mild-mannered man, but his English isn't strong enough to convey any real emotion attached to his garden.

As there is no one else around I drive to Nir Am, a kibbutz closer to Sderot. Emboldened by the sight of cars in their drives I park, and when I take to the kibbutz on foot it is with a spring in my step. The municipal flower beds are in bloom with pansies and there is a heady smell of pinesap from the trees in the centre of the kibbutz.

I come to a white gate. Behind it the grass is overgrown and an old wheelbarrow has found a new lease of life as a bed for fuchsia-pink geraniums next to a fruit tree. There is a shelf next to the front door full of well-used tools and spades.

When I ring, there is no answer. I am about to turn away when I hear a voice. 'Ken?' Hebrew for 'yes'.

'Oh. *Shalom*,' I stutter. 'Do you speak English?'

There is a crash and a series of shuffles and the door opens as wide as the security chain allows it.

It is dark inside and I can only see the shadow of a man peering out, crossly. I am nervous now and start to falter when I ask again if he speaks English.

'A little. What do you want, lady?'

I smile broadly and tell him I would like to talk about his garden.

When he opens the door he is wearing ragged boxer shorts and a string vest.

'Come in,' he barks and turns on a light.

It is messy inside, and I mean really, really messy. Piles of old newspapers sit dejected on a draining board. The sink is so full of washing-up there is no space for the grimy saucepans and they fester on the hob, one of the elements of which is loose. A fridge hums, just, in the corner next to a bag of rubbish. A television blinks with a basketball game. He turns down the volume, moves some cups from the table and tells me to sit.

I can just about see his garden through the filthy kitchen window. It sits at odds with his squalor and when I compliment him on it, he relaxes a little and smiles.

'I made it because I love gardens,' he says. 'I only grow flowers, never vegetables – the kibbutz has land for vegetables.'

From monosyllabic answers I glean that his name is Avi and he is fifty years old. His parents originated from Bessarabia, a historical area in Eastern Europe which is now part of Moldova and Ukraine,[6] and he was born in Nir Am. When he was old enough, he started farming. He is divorced and lives alone.

He is suspicious of me and very difficult to interview. He sits with his arms crossed and one eye on the flickering television.

'Did you enjoy the farm work?' I ask.

'It was easy,' he barks.

'What was the kibbutz like then?' I ask.

'The situation was easier.'

'Could you tell me how?'

'The Palestinian labourers were my friends and we shared ideas about farming. They would sit and drink tea with me. But since they started throwing rockets, we can't call each other. No, it is not good when they are fired. I do not have anywhere to go when there is a war and have to stay here.'

'Did you garden in the last war?'

'I can't remember.'

'What about your water?'

'There is a well. It is so fresh.'

I continue questioning him about his garden but, making no headway, ask him instead about his life. He doesn't expand much but I learn he had been a basketball referee.

'But you garden now?'

'Yes.'

I become a bit exasperated; the sour smell of the kitchen is making me nauseous and I suggest we go outside. I inhale the fresh air deeply and compliment him on the roses framing the garden. They are, he admits, his first love.

His suspicion and hostility melts away as he shows me more and more of his flowers like a child. 'This is a daisy, a nasturtium, and *this* is a present.'

He reaches into a tree and picks an avocado which he gives to me. When I take it, he holds onto my arm firmly. I don't notice his other hand gripping my shoulder and he pulls me towards him while leaning forward with his mouth open for a kiss. I am able to turn my cheek at the last minute and jump away, screaming inside.

I don't want to create a scene or anger him but extract myself as quickly as possible from his futile embrace. Thanking him politely, I immediately leave. When I am out of sight I run to the car, lock myself in and burst into tears. 'Stupid, stupid girl,' I say to myself. I am probably the first company he has had for a very long time and should never have sat in his filthy little house for so long, desperately extracting details about his sad, cold little life.

Feeling physically sick, I realise I am all alone; there is no one to call, no one to ear-bash about what happened, and I begin to shake. I grip the steering wheel and clench my jaw. As a sole operator it can be easier to work alone because I do not look threatening, I do not look like trouble and I listen. The drawbacks, however, are huge. There is no one to laugh with afterwards and there is no one who can identify with your experiences or journey. But there is something in my blood which compels me to do it, to gather stories. Or maybe like Ghada, I think, I am just nosy. Either way, I never imagined photographing gardens would leave me so vulnerable.

I un-grip the steering wheel and light a cigarette, inhaling so sharply I splutter.

I let the wave of revulsion pass and drive to the pine trees at the edge of the kibbutz. Amber tears of sap drop from the needles. Before me the land endures, above me faint cirrus clouds rib high, and white jet tails intersect as a perfect X.

Storing the incident away, I reverse back to the kibbutz and park on the furthest side.

A Mediterranean bundle of colour and glass ornaments catches my eye and I knock at a door. The woman who answers has a mop in one rubber-gloved hand and a bucket in the other. It is her husband, Schlomo, who is the gardener of the house, but he is at work, she says.

'I keep telling him we should get a fake garden but he won't hear of it.' The woman shakes her head and tells me I will have to come back tomorrow morning.

Frustrated, I drive out to a service station for a feeble lunch of rice cakes and Diet Coke. I decide to try my luck in Be'eri, a kibbutz fifteen kilometres south I had noticed from the road that morning.

With its chalet-style two-storey homes Be'eri feels affluent, and it is certainly greener than the others I have visited. I pass a hammock hanging between two trees framed by jasmine and, rounding the corner, arrive at a small path leading up to an open patio area. There is a terracotta statue of an eagle, another of a roe deer and a cluster of purple pansies.

Simcha is wearing a purple T-shirt depicting a silver butterfly. She has short grey, cropped hair and an impish, expressive face.

The house behind us has been her home for eleven years but she has lived in Be'eri for thirty-eight, moving there just after getting married. Back then it was a traditional kibbutz and her son and two daughters were housed in a *beit yeladim* – a children's quarter separate from the rest of the commune.

Gaza then was just a dusty fishing village, but at eight kilometres from the official border now, Be'eri is within the firing line. 'We had a rocket just two days ago. We try to make it normal for the grand-children. They are easily scared so they sleep in the shelter every night,' she says.

'Gaza makes me sad. Peace would be good for all of us. Palestinians, Jews – we are both Israelis together and were happy friends before the wars started and loved each other. Every year we have a collection and send funds to a few people who used to work here. I know how poor they are and how much they are cut off from the world now.'

I ask what it means to be Israeli and she pauses. 'It is to be able to talk with anyone and everyone. To love people indiscriminately: Jews, Arabs, Muslims, Christians. It doesn't matter. To be Israeli is to be able to feel free.'

It is a beautifully poetic answer: to feel free. Isn't that what we all want? Whether you are Afghan, Palestinian, British, Jewish, young, old, male, female, to feel psychologically or physically trapped is to have lost control. It is the thing that drives so much conflict, and perhaps gardening in extreme circumstances is a way of taking back control and feeling that freedom. Naif, the shopkeeper, knew that. The first thing he did upon finding his house and garden destroyed was to dig.

I remark on how green the kibbutz is and she explains that the kibbutznik of Be'eri take it upon themselves to look after the community spaces together. There's even a library dedicated to gardening where families congregate to read. Simcha herself favours the roses and points to one climbing through a lemon tree. Against the green leaves, its petals are an oversaturated velvet.

Her favourite cactus is a golden barrel, and I tell her about 'Sabaar', the cactus man in Gaza. He favoured the same species. She nods earnestly, 'it is a good cactus.'

I ask if she knows any other gardeners in the kibbutz and immediately she dispatches me to Mimi.

I see Mimi's garden long before her house. A crest of orange and green nasturtiums acts as a border beneath a weeping willow. The chalet-style house, similar to Simcha's, is almost entirely hidden by foliage from citrus trees, a Virginia creeper and a vine.

Mature beds of pansies, cornflowers, poppies, evening primroses, lupin and artfully arranged wooden fruit boxes with rope handles sprouting forget-me-nots line the path to the front door. It is a carefully cultivated and contained wild-meadow style look that only the very green-fingered can really master.

I am just about to ring the bell when I notice that the ripening fruit of the citrus tree is encased in glass bottles.

'My husband makes fruit vodka,' she explains when we are sitting in a secluded area of decking surrounded by dark ferns just next to the house. I am puzzled as to how he got the bottles over the fruits and she laughs. 'The young fruits ripen *inside* the glass and then you pour in the vodka and hey presto! Schnapps! It is really good.'

As a music teacher in both the kibbutz and Sderot, Mimi is always able to run to her own timetable, and devotes large portions of time to gardening.

There are bay trees, palm fronds and tropical fans cooling bamboo shoots. A slight breeze shivers through the willow. She looks up and smiles. It is her favourite tree and one she planted herself. The fruit trees – orange, pomegranate, clementine and guava – are the domain of her husband, the experimental spirit maker.

'I love having colour throughout the year but I try to work with plants that are relatively simple and easy to take care of.' She points at the nasturtiums. 'I first saw them on holiday in San Francisco and, after a bit of research, found out where to get them here. They just grow on their own.'

She installed an automatic irrigation system and adds fertiliser to the rather thin soil.

At the back of the house there is a grassed area and I imagine children playing tag or hide and seek in the bordering evergreen bushes on languid summer evenings.

Her son lives in Boston now and is contemplating a move back to Israel, 'but with the security situation he is afraid. When the sirens go off you have to run as fast as you can to the shelter. I'm trying to convince him that it really is OK and that you can live normally.'

Mimi apologises but has to give a music lesson to a neighbour and we part company. I rather like Be'eri and these two gardeners, Mimi and Simcha. They wear the heaviness of the conflict and unrest quite lightly but with a practical, no-nonsense attitude to surviving it.

I drive back to Sderot with the sun sinking orange into the sea. The rich and deep sky is slowly changing with all the unknown things happening beyond the water's horizon.

Mikhail is pottering beneath the pergola when I arrive back at her house. The evening light glints through the Star of David bunting and makes translucent the young vine leaves. There is an eternal stillness right there and Gaza feels like it is a million miles away.

We go inside to make supper. Or rather, Mikhail rustles something out of her garden and I run through the stories of the day while she interjects with a few titbits of detail like the meaning of the kibbutzim names or the history of the Nahal and juggles rice and courgettes, occasionally asking me to cut a few ''erbs', from the garden. I tell her about Avi and she tells me to be careful. 'Some of the kibbutz people can be kind of weird, I guess.'

After dinner we say goodnight but I struggle to sleep. I am missing the Gazan sea.

3

When I arrive in Nahal Oz the following morning, I recognise it immediately. It was from here that I ill fatedly tried to drive across no man's land in 2009. The car became wedged on a rock in an irrigation ditch but Israeli soldiers were deploying into Gaza a few hundred metres either side of me and an airstrike was about to be launched. The only way I could shift the car was by sitting in the middle of the ditch, up to my waist in mud, and kick the rock out. With the first jellyfish tentacle explosion of phosphorus hanging over Gaza and one sharp kick, the car was free.

The soldiers using the nearest kibbutz as a forward operating base looked at me incredulously when I drove into the back gate pretending to be a lost tourist on the way to Tel Aviv.

'But that's Gaza. Don't you know there's a war on?' they asked.

I shrugged my shoulders and feigned ignorance. Taking me for a simpleton, they allowed me to use their washrooms. When I was driving out and back to the main road, I had noticed that a very large section of their own protective wall obliterating the burning Gaza skyline was painted with a garden mural. I wanted to find it once more.

Nahal Oz is not a large kibbutz but, try as I might, the whereabouts of the mural remains a mystery. Finding no one at home when I knock at the homes of the really pretty gardens, I drive a few minutes up the road to Kfar Azar thinking that perhaps the mural is there.

It is not, but I spot one or two well-tended gardens, park beneath a tall tree and walk around to investigate.

Aviah is in sports kit and standing with his hands on his hips looking at his grass intensely. He looks as though he could beast himself up a mountain and back without so much as breaking sweat and it is obvious he is – or was – a military man. A wooden sign on a cactus reads 'Family, friends and flowers gather here'.

His garden is a regimentally neat trimmed patch of lawn enclosed within a privet hedge. Crimson geraniums, low-maintenance ferns, bougainvillea and a terracotta-coloured rose sit beneath it, orderly. There is a precise order to things; nothing is out of place, not even a blade of grass.

'We moved to this kibbutz twenty-two years ago in order to have a better life. Before, we were living close to the border (Ein HaShlosha, near Nirim) and suffered a lot under the bombardment. It wasn't a good place to bring up a family. It was more developed here, there were more jobs, life was rosier. But the rockets keep falling. The problem is, you get used to it. I am fed up with it, we all are. It is all we ever talk about. You Brits have your weather, we have rockets.'

Aviah has fond memories of Gaza. 'It was the nicest place in the whole of Israel; the best fish, the best hummus. If they were smart, they would invest in tourism instead of getting people to fire rockets all day long, but we are not just going to leave. This is our home.'

As a Yemeni whose family was uprooted and moved to Israel in the forties as part of Operation Magic Carpet, a secret operation which relocated over 49,000 Jews from Yemen after increased persecution, home is important to Aviah.

'I will always be an Israeli. I can travel all over the world but this is where I am from now. I couldn't live anywhere else. It's warm, comfortable, happy, friendly. There is something special here, something that binds us. If we are attacked, we unite.'

He buys his plants in a nursery and grows herbs from seeds but he values his lawn above all. 'I take a blanket and sit on the grass with friends or my family and we just talk. That's what a garden is all about – having a space in nature.'

His garden is a place for gathering but he admits he is a relative newcomer to gardening. 'I started four years ago. It was just something that came to me and now, when I come home from work, I deadhead, water and make cuttings. My parents always lived in a busy apartment and never had a garden. It was something I really craved as a kid. Having a garden stills your mind. You become aware of birdsong, smells, colours, much more so than in any other part of life.'

A young grey and black hooded crow swoops down from the bougainvillea and hops two-footed over the grass towards us. 'It fell out of its nest as a chick. We kept an eye on it and now it keeps coming back for treats,' Aviah says, grabbing a handful of seeds from a pot next to him and scattering them on the grass.

I suddenly realise that I am late to meet the gardener of the garden glass and ferns I had seen yesterday and make a note to return to Kfar Azar later.

Schlomo is standing beneath the wooden veranda roof in a sky-blue T-shirt and jeans. He has a kind face, with eyes creased from smiling. An abundance of nasturtiums lead up to the house. Purple and pink pansies in pots raised on iron stands poke out of them.

Blue and green glass baubles hang from the gabled veranda rafters, playful metal figurines lean back on a swing suspended from a tree. Further around the side of the house the light-hearted colours fade into dramatic forest greens and white hybrid lilies.

There is a faint tinkle in the breeze from a hanging mother of pearl ornament. He brings me a cup of coffee as we sit.

I am expecting a gentle patter from Schlomo as he fondly describes a youth in the kibbutz, working the fields and helping to found the state of Israel.

Instead he starts with a sad story of detachment and isolation.

In 1959, when he was just fifteen, his parents brought him to Nir Am from Cordoba, Argentina with his sisters, and left them to fend for themselves.

His English falters and I tell him in slightly clunky Spanish that I lived in his home country many years ago but he shakes his head. 'I do not speak it any more. I have no reason to. It is not my homeland. Spain is the motherland but I am an Israeli through and through.'

It took him a long time to come to terms with the abandonment and, combined with the hard living conditions of the kibbutz, it did not make for a happy childhood, although he understands the reason why he was sent: 'To build a nation for the people without a country from all over the world after the Holocaust. We are the sinew of Abraham's promised land.'

He is, however, fed up with the situation and the lack of any solution so is not positive about the future. 'The Palestinians were here before us, we know that. It is not logical that they are now locked up inside Gaza. Of course they want their land back. We Jews have never existed in one place for more than one hundred years in history. We have been *here* for sixty-five so far so it seems logical that we have only thirty-five years left.'

He is more of an optimist about his domestic life. 'At the end of the day, what matters are my children and grandchildren, my wife and my garden. No matter what, no matter where.'

The sun is fragmented to emerald and sapphire shadows by the glass ornaments. 'This bit is a Mediterranean garden,' he says. 'Maybe it is the Spanish influence. I like to keep things relatively simple and chose plants that did not need too much work.' He tries to plant seasonal flowers despite the searing summer temperatures. Many of the pots are raised for practical reasons; a neighbour has an irritating and uncontrollable dog which we can hear barking.

At the back of the house he has an orchard of apricot, guava, plum, pear and orange trees which he estimates are around twenty years old and are still fruiting. He has painted their trunks with a peach-coloured solution of zinc to avoid infection or blight, and the overall effect is like looking at a half-finished surrealist painting. 'If it doesn't work, the trees will let me know.' He slaps the orange tree trunk affectionately.

Schlomo explains that his garden is his sanity. Since retiring, he has spiralled into a deep depression and is currently seeing a therapist whom he does not trust. 'The past and my childhood is what it comes down to. It was not very happy. To wake at five or six in the morning and hear the birds in the trees outside your window. Nature, it's the most naturally calming thing in the world. Gardening, getting my hands in the soil, it lifts my spirits and it is a lot cheaper than psychotherapy.'

Mycobacterium vaccae, I think, the bacteria in soil believed to reduce depression. It is said to mirror the effect on neurons that chemical drugs like Prozac can provide. Schlomo is getting his dose of nature's happy pills through his garden. Mikhail will be delighted when I tell her.

'My plants are lucky – they do not have to deal with sadness like me, only the dust, which feels like it is encroaching from the desert.'

When I am thanking him and saying goodbye he says, 'I almost forgot, I had a dream last night that I met [Yasser] Arafat[7] and his ministers – those simple Arab farmers who became terrorists. We ate herbs and potatoes sitting in this very garden and I was telling them that peace is actually a very reasonable objective, so long as we keep trying.'

Schlomo suddenly appears shy and uncertain and wrings his hands. 'It sounds stupid but I thought it important to tell you, that you might want to know that a dreamed peace happened in a garden.'

I return to the car and drive back to Kfar Azar. Aviah the Yemeni had mentioned a garden on the other side of the kibbutz.

In her bright turquoise top and loose three-quarter length trousers, the lady at the other end of a lane is hard to miss. She is pushing a wheelbarrow almost twice her size up the path to the raised beds she has been weeding. Like Schlomo she has Etruscan-style terracotta urns dotted around. The majority of the paved area outside her house is given over to pots – in almost every size, shape and colour.

The colour palette is feminine, with soft pink roses, pastel-yellow snapdragon, pink hollyhocks and purple foxgloves which sit like surf on water over the smaller, bold blue border flowers at their edges.

The lady in turquoise is Esti, a seventy-year-old with the strength and agility of someone decades younger.

When she first moved to the kibbutz there were just fifty people living and working there, and the trees beneath which I am parked were just tiny saplings.

Unlike Schlomo, Esti recalls the early halcyon days working the fields and the poultry farm fondly. 'We grew a lot of produce then, like potatoes, corn, watermelon, chickpeas,' she says, 'and we fed ourselves well.'

Now things are slightly different. 'This house belongs to the kibbutz, I belong to the kibbutz but this garden is just mine.'

I recall a rocket landing in Kfar Azar during the war and she shrugs. 'Many did. Some in the fields, some on the homes. My neighbour's garden was hit quite badly, all the windows blew out and he died. I went north to stay with my family. I was not going to stay around here and let the same thing happen to me.' She points to an old olive tree which she planted, with her then-boyfriend, in memory of her neighbour.

Behind her is her bomb shelter. She is growing things up its sides and trying to make it look like an inconsequential part of the house and garden. 'Of course it is scary when there is attack but if the shelter is part of the garden, well it is the safest place I can be. When you come here and work with the flowers all the rubbish from the world just melts away.'

Esti's garden is her mental escape from danger. If she can incorporate the shelter, her physical protection, then so much the better. 'Just look at the colours here,' she marvels, picking up a cyclamen, her favourite flower. 'How can you not be happy and safe when you see this?'

She never stops working while she talks. 'I want peace and quiet,' she says. 'The people of Gaza want that too. They are good people just like we are. They have the same daily fears, hopes, dreams that we have – that the rest of the world has. But the problem comes down to men. They can never say "sorry" and they are the ones in power. If women were in power we wouldn't be in this mess. There would be no war.'

I wonder if this is true. Maybe ten years ago I would have agreed, but I have grown cynical. Here there is so much at stake and too much blood has been spilled.

We shake hands warmly and I leave her hauling another barrow full of earth across her garden. A wave of exhaustion crashes over me. It is as if I haven't slept in weeks and, despite the warmth of the day, I am cold.

I can probably muster the energy for one more garden today but I need a break. My head is too full of noise.

I purchase another dreadful non-lunch of Diet Coke and pumpkin seeds from a nearby gas station and hit the road to the far south, to the empty desert where there is only sand and sky, to organise my thoughts. When I walked the kilometre or so through a caged

walkway to the border just a few days ago it was with a semi-reluc-
tance. I did not want to return to the real world – least of all one
belonging to the violent oppressors treating the Palestinians exactly
as they themselves had been treated when the lights went out over
Europe in the Second World War. But having listened to the different
versions of life in the shadow of war, now I am not so sure which side
is more at fault. War, of course, is never symmetrical.

I drive towards the Egyptian border and the landscape changes. I
feel as if I have arrived in a wilderness. I am restless and want to get
out and walk but the empty landscape is by now, visibly militarised
and hostile with wire fences and beacons on hills.

I drive slowly north again and alight at a kibbutz with an open
gate. Everything looks abandoned and shut up against the ferocious
heat beaming through the desert. I am beyond tired now. Just one
more garden, I think to myself. Just one more.

The garden I find is of rusting metal, stone and plastic toys.

Two flower beds in front of a low bungalow burst with rusting
farm wheels, old sewing machines, china gnomes, terracotta eagles
and gnarled rockets. There is a painted cartoon mushroom, a
rearing plaster horse and a jagged strip of what was possibly once a
bit of car.

Cacti grow out of pots perched on flat edges, mellow catmint
grows from a window box on one side. The overall effect is fantasti-
cally messy, yet somewhere in between being the garden of a stately
home and a modern suburb. Despite the sporadic planting, however,
there is something very static and immobile about it. At the edge
of the garden is a bright green plastic caterpillar perched on the

twisted contortions of metal of a rocket. It reminds me of the hook-ah-smoking caterpillar of *Alice in Wonderland* who will never turn into a butterfly.

The house behind it looks empty but I knock anyway. When an elderly man opens it, my heart sinks. Another Avi, I think; another lonely old man with nothing left to give and nothing much to live for. But the interior behind him is well kept and smells as if it has just been cleaned.

'Yes?' he says.

After an introduction and explanation he says he will talk to me providing he doesn't have to give me his name. 'Some people don't agree with my politics around here,' he adds ominously.

We sit in the kitchen. With the blinds drawn low to keep out the heat it feels almost as if we're sitting in a light-sensitive archive.

He begins. He was a Nahal soldier when he first came here in 1963. 'It was a smaller place then. Quiet too. Egypt was in control of the Gaza Strip. You see? They were clever when they left us with that problem. Even the other Arab countries don't want the Palestinians! Personally, I don't like them either but I think we should give them back their territories. If we weren't here they'd probably kill themselves fighting but we badly need peace so let's just give them the land they want.'

He has started to make us both a cup of instant coffee and the spoon clatters loudly.

'Most people say it is horrible here. That their children cannot sleep, or wet their beds, that it is not worth staying, that they are afraid. So why don't they leave? You cannot live in this place if you are in constant fear. Most people in this kibbutz are afraid. They say the army does not do enough, that the government does not do enough.'

He and his wife have become used to the drama of border living. 'We made a conscious decision to normalise the danger and fears so we live easier than the rest of the kibbutz.'

His garden, when he first moved to this house thirty years ago, used to be full of flowers, but it became too much hard work and he phased them out with cacti and stones and started experimenting with the old farm machinery he used as a soldier.

'It's my sport. After spending some time in the garden I have the same feeling as if I had been for a run.'

He adds children's toys as and when he finds them. 'It is just a rule of terror the Palestinians are trying to impose on us,' he says, 'so I am poking fun at them by gardening with trivial things.'

I ask if he is religious.

'No. Not any more.' I put his despondency down to a frustration with current politics but have a niggling feeling that there is something more.

I had noticed four rocket shells in his garden used as pots. 'When the sirens go off, instead of going to the shelter I go out and wait for the ground to shake.' It sounds like a suicide mission but, as I was to find out, he was no stranger to the roulette of death.

His daughter had been dating a Druze – a member of an Arabic-speaking ethno-religious group. 'I think he must have had mental difficulties because he murdered her. He murdered our little girl.'

There are some details he asks me not to note down about the circumstances of the tragedy and he asks again for total anonymity. I am stunned by the revelation. I want to say something about peace, or making peace or something, anything to somehow alleviate his pain, but I cannot find the words. I tell him 'I am sorry.'

A shaft of light blazes through a chink in the closed blinds over his eyes and his pupils shrink. The tick of the kitchen clock slices the empty silence which has fallen.

He says, eventually, looking directly at the light, 'When you suffer a grief like that, it makes a living danger like rockets seem like a relief.'

He won't come into the garden with me, saying it is too hot for him, but he lets me photograph it on my own. I imagine him there statue-still waiting for the rockets to fall and the sirens and his grief to end.

When I arrive back at Mikhail's having driven through the embers of the day, I decide I need to go back to Jerusalem the following morning. I am too tired, too confused and beginning to doubt what I am doing. I am the stranger here and I will never fully understand the complexities of this place. I have never lost anyone I love, least of all a child. I am just an outsider, a tourist. I am ill equipped to understand this conflict. It is beyond me.

I tell Mikhail and she understands, saying something about it not being easy. 'And I'm from here.'

Over a garden supper she tells me about 'a really cool paper', she is working on. 'It's related to children's literature from the late nineteenth and early twentieth century.' My interest is piqued, not only because I think the stories told to children at that time are some of the most enchanting and elegant ever written in the Western canon, but also because I am halfway through writing a children's story of my own.

'It is funny,' she says, 'I've had to reread some things, you know? Reacquaint myself with the classics. Guess what came up today?' She grins and I shrug.

'*The Secret Garden*. Spooky, huh?'

I feel as if something has been staring me in the face when I remember the story.

Two rather poisonous, entitled, stubborn and spoiled children – Mary Lennox and Colin Craven – both parentless and sick (she from cholera, he from a spinal disease) are full of vitriol and hatred for their surroundings, and physically and psychologically trapped. But the walls holding them back are nothing but dust when with the help of a secret garden they learn to see outside their own anger, frustration and contempt for each other and learn to live and love. As they grow, so does the garden. It is a story of friendship, learning to forgive and rejuvenation, and it neatly parallels the situation here.

It is so obvious; if children get it, why can't we?

Frances Hodgson Burnett began writing at fifteen when her widowed mother and siblings moved to America from Manchester in 1865. Her family were on the verge of destitution, but through her work she became the main breadwinner of the family. Her sense of dislocation in a new land (combined with a series of tragic personal events) eventually fed into *The Secret Garden* which she wrote in her own garden in Long Island nearing sixty. She remarked towards the end of her life, 'As long as one has a garden one has a future; and as long as one has a future one is alive.'

My mind is racing by the time Mikhail has finished speaking. I have a splitting headache and am flooded with information, emotion, ideas and theories. So much so that I lie awake, tossing and turning and thinking about a walled garden.

When I eventually sleep, I dream of the walled garden of Gaza.

War Machine, Afghanistan

2013–14

'War is the natural occupation of man . . . war – and gardening.'

Winston Churchill to Siegfried Sassoon, 1918

1

Two American soldiers run past the garden's entrance. Their heads are bowed in earnest concentration and their feet thump the tarmac in time to the rhythm of the rock music escaping from their headphones. Their pounding fades and a pigeon recommences its morning coo from somewhere on the twenty-foot-high perimeter wall.

Water overflows from pots lining the pathways and beneath the dappled sun it perfectly mirrors the iron railings and faux streetlight in front of me. Once comfortable but now dusty armchairs sit at the foot of a veranda. A Native American totem pole teeters on the edge of a patch of grass. A panel next to it states it is dedicated to 'the fighting spirit of those who have served and will serve here'. The carved faces running in relief up to an outstretched eagle look rather concerned. As well they might be: this is the Destille Garden of the International Security Assistance Forces headquarters (or ISAF HQ as it is locally known), the nucleus of the war in Afghanistan. It is late summer 2013 and official combat operations are set to continue until the end of next year. ISAF needs all the fighting spirit it can get.

Soon the sun will be drawing high overhead and it will be too hot for the soldiers to exercise. It will also be too bright for me to photograph so I set about composing pictures. It is not an easy job as the garden is difficult to capture and is not naturally photogenic; purely functional additions to the garden – gazebos and wooden benches – are ugly. The few solitary roses are pallid beneath a layer of dust and dwarfed by the mature pine and plane trees. Small purple pansies grow rampantly next to the garden's entrance, providing the only real colour. A plastic rock juts out of the grass and only on close examination do I notice a small Excalibur sticking out at its summit. The totem pole looks more and more disgruntled with every frame I take.

But in the context of the military base surrounding the garden, which is otherwise dominated by uniforms, a Hesco bastion (reinforced collapsible wire-mesh and heavy-duty fabric containers filled with sand or gravel used as a layer of fortification) and semi-permanent living containers, the Destille Garden is a visual relief. I muddle along searching for pretty or quirky corners through the lens.

The Destille has been a military garden since it first began life as the garden of an Afghan military sporting club in the late sixties. Then, it comprised a football pitch, tennis courts, wrestling and boxing rings as well as gardens with private areas for families to entertain. The jewel in the crown of the club was the 'Yellow Building', which was used as a hotel and restaurant by the liberal elite for parties, dinners and weddings. Whisky and wine was readily available. Like the country, the club fell into disrepair during the civil war and further decayed under the Taliban. When ISAF took over the grounds, the garden was nothing but scrubland. Only the chipped, stone-carved sign over the large entrance indicated its former use as Kabul's Military Sporting Club.

The sign is still there, although the entrance is more commonly used for armoured military vehicles. The football pitch is now a helicopter landing site, and any remnants of wrestling rings and tennis courts have all but vanished beneath a modern military's encampment. The Yellow Building still stands, and is now home to the relatively opulent offices of numerous commanders and representatives of ISAF and NATO.

As one of the only recreation areas for soldiers and civilians working at headquarters since operations began, the garden has been seen as a respite from the drudgery of war administration. It has also been home to some of the most ludicrous stories of the increasingly violent war escalating outside the perimeter walls. When Turkey commanded ISAF in 2005[8] one luminary decided to introduce a menagerie of pet rabbits for reasons still unclear. At the time, the conflict was in its infancy – the world's focus remained on Iraq –and the sum total of troops in Afghanistan was a multinational brigade of just a few thousand soldiers. And rabbits. The next commander of ISAF deemed the (now excessive) number of rabbits to be understandably superfluous to operational requirement and had them 'disappeared'. It turned out to be a regrettable decision a few months later when a visit from the outgoing Turkish commanders was announced. Enough rabbits were re-bought and rehoused to avoid a military slur. The Turks were none the wiser.

Until 2009, alcohol flowed freely at ISAF HQ. In the space of a square kilometre there were at least seven bars, and on Thursday nights one was opened in the Destille – Friday being a 'low-ops' day. There was an official 'two can' rule but it was rarely enforced, and civilians and soldiers were quick to find an easy escape from boredom in oblivion. Inebriation became so much of a problem that the military police began breathalysing suspected drunkards found slaloming through the base in the small hours.

So far, so farcical, but when a NATO airstrike launched from Mazar-e-Sharif killed as many as 125 people in the northern city of Kunduz one fateful evening in early September 2009, things changed. General Stanley McChrystal – then the commander of international forces in Afghanistan – was eager to get to the bottom of this tragedy but found that his troops had been partying so hard the previous evening they were either too hung-over or still too drunk to be of much use in deconstructing the mistake. Alcohol was swiftly banned (along with a string of other non-essentials including burger bars, pizza parlours and salsa classes) in operational areas around the country.

McChrystal also did away with the more peculiar ornamentation of the Destille Garden. It was traditional for each of the commanders of ISAF to commemorate their time at the helm with a national statue, and the garden had come to resemble a miniature theme park, with faux windmills and cannon sculptures. But they too were outlawed when heady nights in the Destille Garden were no more under McChrystal. It became a quiet, leafy outside seating area for the 'Tora Bora' coffee shop next door and an overflow for official flag-waving ceremonies and memorial services conducted out of the Yellow Building opposite. When a friend who had worked there at that time explains this years later, the replica of Excalibur suddenly makes sense.

As I sit out of the way by the veranda, a group of three young soldiers come out of the Tora Bora holding steaming paper cups. One rubs the sleep from his eyes, his friend lights a cigarette saying, 'Another day in paradise.' They begin talking about home. The morning light, one is saying, reminds him of this time when he went camping as a kid. 'The trees,' he says, 'they were kind of like these ones. But better.'

The others laugh. 'Everything's better than here.'

They do not notice me and I am content to listen to their Southern-states accents drawing the morning in like treacle, until my appointment with the head gardener, Mohammed Mahmoud.

The soldiers leave and Mohammed arrives, apologising for his tardiness and explaining that the security check at the main gate for national staff had taken longer than usual.

When we are sitting next to the faux boulder façade of his guard hut he explains that he first started working at the sporting club as a driver twenty-five years ago. 'Kabul was a really small city and only one in ten families had a car so I had a lot of work. It was a lovely place to be. There was hardly any pollution then so it was a really green city – not like today – and the gardens here were beautiful.'

Under the Taliban, Mohammed left for the comparative safety of Mazar-e-Sharif. When he returned to Kabul in 2001 the club's grounds were almost unrecognisable. 'Everything had been left to rot. They used the Yellow Building as a headquarters too but there was no electricity or running water. They left this teapot behind when they went,' he says, waving it at me. 'Nothing had grown in the garden, it was just dust, decay and ruin. The old gardener who worked here before had returned and I became his part-time driver. When the foreign soldiers took over the buildings here he was worried I wouldn't be allowed to stay so he put a hammer in one of my hands and a spade in the other, and dragged me over to the senior British soldier. "Look," he said, "this man is my deputy, he has been gardening with me for years. You must give him a security pass so he can continue to garden here." The British soldier gave me a pass and over five years the old man taught me everything he knew about gardening. When he retired I took over from him.

'There are some memorials to soldiers who died in Kabul. One of my American friends died in a suicide attack in the city. His name was Sergeant C. They made a statue for him and I ensured it was built in a neatly bricked area. Every year we remember his death. His wife wrote to me in thanks.'

Kabul, he explains, is a different place these days. Not only is it more dangerous, it is also more polluted. Fortunately for him, the perimeter walls act in much the same way as they did for the Emperor Babur half a century ago and protect the garden from the pollution. 'There are birds nesting up there too. They like the nature.'

A storm erupts as a Chinook hovers overhead, preparing to land on the football pitch. The trees shudder in the whipped and sliced wind and, when a thin orange dust cloud mushrooms towards us, my notebook is quickly covered by a layer of grit. Piles of leaves are flung like playing cards over the garden.

'They come and go all day long,' he shrugs. 'It is incredibly noisy but there is no escaping it here – you block it out. I should have been more careful about sweeping up the leaves. I will do it again later.'

Helicopters are not Mohammed's biggest problem, however. 'To be honest, military people don't like flowers. When they have free time on Fridays and Saturdays they mess everything up and leave chairs all over the place. I would plant flowers everywhere if I could but I don't think they would care. We have signs saying "keep off the grass" but they ignore them and trample all over the place, especially if they are in a bad mood.'

'Why do you bother, then?' I ask.

'The garden is important for them. When you sit behind a computer all day it's good to have a place where you can sit, breathe, drink coffee, meet friends and smoke. Some people say that music is the food of the soul, but *my* soul and my body feed on gardening. I'm forty-six and smoke two packets of cigarettes a day but I think I could scale a wall faster than any fourteen-year-old. It keeps me young. When I garden I think about life and destiny and where it's going to take me.'

Mohammed knows that his position is very much dependent on the continued presence of international troops in Afghanistan, which is already on the wane. His job, he realises, is not for life. But he has a plan; to go to America.

A slightly more realistic plan B is to open a shop in Kabul. 'Either way, the most important thing for me is the education of my children.' Unusually in a country where families tend to be large, he has just two – eight tragically dying at birth. 'I concentrate on my son and daughter all the time. I think about their lives and their futures.'

He looks up as the Chinook prepares to leave, eclipsed against the sun. 'My son,' he says, 'wants to be a pilot so I am working for his dream.'

*

'Of course this is just between us two but the British government is desperate for Afghanistan to go away.' The Foreign Office official whispers conspiringly when the group of journalists are out of earshot. 'It has cost God knows how much and how many lives already. It is an embarrassment really.'

We have just returned to the Provincial Reconstruction Team (PRT) headquarters in Lashkar Gah[9] from a graduation ceremony at an Afghan police training centre. I filmed the event as part of the Legacy Project, a joint initiative from my employers – NATO and the Cabinet Office. The Legacy Project is to be a congratulatory back slap to illustrate the successes and gains made in Helmandi security by the international community since operations began and before the PRT closes in a few months. The irony being that the security situation in Helmand has deteriorated so much that not only did another, more junior, official naively warn the group, 'it won't be safe, there *will* be Afghans there', we are not allowed to travel anywhere by road and instead are ferried ludicrously short distances at exorbitant expense in Osprey aircraft.

I hear a thud in the far, far distance; the war is rumbling on, tangentially. The departure and closure of all these bases, I think to myself, all feels so impossibly premature. The cynic inside me can't help but feel that the Legacy Project is just the final attempt at legitimising an unpopular war. Worse still, cash-strapped and working as a propagandist for the very organisation all journalists have hitherto derided, I am complicit in this.

The Foreign Office official turns to answer his tinkling telephone and mouths 'sorry' at me, before retreating to a corner beneath a hanging basket of begonias still swinging from the recently departed helicopter.

I feel suffocated and irritated. Everything and almost everyone I have spoken to here is so alarmingly disconnected from the reality of Helmand it would be laughable were it not such a crying shame.

The neatly decked FCO garden with its opulent if sterile plants and members of staff fiddling with smartphones and warning against talking to Afghans is just wrong. The war – and the country – feels very far away.

Outside the PRT gates is the rest of the military base, a more familiar, austere and significant landscape of tents, gravel and uniformed purpose. I have no business being there until supper, but when the Foreign Office official disappears into an air-conditioned building, I slip unnoticed through the gate to the military side.

I have been here before, but fleetingly, and it looks different now; it looks lovely in fact. It is early autumn but the remnants of summer remain in the flower beds flanking the pathways either side of the blast walls and in the cheery yellow sunflowers and black-eyed Susans. A cloud of purple and yellow Michaelmas daisies surprises me outside the British Forces postal office.

The sun shines through a bulbous head of bougainvillea like a Chinese lantern, and in the weapon-loading and unloading bay, there are healthy purple and red roses smothering the instruction panels. There is even a pergola covering a path to the tented church in one corner and, when I walk beneath it, I see that on the other side of the blast walls is a sheltered area of rough plywood benches.

Empty ammunition tins serve as ashtrays on low tables made out of oversized wooden cable bobbins. There are flower beds of rich russet marigolds, rose bushes and more sunflowers lining the plastic walkways, protected by a simple rope fence.

I lean against a pomegranate tree dangling its ripening ruby fruit. A vine next to it uses the wire mesh of the Hesco bastion as a trellis. The vines' grapes are dark and glaucous in the sinking light but they taste ambrosial. This place is built for war, I think, but it is paradise for these plants.

I sit on a splintered bench to smoke beneath a variation of a weeping willow. Someone had been reading a very old edition of *Country Life* and it falls open at one of the property pages; a vast Tudor mansion is for sale in the Home Counties with a mature walled kitchen garden. I look around me. The pictures in the magazine don't look half as nice as the garden around me right now, I think to myself as the evening light glows marmalade.

I begin to look for the gardener the following day. The Foreign Office man could easily help me find him but I would be required to submit all photographs and words for approval and I simply can't be bothered.[10] I find him at the back of the base sitting on his haunches beneath an old-fashioned military tarpaulin stretched between a corner of the perimeter fence surrounding another secret oasis. If yesterday's garden in the middle of the base was surprising, this one is overawing.

There are rows of heavy-headed dahlias, flame-shaped celosias and overgrown flower beds. Beneath figs and pomegranates are foxgloves and hollyhocks. Pelargoniums line the paths of head-high rose trees entangled with trailing ivy. The colours are often garish but there is something familiar about the plants.

The gardener, Ghulam Hazrat, pulls two discarded and broken office chairs out of his tent – the walls of which I notice are painted with birds – and we sit next to a rose bush. He holds a length of hose in one hand, ready for action.

The garden, he explains, came into existence before he started working here a few years ago. 'The soldiers started it. They brought plants with them from their own countries and planted them here. I think it reminded them of their home.'

The familiarity of the garden now makes sense, as do the gardening soldiers. In the First World War, soldiers fighting in the obliterated landscape of the Western Front sought (and often found) peace in the natural world. Nature was steady and certain and a reminder that life goes on. As the war dragged on, and trench life became increasingly primitive, they came to understand that the man-made destruction mortified the land, but a few still clung to nature's alternative reality of hope. A century later, that alternative reality is still sought, right here in the middle of southern Afghanistan in the heart of a base whose sole purpose is for war.

Ghulam continues, 'The other gardener was working here as a cleaner but he saw the soldiers didn't know how to look after the plants, and so started watering them from the well. The garden grew and grew and he could not do it all alone. I had a nephew working as an interpreter and he told me that they needed another gardener. I let the flowers in this garden self-seed now but the soldiers still bring me seeds from their own countries, which is always interesting. Most of the time I don't know what they are, but I enjoy working out where they grow best, what kind of soil they like and if they can take the sun.'

He disappears into his tent and returns with British garden centre-bought packets of asclepias, nasturtiums, garden radishes, zinnia and numerous marigold varieties. They are sealed shut with pale duct tape more commonly used by snipers to conceal their weapons. He shrugs. 'Sometimes they grow well, sometimes they don't.'

He replaces the packets in an old ammunition box and points to a group of soldiers sitting in the large gazebo at the end of the garden. 'If they are working here they can never leave the gates so it must be like a prison for them. At least they can come to relax here and enjoy the flowers. It reduces their stress. Mine too.'

When the base closes in a few months Ghulam will lose his job and, with few opportunities of employment in Lashkar Gah city these days, he will probably remain unemployed. But his main concern is his own security. As an employee of ISAF, he is at risk from accusations of collaboration if the wrong people find out who he works for – even as a gardener.

'I feel I am being watched so sometimes I don't go home but sleep in the work tent. I feel a bit like the soldiers here now – as if I am in prison. People outside in the city, they don't like where I work. But at least there are flowers here,' he smiles calmly, 'and for now, there is enough water.'

'Don't let them leave us,' he says, suddenly unsettled, 'If you do, the Taliban will catch us and cut off our heads.'

I want to say that he is wrong and that peace will endure but I do not even believe it myself.

'I love this garden and it will die without me,' he says. 'I am losing sleep just thinking about it. I have tried to plant flowers that like dry soil, because who else will water them if I am not here?'

Helmand

April 2014

'And far and wide, in a scarlet tide,
The poppy's bonfire spread.'

Bayard Taylor, 'The Poet in the East'

1

When Gul Habib was arrested it was a good day.

'They apologised and gave me $10 for the trouble! I told them if they were going to give me $10 again, they could come back tomorrow,' he laughs.

In a rather embarrassing case of misunderstanding, Gul Habib was accused of being a Talib by British soldiers surrounding his house two years ago. They were looking for a known insurgent and carted him away for DNA testing.[11] He laughs about it now but I wonder if he did then.

I am sitting in a large but ill-lit room in Shin Kalay, a small village in Helmand's Nad-e-Ali province with Dr Mohammed Kharoti, a Canadian Helmandi who divides his time between North America and Afghanistan. We were introduced by a mutual friend and he immediately offered to host me for a few days and introduce me to Helmandi gardeners.

The journey from Kabul yesterday was easy enough on a domestic flight in a better-than-the-national-average plane. With my head leaning against the window, I became a bird circling the world on air currents and whimsy over fantastic spines of snowy mountains, through an unfamiliar horizon of icy cirrus clouds, almost invisible from the ground.

In arrivals (a scrap of land delineated by a chicken wire fence) Dr Kharoti spotted me easily – 'the only blonde!' he laughed. I was also the only Westerner in a passenger cargo of – largely male – Pashtuns as we drove into the provincial capital.

Winter had been reluctant to leave Kabul; snow still menaced. Lashkar Gah, 630 kilometres or so further south and 1,000 metres closer to sea level was ten degrees warmer, and I opened the car window to let in the warm spring air. Time slows in Helmand, and Lashkar Gah had changed little in the few years since my last visit. Shops were slightly more abundantly stocked with Pakistani-branded soft drinks and snacks, but it was only when a call to prayer fizzled through the mosque tannoy that I realised it was Easter Sunday.

Dr Kharoti had taken me to meet the provincial governor, Naeem Baluch. As his guest and as a visitor to the province it was a matter of courtesy, he had said – although I privately wondered if I was not just being shown off to add further leverage to the doctor's status as an important man. Regardless, when the salutations and meetings were over, I had wandered around the governor's official garden. Policemen patrolled the perimeter wall but I was excited to see so much in bloom. Bamboo ladders lay in the grass beneath pomegranate and apricot trees. Yellow daisies, misty purple petunias, orange hybrid tea roses, poppies – desert flowers, he had called them – lemon balm, honeysuckle, marigolds and wallflowers. It all boded well for the week I had planned to spend in Helmand.

For the United Kingdom, Helmand province *is* the war in Afghanistan. Between 2001 and 2014 the majority of its combat troops were deployed to the southern province as part of NATO's contribution to the newly established International Security Assistance Force, ISAF.

ISAF's mission, Operation Enduring Freedom, was simple: win the hearts and minds of the local population, help to develop the country and keep the baddies at bay. The mission, however, was riddled with blunders and mutated into one of the most needless and misunderstood conflicts of the twenty-first century.

The violence which erupted cost 453 British soldiers their lives and over 7,300 their limbs. Today the body count of those suffering the after-effects continues to rise as more and more soldiers take their own lives.

The land I saw as an embedded journalist years ago was a land of opposites. Inside the military bases or compounds taken over by ground troops, miniature domains existed – extraneous communities of soldiers, independent worlds without the world. And understandably so; for the soldiers, the environment outside the base walls was a purely hostile one.

Filtered through the dust-smeared windows of armoured vehicles nature and war were compressed into smudges of ochre and watery glass greens. Or, through the crack in an open truck door the outside world was an elongated dusk that feathered the sand dunes pink and purple. During a convoy through Sangin a cracked bulletproof window had refracted the town inside out and upsidedown, obfuscated, repeated, deleted.

And it was a world of subverted nature. Heat and war had emptied the landscape of people – apart from fighters who kept to the shadows. Ditches, paths and fields were planted with IEDs, crops were trampled over, tilled fields exploded, thickets were ripped up, trees were cut down to give troops better views and, on one occasion, an American marine fired so heavily in retaliation to incoming rounds that a tree burst into flames. Its charred remains etched a smouldering fissure in the graphite winter sky.

But when the battles paused for breath and the unnatural noises were silenced, the countryside revealed another, more bucolic, layer. There were wild flowers and thistles hunted by brave butterflies and bees. Dawns broke with occasional birdsong, purple-tinged dusks were mined by darting house martins, swallows or bats. Bulrushes grew out of bogged irrigation canals, home to frogs and toads leaving concentric circles that continued to expand and mesmerise long after they had swum away.

And in the villages, the residential compounds' thorny roses scrambled through mulberry and pomegranate trees in small courtyards. Some had only recently been vacated and the slinking vines and scarlet geraniums coloured the wattle walls. Others had long since been abandoned and grew untamed and wild until, hit by torrid heat, they dried and died.

The desert beyond was a vast and ancient seabed and teemed with weird-looking creatures with too many legs and claws instead of mouths: translucent scorpions, wild dogs, lone wolves, snakes and unidentifiable creatures that screeched into the night. They were home to lonely winds, whirling dust storms full of jinn, harvest moons and complicated constellations splashed across a sky. Oddly, I had never felt so alive in that devastated, diametric land of war.

But that was then. It is April 2014 and combat operations in Afghanistan will end on the last day of the year. The war is nearly over, but before it is, I want to revisit Helmand and say goodbye to the landscape and the war I strangely miss so much.

Gul Habib is Dr Kharoti's older brother. Unlike the doctor, Gul Habib has never left his homeland despite nearly forty years of continuous unrest and war. His grey and brown silk turban trails over his shoulder and rests on his pot belly like the tail of a cat.

Dr Kharoti had promised me that his brother's garden was a beautiful one and I took the literal translation of his name – Gul, meaning 'flower' – to be naturally indicative of his skills as a gardener. I quickly realise that the definition of garden has a much broader meaning in Afghanistan where the same word is used for garden and orchard.

'I don't have a garden,' he says, rubbing his beard. I sigh. It is not a great start.

'At least, I don't have a flower garden. My land is my garden.' He points at the wall behind him beyond which it presumably lies.

It is land the Kharoti tribe were allotted as part of the government's social engineering programme to settle nomadic tribes and different ethnic groups from all over the country in a newly fertile Helmand.

Until the early twentieth century most of Helmand province was an arid and uncultivated desert. In the 1920s and '30s Japanese and German engineers began toying with irrigation projects but they became embroiled in the Second World War and concentrated their attention elsewhere. In the 1950s the United States, determined to establish a modern agro-utopia in Afghanistan as part of their fight against the competing influence of the Soviet Union and Communism, took the reins. The Helmand River Valley Project was at first so successful that the new agro-industrial provincial capital, Lashkar Gah, was known as 'Little America'.

Photographs from that time paint a very different picture to the one we have today. It was built on an American 'grid' design with wide, tree-lined and asphalted streets. Modern white-stucco brick houses were set back from the road separated only by white picket fences and green lawns bordered with flower beds. There was also a swimming pool, a co-ed school and a clubhouse.

Over the years, agricultural projects stopped and started but the communist coup of 1978 put the brakes on everything. The Russians arrived and, during the ensuing civil war, agricultural development in Afghanistan ground to a halt.

Gul Habib's land became an unnatural 'warscape'. 'The rockets just got bigger and bigger and created craters as big as this room,' Gul Habib says, his brother translating. 'They splintered trees to matchsticks, and the smoke and debris blocked out the sun. Nothing grows in darkness and there was neither means nor money to buy anything.'

When the Taliban came to power they brought law and draconian order, which was initially welcomed after the devastation, cruelty and corruption left in the post-war vacuum. For the first few years, life was peaceful in Nad-e-Ali for Gul Habib. But the quiet days were short lived when the Taliban urgently needed men and money to fight the Northern Alliance and conscripted fighting-age men.

As the main breadwinner and, crucially, as a landowner, Gul Habib was exempt from fighting providing he grew poppies. 'I am only a simple farmer and had no idea how to grow it but some people from the mountains came to teach us. I could not believe how easy it was. I earned over five times what I had before, and if I employed more people during the harvest to increase the yield, I could double it.'

He has not grown poppies since 2008 but not due to any moral scruples. 'There are so many people to bribe that there is little benefit these days.' Instead, he grows wheat. The wheat is his garden.

We go outside and walk across a recently ploughed field. Our shadows are short and cling to our feet along with the damp earth. It coagulates over my boots, covering them so completely that they become part of it. In the distance, black smoke rises from a chugging tractor chimney and I notice there is a small building on the far side of the field with a blue metal door.

Dr Kharoti is in front of me and translating something but his voice is lost and I am not listening. The tractor and the blue door feel familiar and I am certain I have been here before. It is at once winter and I am lost in an overcrowded memory of snapping sound barriers and hissing radios. Someone is hiding behind a blue door and firing from a crevice in the wall. I am cold and scared and I can hear someone shouting at me to move, move, move.

'He says the soil here is weak.' The doctor's voice brings me back to the present, but wondering if my memory serves me well or if it is bent on deception, I ask Gul Habib if foreign soldiers ever crossed his land.

'Oh yes,' he says turning to me and swatting a fly out of his face. 'All the time. I gave up trying to farm properly while they were here. Some British soldiers cut down one of my mulberry trees because some [Taliban] soldiers had hidden there. I was compensated with 45,000 afghani (£450) but those trees take years to mature. It wasn't enough.' He sighs, 'I really loved those trees.'

Surprisingly, Gul Habib is not critical of the British presence and the ensuing temporary loss of livelihood. Two of his own sons are currently serving in the Afghan National Army (in a typically strategic move, another is serving as a Taliban foot soldier, thus ensuring safety for the family no matter who wins the war) and he understands the anxiety of families who waited for their sons at home, the sacrifices made and the losses incurred.

'They [the English] gave up their sons and we know there are mothers and fathers grieving for their boys, sisters crying for their brothers, and we weep with them for their loss. A lot of their blood has been spilled on this land.' He describes a specific incident in which an Afghan soldier shot a number of British counterparts in a forward operating base nearby. 'Their lives were ended, cut short,' he says shielding his eyes from the sun. 'The poor families. It is all I can say.'

The two brothers walk to the edge of their field to say goodbye. The doctor will return to Canada soon but his brother will stay in the garden. In a few weeks it will have ripened, been harvested, stubbled, ploughed and furrowed and returned again to earth.

Mullah Issa won't look at me.

I have asked him his age and he shields his eyes with one hand and continues to stroke his ink-black beard with the other, turning his head to the wall to answer, refusing to look at me, a woman unrelated to him.

'I think I am about forty-five or forty-six,' the mullah bellows, half deaf. 'I must be about that age because I'm starting to lose my hair and teeth.' The effect is faintly comic but I stifle a giggle.

I wanted to speak to a Talib Mullah about the religious importance of gardens. It was Jolyon Leslie who sparked the idea when he mentioned Talibs being more interested in their roses than checking his paperwork in the nineties. I have met members of the Taliban in Kabul but for the most part they were relatively indifferent about speaking to female Western journalists. In the provincial south it is a different story.

Dr Kharoti arranged for us to meet in the anteroom attached to the village mosque. The only problem is there is no garden.

It is a mild inconvenience but I am enjoying watching his refusal to look at me – a gorgon of the West – and his faintly ridiculous shouts at the corner, and I feel sure that despite the absence of a garden, he will have his own private space somewhere.

The mullah has only been in residence at the mosque for a few years but he originally hails from the neighbouring district of Narh-e-Saraj.

'My father was in love with God,' he shouts at the wall when I ask what drew him to religion and I smother my mirth with the end of my headscarf, 'and wanted to encourage piety in me.' Issa had run away from home for a day after a beating from said father, 'so I was sent to a madrassa in Quetta.'

His dispatch coincided with the arrival of the Russians and the subsequent war. Unable to return to Narh-e-Saraj, Pakistan remained his home for thirteen years.

He returned to Afghanistan with the Taliban, the ranks of whom he had joined in Quetta as a bona fide religious fighter, settling in a village just outside Spin Boldak on the Afghan border. 'I just wanted to teach religion to the young.' He relaxes a little and lowers his hand with a glance in my direction. The green silk turban covering his thick hair compresses his eyebrows heavily over his dark green eyes, neither of which point in the same direction.

After three years in Spin Boldak he was moved to Lashkar Gah, the capital of Helmand. As a member of the Taliban, his memories of their reign are naturally very fond. 'Apart from the lack of electricity, everything was wonderful. There was no corruption, life was really good; we had peace and everyone was safe.'

When they were overthrown the mullah returned to his family home in Narh-e-Saraj as a semi-'reformed' Talib but was shocked at what he saw. 'It was terrible. There was corruption, murder, theft, and people were having intercourse with little boys.'[12]

The presence of international troops eradicated a lot of this as people fled to other parts of the country or were absorbed in fighting the enemy invaders. But the coalition's agenda was never clear and their allegiances were confusing for Afghans.

'I was teaching in a school and some soldiers arrived. They were looking for the Taliban and some of my students went white with fear that I would be taken away. Luckily one of the other teachers spoke to their interpreter and told them that it was just a school. They apologised and asked what I wanted from them. I said "Peace. And for you to go away." They shook my hands and gave me a turban as a gift.'

The incident is mildly amusing but sadly demonstrates how little we understood the situation not to mention the limitations of some of the military interpreters.

'And your garden?' I ask at length, 'did you have a garden then?' Afghan storytelling is an arduous process, and often to extract just one piece of relevant information can take reams of note taking.

My heart sinks when he says, 'No. I didn't have a garden. The soil in Narh-e-Saraj is too salty.'

It is said that ten centuries ago the lush green fields of Helmand were laid to waste by Genghis Khan. According to some legends he ordered not only for the fields to be razed and the trickling irrigation canals filled in, but in a typically belligerent mood he salted the land, thus condemning it to remain a barren wasteland. Poor drainage and ignorance concerning irrigation methods is a more likely cause for its current salinity, but either way, the mullah has no garden.

Somewhat exasperated, I ask him about the opium trade.

The speed at which poppies grow, the labour force needed to harvest it combined with ease of storage and transportation is what makes opium such an attractive crop, and something which continues to impede billion of dollars of counter-narcotics initiatives.

The poppy was widely grown in parts of the country long before the Taliban were in power and had been for centuries. Its cultivation was declared illegal in the 1970s, but in the more remote parts of Helmand controls were little enforced. And, thanks to instability, poor governance and the irrigation system, the province remained excellent ground for continued cultivation. Cultivation for the international market continued to soar under the Taliban but, fearing market flood and collapse after a bumper crop in 1999, the group's then leader Mullah Omar, banned unauthorised growing, thus ensuring that global prices remained high.

When the Taliban were ousted, the drug lords they had chased away were reinstalled by the US-led coalition – who, incidentally, had more or less backed them when they were fighting the Russians. Between 2008 and 2012 the UK and US governments spent between $12 million and $18 million per year on the Helmand Food Zone, a programme which ran alongside increased troop presence and was designed to bring about a reduction in opium production.[13] Initial successes were short lived, and today Afghanistan still supplies over eighty-five per cent of the world's opium, and the business of the poppy remains deeply entrenched in the agricultural economy of south-western Afghanistan.

The mullah is surprisingly candid and proud about his involvement. 'It is great money and I was good at it too. Very quick!' he uses both hands to mimic the method of latex extraction.

'But,' I argue, 'surely it is irreligious and forbidden in Islam?'

'It is,' he replies and looks me in the eye the first time. 'Everything about the poppy is sinful in the Qur'an; its cultivation, irrigation, harvest, trade, its use. Everything. But the money it provides is *jihad* against the invaders and that is why we do it.'

Mullah Issa begins chatting and chortling with Dr Kharoti. I look out at the mosque on the other side of the courtyard. It is a single-roomed, nondescript building. Had I not been told its use I would have mistaken it for an abandoned schoolroom. A scraggly patch of grass outside is browning beneath a torrid sun. It is not even pretending to be a garden.

The mullah, having claimed the religious high ground, has given up deferring to the wall and follows my eyeline. 'It is sad,' he admits. 'I wish I had a proper garden. We need greenery to refresh ourselves before, during and after prayer. Bread might feed the body but flowers feed the soul.'

He offers to show me the mosque. I poke my head tentatively around the door, but he shoos me inside.

It is a musty, dingy room. A thin, acrylic carpet lines the floor and I can feel the uneven cement beneath it.

On the windowsill are a handful of torn exercise books covered with pictures of the Kaaba, the holiest site in Islam in the centre of the most sacred mosque in Mecca. Qur'anic verses hang from the walls and a few rolled-up, fraying prayer mats are stacked in a dusty corner. A clock stopped ticking at five to nine a long time ago. Much to my surprise, he poses for a photograph in a recessed alcove surrounded by the wall hangings.

Next to the exercise books on the windowsill are two forlorn flowerpots of wire leaves and orange plastic roses. A layer of dust has paled them to beige. The mullah picks them up and blows the dust away with a puff and hands one to me.

'There is a line in the Qu'ran from the Prophet Mohammed,' he says, his manner now bordering on the avuncular. 'If you want to see God, give a rose to your neighbour as a gift.'

The doctor leads me back to the mosque anteroom on the other side of the village and a teenage boy arrives. His shy, adolescent voice has only just broken, and a dusty *shalwar kameez* hangs off his bony frame.

Like a kind grandfather, the doctor pats the cushion next to him and the boy sits, adjusting his sparkly skullcap self-consciously.

The boy is Habibullah, the son of a local cotton farmer. When I ask how old he is he shrugs. 'Maybe fourteen or fifteen, I don't know. I don't have an identity card.'

But it is not his age that I want to discuss. Habibullah has just finished the last day of his first poppy harvest in the fields just outside Camp Bastion, the British military mega-base.

Habibullah begins, 'The work was hard but it was a nice way to spend time with my brothers and friends. I really loved sleeping outside. There are so many stars at night. I use a *nushtar* [a knife specifically used for opium extraction], and scratch notches in the seed head. You have to leave it overnight and collect the sticky stuff in the morning. Sometimes you can go back to the same plant two or three times, but it depends how good you are. It is only my first year but I collected eight pounds.'

For his labour, he earned two of those pounds, which he had to hide under a rock on the way here. 'There were police everywhere and if they found it they would just keep it for themselves. It will be safe until the desert people come to buy it. After they take it, I don't know what happens.'

I ask what he can expect to make with his two-pound yield and he starts counting on his fingers. Struggling, Kharoti gives him an impromptu maths lesson. It is a totally surreal take on a basic school arithmetic class involving citrus fruits. 'I have eight pounds of heroin and I give a third to Simon and a quarter to Susan. How many pounds of heroin do I have left?'

At length he calculates, 'Around 20,000 Pakistani rupees.'[14] This is about $200, but the street value of his yield (once it hits Europe) is close to $20,000, more if cut with other chemicals.

'Have you ever tried it?' I ask Habibullah and he shakes his head. 'No. My friend smokes it and he is so ill and skinny now he can't work. Why would you take something that stops you functioning? And it smells terrible. So does he.'

The domestic toll of opium on Afghanistan is huge. The UNODC (United Nations Office for Drugs and Crime) estimates that the number of Afghans addicted to opium rose by sixty per cent between 2009 and 2014. When the figures were published, a friend joked that perhaps this was boosted by the number of expatriates working for the very same organisation smoking themselves to annihilation at weekends.

I ask Habibullah what his motivation was to work on the harvest, having seen the effects of the drug on his friend.

'My family,' he replies. '$200 will buy new tyres for my father's tractor and he really needs them.'

When Habibullah was about seven or eight Shin Kalay was full of foreign soldiers. 'They came and put a checkpoint in at the end of our road and stopped anyone trying to get through. They kept on destroying our crops with their tanks and then they started coming to our homes at night looking for something.'

'When was this?' I ask him.

He starts counting again, but this time in seasons, and his memory is inexact. 'Four or six summers ago,' he says.

'I don't know what it was they were looking for but it must have been really important because they did some really bad things while they looked.'

'Like what?'

Kharoti and he talk for a minute. 'He doesn't want to say.'

'I am glad they have gone.' Habibullah says. 'The mullah tells us that poppy is a sin but that it helps to fight them so I will do it every year.' He turns to Kharoti to ask if he can leave.

We leave the anteroom too and return to the car parked at Gul Habib's house. He is not there, and when we enter the compound the women preparing supper and washing clothes in the courtyard scatter like jacks, desperate to remain hidden from my camera, which is not even on.

We drive back through the flat sandy tracks of the village, the dusk stretching every shadow, until we reach the road to Lashkar Gah. There is a makeshift petrol station comprising a trestle table, canisters of fuel and rough tin funnels. White chickens are also for sale from a small cage adjacent. A motorbike carrying three passengers overtakes us, a van without a number plate toots us out of the way in the other direction.

We pass an abandoned military base, a former world within a world. Its entrance, once fortified, is open. Three boys on bicycles circle each other. A policeman sleeps and the curious tableau vanishes. At the bridge into the city the traffic begins to congest. The cucumber and tomato sellers are out in force, their produce stacked with geometric precision, shiny bright green and red in the generous evening light.

In Kharoti's city compound, a modest, discreet building down a backstreet of a backstreet, I arrange my notes and pictures, and when the generator comes on I charge my camera batteries.

Moths cluster, drawn both to the bare bulb above my head and the bright blue screen of my computer as I type. They hurtle through the darkness and one lands on my arm, oversized and alien looking and I flick it away, revolted. It leaves a brown dusting on the back of my hand.

Before closing down and switching off my laptop, I connect to the internet and look up the incident Gul Habib had described. On 3 November 2009 five British soldiers were shot and killed by an Afghan policeman they had been living alongside in Shin Kalay. Their lives were cut short, felled like a tree. Gul Habib's words ring in my ears. 'The poor families.'

2

The sun peeks through the thin curtain at the window. At first an uncertain glimmer, it grows vivid and stronger with every minute and it takes me a moment to remember where I am. The sounds of morning are muffled but unmistakable: hushed voices, shuffles, stretches, a pot clatters, a tap gushes with water, a match is ignited, a gas canister opened, a tin kettle rattles. Somewhere a rooster throws out its scratched song. Beyond the courtyard is the city, also yawning into a morning routine. Bicycle bells, car horns, the first fruit and vegetable pedlars, and an ice cream van whistles its arrival.

An hour later I am in the back of the car and can barely see anything at all. The blue mesh presses against my lashes and blurs any view of the world. It is intolerably hot and, unable to breathe properly, I feel half starved of oxygen. The fabric is also squeezing and pinching the crown of my head and I am becoming disorientated.

Until now, Dr Kharoti has waved away my suggestions of wearing a burkha, explaining, 'People know I know foreigners.' Today is different, however. We are about to meet Mirwais Khan, the son of the Kharoti leader and a distant cousin of the doctor. He has both a criminal record and an enormous orchard and the doctor is nervous.

He is an imposing, thickset figure with wrestler's shoulders beneath a starched, creaseless *shalwar* made brighter by an unblinking sun, and the train of his deep-black silk turban dangles next to his left arm like an oversized eel. His beard is short and neatly trimmed, and he moves with the unhurried pace of someone used to having things done for him. I don't ask his age – he probably would not know anyway – but mentally place him in his mid-forties.

We are drinking tea in the fruit orchard of one of his properties on the outskirts of Shin Kalay.

A large faded red carpet has been laid out under one of the pomegranate trees. Its pattern is a repeated 'elephant's foot' of vines and leaves. Fruits above us are beginning to swell and there is a vineyard on our left, but the grapes are still button-small and sour.

Beyond the orchard and the vineyard is a large house of mud and wattle, but sturdy, built to last. It is the largest traditional house I think I have ever seen. Its courtyard is in part covered by a pergola and young vines. A creeper of some description smokes through its branches.

From the orchard I can only see one of the boundary walls of his land and I hazard a guess that the vast acreage around us is not a means of escape or therapy; it is a status symbol, for in such a feudal society, land comes with power.

But sitting beneath a pomegranate tree in a luscious orchard it is hard to place him. He throws a pistachio shell into the grass, hitting a beetle, and wearily describes a series of incidents which convinced him that the British military were untrustworthy. This includes working with the police who were notorious, locally, for being criminals or for having direct ties with the opium trade and the Taliban, and becoming embroiled in a series of Mafia-style vendettas enmeshing Helmandi politics and pissing off a lot of the wrong people. As he speaks, he has the air of a benevolent yet weary king, just waiting for the fuss of war to dissipate so that he can carry on being lord of the manor, or *Shah-i-Qala*.

But at the same time he is a shadowy figure. In 2009 he stole wheat seed intended for his community from an ISAF-backed development project[15] and sold it. Surprisingly, given the level of corruption in the Afghan justice system and that most get off for much worse crimes, he was prosecuted and spent a year in prison.

Criminal activity notwithstanding, Mirwais is also a fighter and comes from the warrior class, duty bound to resist and defend his land and community from outsiders. 'In the beginning, we didn't know where the foreign soldiers were from. All we heard was that they were looking for al-Qaeda,'[16] he explains.

'In *Pashtunwali*,[17] if someone comes to your home or land without the permission of the head of the house, you can kill them,' he adds, and points to the compound walls. 'There was a line of division on the other side there. Most of the villagers left but I stayed. It was *my* land they were trampling over. My *ancestors'* land. I wasn't going to let them do that.'

Ultimately, or course, it is the land which owns Mirwais and he is part of its honour and value. Its invasion meant that he *had* to fight the perpetrators and fight he did. 'The foreign soldiers destroyed the land when they came with their tanks. The soil became so compressed that the farmers couldn't farm.' He explains that had the British engaged in the rules of *Pashtunwali* from the outset, perhaps the outcome would have been different. 'They did not have permission but they entered our homes, they killed, they cut up our land and destroyed our peace.'

I am photographing him in the corners of his orchard while battling the harsh glare of a keen sun when he says, 'The garden is a place of enjoyment where you can refresh your soul. But when there is fighting there is no time for pleasure, only fear and worry.'

Back at the car I replace the nasty blue nylon burkha over my head. It only comes to my calves, and my ankles and grubby trainers poke out of the poor disguise. I feel like a child dressed up at Halloween and suppress the childish urge to prance around shaking my hands like a ghost. Instead I pull the headpiece back and thank Mirwais as deferentially as I can.

As I leave he looks me straight in the eye and says, 'There are many things which happened in Helmand while they were here. Many things which we will never write down to remember, as sometimes it is best to forget. But what would you do if foreigners invaded your garden?'

The road is a straight line of white chalk ahead of us. Poplar trees flash by on either side, bulrushes cool their feet in the waters of irrigation canals. A motorbike driven by a young man transporting a large melon, two burkha-clad women and a child lags behind us and almost crashes when we swerve to avoid a donkey.

When we reach the junction heading out of Nad-e-Ali towards Lashkar Gah city we turn for Marjah, a small town in the heart of the poppy-land where we are going to meet Abdul Hakim, a labourer who has recently turned to farming.

In 2010, Marjah was where it was at for poppy farmers. The surrounding area was controlled by the Taliban and drug traffickers who were exploiting the local population. Operation Moshtarak, one of the largest offensives of the war in Afghanistan led by NATO forces, aimed to free Marjah of the Taliban – and the poppy.

Poppy farmers don't exactly get rich from their crop, but they can make around twelve times more than from legal crops. Straight eradication has never worked. The people most affected are always the farmers, who are already indebted to the Taliban who loaned them the money to buy seeds and fertiliser in the first place. Without a crop to pay them off (and without a viable alternative) poppy-less farmers are left destitute. They are the perfect new recruits for the Taliban who offer a pretty decent wage of $10 a day if you decide to fight.

In the bid to entice farmers or labourers away from its cultivation or fighting, development agencies offer 'Alternative Livelihoods'.

On paper, Alternative Livelihoods is a brilliant scheme which creates jobs and income while doubling up as 'development'.

The reality over the years has not only been disastrous, it also perfectly illustrates how poorly Western governments and development agencies understood the dynamics of subsistence farming and indeed the needs of the population of Helmand province. They also massively underestimated the level of unemployment which the opium trade absorbed, year on year.

Ludicrous projects rolled out over the years as Alternative Liveli-hoods included building a cobbled street out of Lashkar Gah to the archaeological site of Bost (the Ghaznavid[18] capital of the province). It was abandoned after the locals complained that the stones hurt the camels' hooves. There was also a 'women's centre'- an ill-conceived idea given that most women in the conservative south are largely still at the bidding of their husbands. Then there was the cold-storage unit designed to help preserve fruits and vegetables for market – use-less in a country where even the capital city suffers from twice- and thrice-daily power cuts. Wheat seeds and fertiliser were handed out in another initiative. Often the seeds produced grass, not wheat. Not that it mattered; most bags of seed ended up in the markets in Pakistan and the free fertiliser was used for – guess what? Fertilising poppies.

We stop just after a fork in the road at a house – the only one. The smear of faded terracotta is humble even by Afghan standards. The walls look like they might not last the next rain shower.

A small thin man in a frayed *shalwar kameez* the same colour as the earth greets us quickly and hurries us inside, anxious to hide me – so obviously a foreigner beneath a burkha – from prying, suspicious and jealous eyes. The war might be drawing to a close but victory is still up for grabs, and colluding with a Westerner could send the wrong message.

The four walls of the compound enclose a bare and ragged court-yard. A washing line intersects the space, and out of a glassless window behind me I can feel watchful, silent female eyes. It is typical of traditional communities; she – or they – will wait out of sight until after we have gone. A bone-thin cow is tethered in one corner and metal pots and pans are stacked next to a large blue barrel. There is a hairline crack in its side and the water, having seeped out, has muddied the rest of the yard to slime. The ground is uneven and there is an overwhelming smell of ammonia, dung and spent cooking oil.

Abdul Haqib is clearly a very poor man.

He leads Dr Kharoti and me through a metal gate on the other side of the yard and across a dirt track to his greenhouse, a basic metal structure covered in plastic sheets. Inside there are cucumber plants strung up to a frame, lush and fresh, butter-yellow flowers bursting through.

He steps with a dextrous agility between the closely hung tendrils and explains they will be sold locally. 'The problem is that there are cheaper cucumbers coming from Farah or Herat, and if I sell at their prices, I don't make any profit at all.' It is a familiar story. Haqib's cucumbers retail at only three afghani each: just over a penny.

There is a bare-branched dead tree at the end of the greenhouse. Rags have been tied to its branches – to scare away the birds and insects, I am told. Behind it, I notice an enormous marijuana plant. Its elongated jagged leaves are unmistakable.

'It is from bird poo,' Dr Kharoti simultaneously translates Haqib. 'People feed the seeds to fighting birds.[19] It makes them better, stronger, more aggressive. When it passes through their system, it just grows.' It is a plausible theory but I am most interested in how large it is. It is almost as tall as me, and I teeter well over the average. Its leaves hang as large as my own hands, and with the heat of the plastic around us, the heady aroma is quite intoxicating. I wonder how accurate his story is.

Beneath the polyester *shalwar khameez*, a style of clothing popular among good country girls which I had borrowed off a girlfriend in Kabul, I feel nauseous and am uncomfortably hot. I am pleased to be out in the open when we make for his field. Haqib rents it, paying for it in yield; He gets to keep a third of the produce; the other two thirds go to the landowner.

'I will make around $400 in six months,' he tells me. 'I wish I could add some fertiliser to the soil to make everything grow faster, but it is too expensive.'

Four hundred dollars over six months is a pitiful amount and well below the national average. I make a few calculations in my head. The entire family survives on just over two dollars a day. Two dollars for food, cooking gas, clothing. Then there is the added cost of schooling, equipment, medical bills.

When he worked as a labourer in Pakistan as a refugee he earned even less *and* had a worse quality of life. 'Sometimes I would go for days without work. I could never provide for my family and we were always hungry. At least as a farmer I can grow food to feed them independently and sell the surplus. Everyone needs to be able to fill their empty stomachs. It's a matter of survival and pride.' He brushes away some dirt from his sleeve.

Six children smile shyly out of the wattle corner of the compound and skipping over to their father, cling to the hem of his shirt. They are small and undernourished. He lifts the smallest into his arms and holds her head close to his shoulder in the palm of his hand. She puts her thumb in her mouth and sighs – hungry, more than likely, but at least cradled with love.

His eldest daughter picks a cucumber from the greenhouse and hands it to me. She has a cleft lip and a lazy eye. When she smiles there are large empty spaces where there should be teeth, and when she turns back to join her siblings, her narrow shoulder blades almost slice through her *shalwar*.

I notice something else on the edge of the field. Poppies.

Waist high, their petals blush the glaucous leaves beneath them with pink and white. When I take particular interest Haqib is quick to explain that in a previous life the field had been used for opium farming but that *these* poppies are incidental, a by-product of mono-farming.

I am suspicious. Poppies do self-seed, especially when the crops are regularly rotated, but the 'wild' poppies seem to be growing in a very clearly delineated square, and the yield of opium here, although small, could add substantially to his pitiful income.

I ask about his luxuries – are there any? It is a trite question and I know it. There are no luxuries. I expect him to describe the horrors of poverty – perhaps a sick mother or a dying wife – or some other devastating layer to an already sad life.

'I can't afford to *buy* luxuries,' he says rather too brightly, smiling for the first time. 'But come with me.'

He leads us around the side of his house. His sons and daughters trip along after us like the children of Hamelin. Rounding the corner, we arrive in an orchard of fruit trees, with a mature vine and a bright pink dog rose in full bloom.

There are several rows of two-metre-high concrete posts with washing lines hanging between them over which more vines trail their tentacles. They are still growing – and growing strong – and in a few months, Haqib will be able to sell the grapes, but the vines offer more than that. Their leafy canopy will have created a hidden den carpeted by the grasses which already feel soft beneath my feet.

The children scatter and start playing a version of tag between the vines. The height of the posts and the length of the grasses dwarf them significantly and they disappear into another world, chattering and laughing together, unblighted.

I ask the skinny girl if she likes the garden. 'Yes,' she says, 'but school is better,' before running off to taunt a brother.

Dr Kharoti buys a sack of cucumbers from Haqib, giving him a more than generous market rate. They bounce around on the back seat next to me as we return to the fork in the road in a diminishing light.

As the sun dips lower, it pulls its blanket of stars. Concertinas of barbed wire top sandbagged checkpoints. We are one of the few cars on the road, and the Afghan soldiers newly in charge wave us through without looking up. I lean on the side of the car door, window open, letting my eyes follow the straight lines of the irrigation canals, intersecting the fields and roads in an unsolvable puzzle.

Haqib, like Mirwais Khan, is owned by his land, his garden. He will never be duty bound to defend it, but as his only source of income and sustenance, it possesses him.

So what, I think to myself, if he is growing poppy and trying to take ownership of his life by supplementing a pitiful income to feed an undernourished family. So damn what.

We re-enter Lashkar Gah and pull up at a metal door. On the other side is a large tiled courtyard connecting two tall buildings hidden from the road. The white ceramic tiles are dazzling even in the mallow light. In front of me is a set of stairs leading up to a door at which are a pile of shoes and five small children, dressed smartly in a mixture of traditional and Western clothes.

Most of the courtyard is taken up by a patch of grass that is around four square metres. It has been clipped short and it smells summery sweet with a three-foot-wide bed of lilac and white petunias surrounding it.

A fresh-faced man appears at the top of the stairs with a grin as wide as his outstretched arms. Having picked out his sandals he walks down to greet us.

Daram is an old friend of Kharoti's and a gardener, and his garden is a few months old. He created it for the private clinic (the locked building closest to the road), which he built a year ago.

There he treats around thirty outpatients at any one time. 'The garden is for them,' he says, and he leads me through the petunias and onto the grass. There is a military camp bed on the concrete path running along the south side of the grass behind the flower bed – a very tangible reminder of the war and recent military presence. He says, 'I encourage my patients to sit and read here while they are waiting or recovering from a treatment. It is a restorative, fresh place.'

He is not wrong. The combination of greens, whites and purples is calming and radiates a mother-of-pearl light. The flower beds also prove to be a barrier against the sounds of the city's rush hour outside the compound walls.

'My favourite flower is the *shaboo* – the wallflower – and next year I will plant some along the back wall.'

His granddaughter arrives with a metal tray upon which wobbles a pot of tea, glass cups and a bowl of toffee-fudge sweets, and we sit on the plastic chairs.

As a nurse in Lashkar Gah's central hospital he cannot be short of work so I am curious about his decision to build another, and no doubt costly, clinic.

'Security in the city had improved from 2006 to 2010,' he explains, 'but in the countryside, it was chaos. People were coming in with gunshot wounds every day, just regular civilians who were in the wrong place at the wrong time. There were the mines too and so many children who . . .' He notices another granddaughter and grandson hovering near us and shoos them away kindly. 'It was tragic to see and we were overwhelmed. All we could do was give them basic treatment and send them home as soon as they were able to walk.' The clinic is his attempt to relieve some of the hospital's burden.

Patients pay a small fee for treatment but I am curious as to how he funds the majority of the clinic. The answer is paradoxical.

His family owns land close to Gereshk, a town around 70 kilometres north of Lashkar Gah. They were forbidden from growing poppy under the Taliban but its cultivation, he says, is easy thanks to the state of insecurity, and his ancestral land is now entirely used for opium cultivation. 'In a good year, when the smugglers come from the mountains, we can make 100,000 afghani (around £1,000) after we have paid the harvesters.'

We go to stand in the middle of the grass when he says, 'The world is telling us that the United States and the United Kingdom came here to build security and peace but there is neither, so forgive us when we ask "Why is this not working?" Look at the hospitals. They are still full of children missing arms and legs, scarred for life. How is it that, after all this time, there is still no peace apart from in this garden?'

In 1915, Canadian physician Lieutenant Colonel John McCrae wrote his immortal poem 'In Flanders Field' after the funeral of a friend and fellow soldier. It describes the ubiquitous red poppies which grew in their thousands despite the destruction taking place in the countryside of Western Europe during the First World War, 'the war to end all wars'. After the armistice, the poppy became the symbol of remembrance, sacrifice and futility.

A century later the dynamics of war have changed but the poppy, as a symbol, remains the same. Every year hundreds and thousands of paper poppies are sold across Britain and pinned to lapels so that we can all remember the sacrifices made by our armed forces through all wars. It is bitterly ironic, therefore, that the remembrance of 453 lives lost in *this* war is with a paper version of the very thing that funded the people who killed them.

There is a second irony. For the soldiers readjusting to limbless lives, their bodies crisscrossed with scars like contour lines on a new map, morphine – an opiate – would have been the initial pain relief administered. After the discharge papers have been signed, some newly civilianised soldiers find themselves resorting to opiates and alcohol in an effort to escape the horrors and memory.

I look at the cot bed beneath the clinic's windows. The clinic he has built to treat the civilians caught in the crossfire he believes is brought by the presence of international soldiers who are fighting an insurgency funded by the crop he insists on growing . . . to fund the clinic which props up the province's reputation as a narco-state . . . which only perpetuates the cycle of poverty, escapable by growing the poppy. And so on.

It's an Escher drawing of never-ending and interconnecting ladders and doors which open onto themselves. And here we are in the centre of the clinic's garden. Daram turns to talk to his old friend but I remain beneath a nacre lamp, deflated. Next to a stump of a fruit tree against a wall, I notice a white poppy growing wild. Paper-thin petals which will not last long, a bursting seed head which will.

Arlington Cemetery, Washington, DC

March 2016

'Certainly flowers have the easiest time on earth.
"I shall be one with nature, herb, and stone,"
Shelley would tell me. Shelley would be stunned:
The dullest Tommy hugs that fancy now.
"Pushing up daisies" is their creed, you know.'

Wilfred Owen, 'A Terre'

1

Kelly is planting daffodil bulbs beneath a tree when I find her in the stone garden.

'They bring such spring cheer on a day like today,' she says, wiping her hands clean and shaking mine and smiling. 'Plus, they kind of look after themselves.'

She leans down to pick up a leaf from the stone floor. 'As a gardener here you are very much dealing with life in a place of death and it is my job to ensure that what grows here brings joy to visitors and offers them a space to grieve.'

We are in the columbarium at Arlington National Cemetery – America's national burial ground on the outskirts of Washington, DC. The columbarium walls are lined with niches for funeral urns.

I had risen early to catch dawn rising from the Potomac River to meet Kelly Wilson, a horticulturalist working at Arlington. I am in Washington for other work, but I wanted to visit that most grand of final resting places and maybe to pay respects to the soldiers who had uttered their last in a land I had once called my home.

Kelly pulls her thick fleece around her as the March wind starts biting through the concrete and granite corridors and I envy her jacket. A flour-fine drizzle begins to fall and I sneeze. Yesterday was so warm I was too hot in jeans and a T-shirt, but winter has returned today and I am not dressed for it. I am not even wearing socks, and can feel my feet begin to freeze in already soaked canvas shoes.

'You wouldn't believe how hot it gets here in August,' she says. The columbarium stones absorb the heat and she and the team are constantly playing with creative horticultural ideas to keep the few plants there healthy.

We walk onto a pathway to join an asphalted road surrounded by headstones. It is a still and beautiful sight; there are more soldier-straight verticals and horizontals of stone than there is land, and they shiver into new geometric shapes with each step. There must be at least 10,000 of them marching up and over a hill a kilometre or so away. The brow is broken by solid silhouettes of trees not yet ready for spring.

'There are over 8,600 trees in Arlington,' Kelly tells me. Most of them are oaks which are indigenous to Virginia and a lot of them are as old as the cemetery itself, which dates back to the late 1860s. There are also basswood trees and peeling river birches and 'milkweed for butterflies, they love the leaves and hummingbirds love the nectar.' Somewhere behind us I can hear crows squabbling. 'We have lots of wildlife. Birds, coyotes, deer, foxes, squirrels, chipmunks. There is twenty-seven acres of them to play in so we plant with them in mind too.'

The land was originally owned by George Washington's step-grandson, George Washington Parke Curtis, who bequeathed the land to his daughter Mary and her husband, Robert Lee. The Lee family fled their home in 1861 after the eruption of the Civil War, and federal troops occupied the property and land as a camp. It became a burial ground out of necessity after the number of casualties exceeded the capacity of civic cemeteries.

Since that war, over 400,000 active duty American soldiers, veterans and family members have been laid to rest at Arlington. Today, there are currently thirty active burial grounds, or 'sections', as they are known here out of seventy-six – and there is a constant traffic of funerals.

'We concentrate on those areas and ensure everything is immaculate for people visiting loved ones. In the summer it is a challenge; we have a whole month of drought and the turf irrigation here is poor.'

I notice that the 'section' we are passing looks incomplete. The headstones come to a stop in the middle of a row. It is as if it is waiting to be finished.

'Oh. That is Section 60. It is the burial ground for the current wars and KIAs – killed in action. Most of them at the moment are from Afghanistan.' She goes on to explain that things are a little bit quieter there now since the withdrawal of troops but that '2011 was a busy time in Section 60.'

I know, I nod. Between 2009 and 2011, an extra 30,000 US troops were deployed to Afghanistan as part of the US government attempt to prevent the war being lost.

'There must have been a funeral a week then. Often more. We had a problem working out where to put the earth dug out for the coffins.' It is a poignant problem. I notice a mound of earth on the other side of Section 60.

'There were a lot of visitors coming then too. Other soldiers paying respects to their buddies, young wives, parents and children. It was a really sad time. Now, if ever I hear there is a funeral for a soldier killed on active duty, I take the time to look them up so as to feel more connected to them.'

I stay in Section 60 after Kelly returns to work, my feet now numb to the cold, and walk between the headstones, recognising some of the names and battle dates. Unlike the war cemetery in Gaza, it is forbidden to plant anything at these graves, but loved ones are free to leave cut flowers and offerings. The cold expanse of headstones is intermittently broken by a handful of red tulips, a cone of pink-fringed carnations, a bouquet of yellow and red roses, white lilies. Four bouquets of carnations, roses and primulas sit on an unturfed, unmarked grave, the most recent addition to Section 60.

The fine drizzle falls faster and harder and I retreat to shelter beneath a bare oak, keeping my eyes fixed on the headstones. Names read out in memorials, listed in newspapers or carved into stone become almost meaningless statistics. But seeing the final epitaphs of so many who died in some godless corner of Afghanistan I feel like I am seeing ghosts.

Ukraine

August 2014

'You look and see nothing, and you might think there wasn't a garden at all; but all the time, of course, there is, waiting for you.'

Philippa Pearce, *Tom's Midnight Garden*

1

The motion of the train finally rocks the other women to sleep. Very quietly, from my top berth, I lift a corner of the curtain, eager to catch a glimpse of the world outside. There is a bright pearl moon creating a midnight twilight in which the fields of wheat glow pale rose-gold.

A few hours later the sun is kissing the morning horizon. Lucid light, fragile day. Most of the other passengers, including my cabin mates, have already disembarked and disappeared into the pre-dawns of unpronounceable towns. I open the curtain fully and lie on my stomach, head resting on hands and look down and out through the smudged glass and candescent light.

The hedgerows are trying to overwhelm the train tracks and I am convinced I see a pair of fox's eyes staring out at me. Beyond the thickets is undulating farmland, acres of wheat, maize, barley, sunflowers. Only the telegraph poles interrupt the land with a lyrical rhythm. My eyes follow their wires as they whizz up and down, connecting lives with energy and light.

A lurching stop wakes me from a doze. The landscape outside has changed and is now an entirely man-made vista. Slag heaps, improbable dunes of the underworld, rise from the ground. Centuries ago this was a rolling, monotonous plain, scarred only with gullies and natural ravines. But the surface beneath was ferrous and coal-rich, and a century of mining and fast extraction has left its mark on the pastoral hinterland. Railways and highways, heaps of slag and factory chimneys now break the middle distances. The natural river systems were affected too; the gullies gave way to reservoirs and subsidence, and the collapse of the old mine shafts has given rise to ponds.

Today crop fields skirt around the Mordor-like pyramids of mine waste for it is a landscape where agriculture and industry still sit shoulder to shoulder: it is the landscape of the Ukrainian Donetsk Oblast, and this is a unique journey: I have never taken a train to a front line before and I am oh so excited.

I check my watch. It is past eight o'clock and we should have arrived in the province's capital, Donetsk, two hours ago. The GPS map on my telephone indicates that we are still miles away.

The delay is disconcerting. I had heard that the railway line here is vulnerable to shelling. I make for the end of the carriage and stand at the join with the next one, smoking a thin cigarette with two other bleary-eyed passengers seemingly unfazed by the delay. A conductor approaches and I prepare for a telling-off (there is a 'No Smoking' sign next to us) but instead she asks for a light.

The engine squeaks shrilly and the nuts and bolts rattle as we edge our way, incrementally slowly over short metres of track at a time. When we pull into the station at Donetsk we are three hours late, and the whole city feels weirdly deserted.

*

Against an urban skyline a thin fog clings to the surface of the reservoir like a veil the following morning. Fishermen sit at the water's edge next to poplar trees between the bridges, their long rods already planted in the ground, with coffee, cigarettes and expectation in hand. There is no humdrum, no sound of traffic, no commuters rushing, nor are there eager joggers pounding the pathways. Just the miserly fog and weeping willow leaves dipping their tips on the surface of the water.

I see a bed of colour ahead and my idle step quickens. There they are: hundreds of deep, velvet, royal red roses. Strong, sturdy and indifferent to time. Next to them is a bed of fragrant white ones and beyond are the pink and yellow ones calling for attention. The light is downy soft and sublime-perfect. I lift my camera and begin to photograph.

A white van hurtles around the corner, screeches to a halt and the passenger door slides open to deposit a handful of militiamen in front of me. They are all armed and some sport bandanas. Three immediately light cigarettes. The rebels.

The shortest one shouts something at me in Russian and the smokers look on with a combination of mild curiosity and disdain.

I look back blankly and casually sling my camera over one shoulder hoping that the combination of shorts, T-shirt and flip-flops I am wearing makes me look more touristy than terror-isty. 'Just don't piss off the rebels,' I remember the advice given to me a few days ago by John, an old friend from Kabul now living in Kiev.

'*Dokuementa?*' says the shortest one, holding his hand out. This at least I understand.

I delve into a pocket for the A6 piece of paper date-stamped the previous day and a fake identity card from an obscure but official-sounding journalists' association in London. While the rebels gather around it searching for anomalies, I light a cigarette.

'Camera,' the shortest one barks. I show him how to scroll through the images and step back, letting the group peer over his shoulder. The memory card on the camera is filled entirely with roses. Frame after frame blinks up from the screen. They mutter to each other but the only word I can discern is '*Rozy*? Something something *rozy*?' Two peel off and start to joke with each other like gawky sixth-formers.

'*Pressa?*' asks the shortest one, not without incredulity. I nod. He takes the camera again to check I haven't deceived him, then returns it to me, shaking his head, bemused.

He barks something rousing and, less than a minute later, both van and rebels hurtle up the empty Shevchenka Boulevard and into the morning. With the sun now a little higher in the azure sky, the scarlet roses around me cut through the morning like a shout.

It was Roland Oliphant, the *Telegraph*'s then Moscow correspondent, who had first told me about Ukrainian roses. We had spent a week being fake-kidnapped in simulated bomb blasts and road accidents by former SAS soldiers during a 'hostile environment' training week where newspapers are obliged to send their foreign correspondents. I was describing the gardens I had already encountered in unlikely wars when he interrupted excitedly. 'Go to Donetsk,' he said. 'It's the city of a million roses. And Ukrainians are crazy about their gardens.'

The conflict which had been sweeping Eastern Ukraine since early spring was one I had watched on news in Kabul with benign indifference. But I must have lodged Roland's idea somewhere at the back of my head, for when civilian Flight MA17 was shot down in late July by a Russian BUK missile and everyone on board was killed, their bodies scattered like seeds over a land they only came to be part of in death, I knew I had to go and find the garden-crazy Ukrainians and the million roses. Besides which, I had finally left Kabul but I missed the rawness and netherworld pulse of war.

On a cold, grey March morning, in the square in front of the Donetsk Oblast administrative building, the still skeletal birch trees defied the spring to come. Thorny, leafless rose bushes lining Donetsk's Pushkin Boulevard scratched at an overcast sky and the birch trees began to shake with protest. Eastern Ukrainians had grown sick of being dictated to by a government which alienated them. Feeling naturally closer in spirit and ethos to Russia than Kiev, demonstrators, wrapped up tightly against the brutal wind, tore down the sky-blue and sun-flower-yellow Ukrainian flag and shouted for Putin, for Crimea and for independence.

A statue of the poet and writer Taras Shevchenko looked on as activists stormed the building. By the end of the week, the government had retaken control but, over the following weeks, more and more anti-government demonstrators took to the streets with flags, fury and a mind for a fight. A month or so later, against an uncertain April sky, separatists had taken control again.

Spring exploded in the city as quickly as the unrest rampaged through the east, enveloping other towns and urban centres in the most easterly regions of Ukraine. The industrial city of Donetsk quickly found itself the de facto capital of the self-proclaimed Donetsk People's Republic, and the city's budding trees and thorny rose bushes, of which there are one million – one, supposedly, for each member of the population[20] – were at the heart of one of the most unexpected and violent conflicts of 2014.

Those who had the means to, fled. Some to the Black Sea coastal resorts of Odessa and Mariupol, others over the border to Russia.

But not everyone was able to leave and not everyone wanted to. Their roots, like the roses, lay firmly in the East.

Artem – an English-speaking chemical engineer doubling up as my fixer – and I are walking up Pushkin Boulevard towards an austere, 1960s tower block. It is surrounded by sandbags, razor wire and rubber tyres, and a rag-tag crew of separatist supporters and soldiers in mismatching uniforms mill about in the forecourt. I can identify some old British army desert fatigues – the kind used in Iraq and Afghanistan before the multi-terrain pattern was brought in – and a few Macedonian army smocks. Tall birch trees, now leafy, are pulled with a rustle by a slight breeze. Black, blue and red flags of varying sizes hang limply at corners and from poles, and a banner written in Cyrillic sags over the building's entrance. The scene looks very familiar; we have arrived at the headquarters of the Donetsk People's Republic where I need to register as a visiting journalist.

The boulevard is a paved, tree-lined walkway in an upmarket area of Donetsk. There is a children's play park, a number of cafés, boutiques and large metal sculptures of trees whose jagged leaves catch shards of light. There might be a war going on, but to look at the flower beds you would never know it.

A platoon of women of all ages, aproned and armed with rakes, brooms, gloves and pairs of secateurs – the municipal babushkas – tends to them. I ask around for the 'head' babushka. Katerina, we are told, is up by the white roses.

A tiny lady with short white hair, cropped trousers and a flowery apron looks up when we call her name. She squints at me through thick, heavy-rimmed glasses and shakes her head when she finds out I am a journalist.

'No,' she says, 'I'm not going to talk to you.'

Artem is not surprised; not only does her age indicate a natural wariness of foreigners from the West, but Katerina is a survivor of the Soviet purges and knows from bitter experience that to be pro or anti war, independence, unification, Russia or Ukraine, is to be condemned, one way or another. Right now, opinion in the city is polarised; civil war is simmering and she is very anxious not to self-condemn.

Roses provide us with common ground and she agrees to speak to me about them. She puts down her broom and sits on the bench next to me. I take out my notebook and ask for her full name and age. She laughs and says something to Artem who translates with a smile: 'I am Katerina and I am over sixty. Let's just leave it at that.'

I ask her about the roses and how she came to work here, and she paints a picture of an older Donetsk.

She has been a gardener for forty-five years, thirteen of which have been spent working for the Donetsk municipality. She had no formal education in horticulture but when she began working in the city hothouses, she took to it immediately. 'I know every plant I work with, what they like and how they should be pruned.' Her initial hostility has dissipated and she is jovial and at ease. 'Working with plants gives you spirit. Forty-five years, after all – you'd think I should know a thing or two by now!'

Katerina describes a modest upbringing with her mother and grandparents in the countryside. They arrived in the city in 1966 shortly after it had been renamed Donetsk – after the Severesky Donets tributary from the River Don. Until then it had been known as Yuzovka (the Russian translation of 'Hughes'[21]) and for a brief time, Stalino. When Katerina's family moved here, the newly de-Stalinised Donetsk was expanding fast.

'Now life here is even better,' Katerina adds as she pushes her glasses up the bridge of her nose.

National Day is in a few weeks and she is working hard and diligently to ensure the city's municipal gardens are ready for everyone to enjoy.

But she is not worried. The roses will do most of the hard work. 'You couldn't get anything more perfect than Donetsk roses!' She has to get back to work and stands to resume her sweeping and pruning, a curiously small figure, swallowed in chest-high rose bushes.

We walk back down the boulevard. Shops are boarded up, empty trams tinkle past, walls glisten with freshly spray-painted Donetsk People's Republic flags. We cross the Kalmius River at a narrow point of its reservoir. The sun is hot now and bleaches the world white. In the Scherbakov Park, one of the public leisure parks bordering the reservoir, surrounded on all sides by concrete high-rises there are more gardeners still, cutting this way and that with wheelbarrows and hosepipes. The water spray catches the light chased by rainbows.

A sonic claxon booms and bounces over the water – a mournful, strange, siren. They are the hourly alarms from the metallurgical factories which have been closed thanks to the war and continue to echo into the city, vacant apart from a brigade of gardeners.

We drive out of the city centre in the afternoon to meet Alexander. From the back of the car I get a sense of the size and scale of the city with its long wide avenues and large public squares watched over by enormous bronze statues and brutalist twentieth-century tower blocks, the concrete skyline of the city's utilitarian factories rising even higher above them like fingers. Almost empty of its residents it is an ordered city, neat but eerily calm, post- or pre-apocalypse.

Reaching a suburb on the outskirts of Donetsk, we stop at a tall, slate-rendered apartment block, one of several belonging to a housing estate of industrial menhirs. A concrete courtyard is strewn with litter and debris and lined by a few straggly trees. Washing hangs between windows nine floors high.

Inside the fifth-floor apartment brown velour furniture dominates the floor space, and the green walls of the living room are crammed with the debris of a life of books, papers and thoughts. It is a dark and musty room, broken only by the natural light from the window. The balcony that it belongs to is stuffed to bursting with tomato plants.

Alexander is in his sixties. His most recent job was in one of the local steel factories, and before that he was a member of the intelligence services. He has lived in the apartment for twenty-two years. 'I don't have an outside garden but I keep over thirty plants on my balcony,' he says proudly. 'In the spring I grow green onions and in the summer green peppers and tomatoes, which my granddaughter enjoys looking after with me. I like seeing my tomatoes against the clear sky but I suppose I will have to put tape up on the windows if the explosions and fighting continues.'

He has been showing his five-year-old granddaughter, Sonia, how to keep the tomato plants damp and fresh with a fine spray. When he sets the bottle down to greet me he does so with such care it is as if he is trying not to wake sleeping children. He sits in a deep velvet armchair and she perches on one of the arms, twirling a strand of hair around one finger.

Times are lean now but he describes with fondness a bigger family house, a dacha[22] and a more prosperous youth. He had to sell everything to pay for his wife's medical bills. 'When we had the dacha, we grew what we needed and preserved for the winter. It was convenient and we never needed to buy anything. Everything is different now, but lots of old people like me still try to live like that,' he says, pointing to his balcony.

Now Alexander finds therapy in tending his plants. 'I have had a kidney problem for over ten years and the drugs make me stressed and super nervous. Gardening counteracts this; it relaxes me. There is a micro-climate around plants too which helps to clean the air and the colour green calms the nerves.'

Unlike Katerina in the city, Alexander has much to say about the current situation. 'It is an artificial war. In February, no one would have said it was possible to divide Ukraine in two. We in the south-east have our roots in Russia, while those in the west, in Kiev, have more links with Europe, but we were still one multicultural country and we were all friends. Now the government is trying to destroy our infrastructure, cutting off our electricity, gas and roads and killing our civilians.'

He becomes agitated, begins to spray his tomatoes again. 'Since the war started supplies have dried up, people have lost their houses, jobs, lives. I can only get the medicines I need to survive from Russia.'

As the shelling encroaches he anticipates fighting will arrive in the city before too long, but it is his children and grandchildren he is most afraid for, and not just because of the imminent battle; the influence from Western Ukraine is far more dangerous than war, and his garden has become an extension of traditional Ukrainian values. To understand vegetables and growth is by default to understand what it means to be a 'good Ukrainian'.

'I am teaching my granddaughter how to grow tomatoes. It's important to make our children love gardens; it teaches them old-fashioned values to enable them to be good Ukrainians in the future and understand how we had to grow things when we were younger. I don't want my children or grandchildren to be like the youngsters of Kiev who cannot think for themselves and who succumb to fascist propaganda.'

I look at his granddaughter on the other side of the room. The orange and pink flower pattern of her summer dress punctuates the brown sofa – unlikely periwinkles in a woodland floor. She adjusts her pink hair band and smiles at me, revealing a small row of milk teeth. Very confidently she springs into life to spray the balcony tomato plants.

I ask her what she enjoys most about gardening and she replies earnestly, 'I like how things grow, smell and taste. It is different to what we get in the supermarket . . . more sweet and juicy. When I'm helping my grandfather, I think about how tasty the little ones are going to be when my grandmother adds them to borscht. When I grow up I think I want to be a painter.'

Back in my hotel room, ten floors above the earth, sleep evades me yet again. I lie awake in the darkness for hours, thinking about roses and war. But despite the war's proximity I feel mostly absent from here and take little comfort in anything.

About thirty kilometres east of Donetsk is Khartsyzk, a small industrial city, home to a number of factories and foundries. In April 2014, Khartsyzk was taken by armed men and quickly absorbed into the newly formed Donetsk People's Republic. The outskirts of the city had suffered under heavy fighting and, given its proximity to Donetsk and that city's own current unrest, served as a foreshadowing of things to come.

There I am to see an unusual garden, Artem promises me.

We arrive at the home of Anatoly and the buttery morning thins. The single-storey house sits in one corner of his plot of land and he is standing outside in shorts, T-shirt and flip-flops, waiting for us. A small sheet of hessian sacking from which hang rows and rows of brown plastic bottles shades the garden patio.

A chicken wire fence delineates the space of the garden proper into an orchestra of flowers, vegetables and fruit trees. It is a delightful oasis of plenty. But I notice something else. Palm trees made out of plastic two-litre soft drinks bottles.

'She likes making things, my wife,' he says as the bottle-bottom sheet ripples a translucent shadow across his face. 'Hates to throw things away. It is important to have space for beauty, otherwise, what else is there?'

They have lived there, he explains, for fifteen years, first moving when he found work in the local steel factory. The garden represents everything they have worked for and built up together, but Anatoly is modest and credits the garden's success to his wife: 'I just help her out with manual labour.' But having sent her away to her sister when the fighting came too close, he is now the one responsible for everything.

In gardening he has found a new escapism. 'When I am here, I let my mind wander over the borders into the past and the future and away from the present troubles here. The situation is becoming increasingly difficult and living is harder, but the garden calms me down and keeps me connected to my wife.'

We walk up the central pathway between the garden beds. There are swollen cabbage heads and cauliflowers under pear trees and a proliferation of marigolds which have been planted 'to keep the bugs at bay'. The sun is hot and dry and the cosmos and zinnia petals hang still, preserving their energy.

Last year, he tells me, he and his wife were planning their retirement and future, but this year they don't have one. 'Too much blood has been spilled already in this war, so Ukraine will never be united again. I thought we lived in the most calm and quiet country in the world – no one could ever have imagined this war.'

Anatoly can hear shelling every night, and knows there is more to come. 'I'm just waiting for it to arrive, and I think this time next week there will be a battle here. I have already made the basement ready. There is a mattress, food, water and tools in case I have to dig out of the rubble.'

At fifty-seven he says he is too old to be scared, but Anatoly is worried about how he and his wife will survive financially if Donetsk falls. 'We don't have the savings to start all over again and it's not like anyone is going to buy a house in this region now, even if the garden *is* as beautiful as this one.'

By the time we return to Donetsk, the light has mellowed a little. We take a tram and hurtle across the city to another empty suburb.

But not everyone has left; I am going to meet Helena, a grandmother with a garden next to her house. We knock and a shell thuds softly in the distance.

A vine- and rose-covered pergola lead to four allotment-style beds in which, at a first glance, I can see growing keen runner beans, solid courgettes, noisy nasturtiums and frilly lettuces next to bee-loved sunflowers.

Helena shakes my hand nervously. She has a neat bob, which she smooths with her hand, and readjusts a pair of blue-rimmed spectacles. We sit at a table beneath bamboo-slatted shade and she scuttles inside the house to produce a magnum-sized glass bottle that had once held Smirnoff vodka. She pours a rust-coloured treacle syrup into small thimbles and announces proudly, 'My most recent batch of rose petal wine! Drink!' I sip.

It is enamel-scrapingly sweet and the alcohol catches the back of my throat, but the infusion of tea roses is comfortingly familiar and reminds me of a rose tea I had once sipped in the souk in Aleppo, many, many years ago. She takes a sip too and sits back in her chair with a loud sigh.

'No one has ever cared about politics in the Donbass. It has just always been a mishmash of Russians, Ukrainians, Greeks, Jews and Georgians. The pro-Russians have always just been "the pro-Russians" and the pro-Ukrainians were always just "the pro-Ukrainians". The rest of us were just people in the middle, not really caring about either. Now we are all divided and we don't know what to do or where to go.'

She is monumentally distracted and is continuously moving cups and papers around the table. At one point she jumps up to pick some radishes but forgets the task in hand after a few minutes and returns empty handed.

She wrings her hands – hands, she says, which were in the soil for most of her youth. Like Alexander, her family had a dacha, which they used for growing their own fruits and vegetables, preserving what they could not eat for winter. And also like Alexander, they sold the dacha.

In any one year they would harvest apples, pears, beetroot, carrot, cabbage, strawberries, raspberries and grapes. 'Oh, and potatoes,' she grins, 'lots and lots of potatoes for the winter.' They would also grow flowers and sunflowers 'like you've never seen!' and deep red and pure white roses, from which she learned how to make the rose-petal wine. She pours me another thimbleful.

The rise of convenience foods and the ubiquity of supermarkets has done away with dacha-style vegetable gardening. Until this year, her garden was full of flowers only, which she grew purely for her granddaughter to play in.

The war has changed all that.

Supermarkets and grocery shops, she explains, are no longer being restocked with the cheap imported vegetables. Many stores have closed indefinitely and the prices of produce in those that have remained open have soared.

As a result, she is falling back on the old ways and growing her own produce: tomatoes, lettuce, carrots, radishes, beets and potatoes. 'Enforced gardening like this doesn't relax me, but when I see something growing it does make me hopeful. If it's something I can show Sasha, then so much the better.'

Her granddaughter is only five, but is aware of the war. 'She sees the soldiers in the streets and her mother has to work long hours as a translator so she knows something is up.'

Gardening with her granddaughter gives Helena the greatest pleasure of all. 'When she sees things growing in the ground or in the undergrowth, she cries out, "Look, Babushka! Look how big they have become!" It is like magic for her.

'Am I scared? Yes, I'm scared. I never expected this. When I was Sasha's age we were locked into a cold war between the Soviet Union and the United States of America. Back then, there was always *talk* of war. But I never thought I would see war as an adult. The city is so empty now it is not even eerie or strange any more, it is just horrible. You used to have to be careful when you crossed the street, there was so much traffic. Now there are barely any cars on the roads at all.

There is another thud in the distance and she takes another sip of rose wine.

Sasha, oblivious to the noise or the heat, runs between the flower beds, skipping freely amidst the dark green heads of Swiss chard, her brown pigtails bobbing on her shoulders before joining us at the table, gulping a glass of water between gasps. 'I like growing things with my babushka,' she pants, when I ask. 'This afternoon we were gardening cabbages and I like it because I like growing vegetables you can eat because I like eating. I also like picking flowers for Mum to have when she gets home from work and she is tired. When it's hot I like to play and ride my scooter and bike in the garden. My favourite flowers are roses and camomile.' She turns to her grandmother, 'Please can I have some sunflower seeds now?'

Helena chuckles, instantly calmed by Sasha's unfiltered youth and innocence.

The shelling intensifies that night. From the relative safety of my hotel room I see puffs of smoke appear on the near horizon accompanying dull thuds of the doomed and damned. The sky above is cluttered. The stars are crowding round to watch as the cross hairs of urban conflict close in on Donetsk, a forgotten corner of Europe.

The morning shines bright. It rained in the night and I imagine hissing embers of burned-out craters. We drive to Leninskyi district, at the intersection of the Durna and Kalmius rivers. The district has borne much of the brunt of the shelling and been badly hit. Most of the residents had left in the spring. The whole place is deserted: no cars, no stray cats, no ne'er-do-wells looking for a quick loot. The plots of land – the gardens – surrounding the single-storey houses are unkempt and scraggly.

Igor is a friend of a friend of a former colleague of Artem. Apparently his reputation for gardening amongst his work friends is unsurpassed, and when we arrive, I can see why. While the house is a modest-sized building of old stone and terracotta roof tiles more befitting a farm and distinct from the neighbouring bungalows, Igor's garden stretches behind up the sides of a steep stone-terraced hill from the top of which can be seen faint glimmers of city life. But looking up from the lowest level, it feels more dingly-dell-Dorset than downtown Donetsk.

Each terrace is contoured with vines, lines of runner beans, fruit trees, lettuces, aubergines and courgettes. Every shade of green imaginable has been scrubbed and polished bright by the morning's rain.

Igor, dressed in gardening shorts, T-shirt and holding a ball of twine, takes us up to the second-last terrace to sit on an upturned log next to the vines. It is his favourite spot in the whole garden, he says. From there he can see everything he is growing, but the city – and the war – is part of another world.

The organisation of the terraces of his garden is of individual mini worlds within worlds. At every level there is something new and beguiling. The neat vegetable garden is a palette of ripening tomatoes, aubergines, peppers and cabbages. Roses snake through apple and pear trees, marigolds and chrysanthemums at their roots.

Plump ruby strawberries nestle beneath its dark green leaves next to a substantial rockery of ferns.

Igor was born and raised in the house and has never left. 'It is my pride and joy,' he says looking fondly at a spray of pink and white petunias.

He works as a supervisor in a metal plant – one of the few still open. However, as so many have left the city, his staff of seventy-five has depleted to five and his workload had decreased accordingly. 'It is a good thing,' he says, 'I can devote more time to my garden.'

His garden is the greenest – and objectively prettiest – of all that I have seen so far in Ukraine, and the most mature. Over eighty per cent of the garden is productive but he is always rotating his crops, vegetables and flowers in search of the most beautiful combination.

'I mess around with colours. The purple cabbage and orange trumpet flowers kind of complement each other. I think the only things I don't grow are potatoes and onions. I love the combination of roses and vines and often sit up here or under a plum tree in the evening. It makes me feel wonderful at any time of day. Even in winter! It is full of life. My youngest sledges down the hill and the snow-covered garden is full of his laughter and delight.'

His children are with his wife in Kirovograd (a city 500 kilometres west of Donetsk) where he sent them as soon as the shelling started. 'I wanted to go with them; I miss them. But I couldn't,' he says, his arms outstretched as if embracing his land, his garden. 'The war is eerie and unsettling, but here I do not notice what is going on and it is easy to forget the war. I could never have left all this. It is my home.'

When we leave Igor's hidden garden world, the world outside looks like a crueller place. The sun has burned off the morning clouds and everything is sharper, hotter. The empty houses are more hostile, the electricity lines more frayed. Nearing the city centre there are a few people and traffic and hustle has amassed. It seems as if there is an urgency, a frightened energy there; no one wants to be trapped in traffic if the shelling starts.

We continue west to meet Alexi, another factory worker at a loose end. On the way we pass a crater where a shell had landed during the night and, although no one was hurt, half a building now teeters in the rubble, greying with smoke. The sky has clouded. War is coming closer.

Alexi is carrying a spade over his shoulder and a large green children's buggy in his hand. He is, he admits, bored. The factory where he works was closed over a month ago. Although at first delighted with the spare time he had to fix up his house and garden in preparation for his wedding, he is now listless. He is also worried and afraid. The city power usually cuts out at dusk, and for the previous few evenings he has sat on his porch with candles and a bottle of beer, pretending everything is normal.

But the previous evening's barrage was so close and loud that he slept in a corner of the room beneath blankets. 'If you hear it during the day it is somehow less frightening . . . you can kid yourself it is a car backfiring or the TV. Unless of course you see planes or hear machine-gun fire. At night it is harder to normalise the sounds.'

Alexi is an average guy in his late twenties trying to get on with his adult life, and does not understand the conflict. 'Why are Ukrainians fighting Ukrainians? I don't know who started this war any more or who to blame. I have heard propaganda from both sides. I just don't know what to think, but I do know that I don't want to die or continue to live in fear like this.'

He has spent the day clearing out a storage cellar and ensuring it is well stocked with blankets, food, water and a torch. Extreme but necessary measures. Dark circles of sleeplessness frame his eyes. 'This house could easily have been hit,' he says. 'Tonight I will sleep in the earth like the garden.'

The house used to belong to his grandmother and he remembers playing in the garden. 'I was about three years old and used to drive this buggy up and down the pathways as she gardened. Now I am the one gardening – and it is my nephew who races around the garden in the green buggy. I hope one day it will be my own son or daughter.'

Before he started work, the garden was scrappy, he says. 'At least it is doing all right during the war.' He has planted petunias, roses, yellow daisies, geraniums, phlox, orange gladioli and pink rudbeckia. The cabbages are twice the size of rugby balls beneath giant asters, and the tomatoes are bursting scarlet-red and ripe. He has tamed a white hydrangea and now the garden is so neat that neither leaf nor bloom is out of place. The impending mortification of war might loom but this patch of land is alive.

But, he says, he derives little enjoyment from it now. 'Before the city changed, I would be at work all day and only be able to enjoy the garden in the evening. My friends would come over and we would chill out here with a few beers and talk about the future. There was always stuff to do in the garden but now that I have done it, I can't enjoy it on my own.' He deadheads a wilting black-eyed Susan, its black centre a solar eclipse against the yellow petals.

The distance rumbles.

'I do not want to live in a country where citizens are killing each other and I have to sleep in a hole in the ground, but this is my home.' He pushes the buggy down the path. 'It is where I've spent most of my life and where my memories are found. Where else could I go?'

He stops abruptly and looks up in alarm when we hear another loud clatter.

'There's another shell right there – did you hear it?'

The cottage garden sits at odds with the ultra-modern train line of cables and shiny steel track slicing through the countryside. It surrounds the single-roomed railway cottage office with a moat of marigolds and beds of white potato flowers. The stairs leading up to the front door are well worn, which only adds to its old-world charm. The meadowsweet flowers either side are dandelion soft. I knock at the blue steel door but there is no answer. A pane of glass is missing from one of the windows, and when I poke my head through, I see a cup of tea still sitting on a desk of papers and timetables and a half-completed sudoku puzzle. It has the look of having been abandoned in a hurry – presumably when the railway was shelled – and judging by the layer of dust, more than a few weeks ago.

But someone has been defying the shells and maintaining the garden. The soil is damp and I notice a watering can next to one flowerpot. Some of the daisies have been recently cut too, and at the back there is a shed, padlocked, accessed through the grasses via a well-trodden path. I press my nose against the door and try to see inside but instead am met with the heady smell of creosote.

I turn back to the garden of trumpet flowers, daisies and two fruit trees. There is no sign of human life, no distant rumble of a car engine, no echoing electricity whispering through the cables over-head, no murmur of chatter. Only a bumblebee stuffing itself with pollen and the outline of a buzzard, hovering on a wind current in the field beyond.

We have just crossed into Ukrainian-held Slavyansk, about an hour's drive from Donetsk, and the railway cottage garden is right on a transient front line. The driver is becoming anxious.

The rebel checkpoint on the road heading out of Donetsk was little more than a pile of sandbags and a few sheets of corrugated iron covered haphazardly in Russian and Donetsk People's Republic flags. They had fluttered proudly above it against an azure sky. Cyrillic lettering spray-painted onto plywood warned drivers to stop. A short line of traffic built up as a few men in mismatching uniforms peered into each car, intermittently checking passengers' documents. They all smoked and two looked especially bored. They waved us through without hesitation.

At a junction further on we arrived at another checkpoint, but the rebel soldiers there were twitchy and kept an eye on the treeline at the same time as checking cars. A bead of sweat trickled from the hairline of the soldier looking at my accreditation documents. He crouched down at the driver's window and appeared to be using the car as cover.

'Go,' he said urgently. 'Just go. The fighting is about to start so hurry.'

The city disappeared behind us and we were out in the open countryside. The car hurtled past a field of elderly sunflowers. In the woods beyond them a line of Ukrainian tanks was preparing to move.

It is the driver's idea to detour over the railway line to avoid them. He had been reluctant to stop when I saw the railway garden and he keeps scanning the middle distance, so we continue on down narrow country lanes and arrive at a Ukrainian checkpoint. The young soldiers check my papers and passport, eyeing my camera suspiciously. One stoops down to my height and says in English, 'Welcome to Ukraine.'

Foot to floor, the driver pushes the car to its limit and bolts from the checkpoint, swerving to avoid the fragment of shell lodged in the tarmac, and up a very long, straight and steep hill. At its summit the pastoral countryside rolls out gloriously and it is hard to imagine anyone fighting here. It is a scene of late summer, fields and farming, sylvan glades and Georgic arcadia. But a puff of black smoke in the far distance and a boom from behind a few seconds later contradicts that; this is a landscape of movable front lines.

And somewhere out in that blurred landscape is the wreckage of MA17 and the bodies which had rained down. I had spoken to Roland about it in London. He had been to the crash site and described the indignity of it all: the bodies lying naked at the edges of sunflower fields, the mangled limbs that had become unidentifiable in amongst the debris scattered over a fifty-square-kilometre area.

In Grabovo, a village where part of the plane had landed, he saw the body of a young girl of about seven, lying deep in the grass. In Rosiponye he met a villager who was tending cabbages when a body fell through the roof of her house. Its head was found later in the cabbage bed. It is a horrible image straight out of a Hieronymus Bosch tableau of hell. I heard later that it was the local miners, used to dealing with horrific injuries and accidents down the shafts, who had volunteered to clear up the body parts.

Until 2014, like Donetsk, Slavyansk was just another ordinary Ukrainian city of industry. A series of counter-offences and stand-offs between the Ukrainian army and the separatists was the first major engagement between the two sides. The fighting intensified in a series of dirty urban battles over four months until Slavyansk was eventually retaken by government forces in early July and the rebels retreated south to Donetsk.

The city has been free for a month, but battle scars remain in its pockmarked buildings, black-burned and crumbling. Glass glints unevenly where once there were windows. Spindly trees stripped bare of leaves stand wearily in the smashed paving stones. It feels oppressive, claustrophobic; a sad suburban Gomorrah.

But a short drive out of the city centre, the sky widens over a flat plain and we arrive at a junction. Narrow, four-foot-deep ditches snake through the ground, too shallow to offer any substantial cover and too narrow to navigate comfortably. There is a fortified lookout at street level cluttered with cigarette butts, a sweat rag and a single playing card. The rest of the trench is littered with food wrappers, muddy rags, socks and boots – small windows into rebel trench life for the rebels who had lived and fought there.

We are in Semonyovka, a small suburb of Slavyansk. A few months ago, Semonyovka was the sort of place where front doors were always left open and nothing much happened. The population lived simply, working hard for a crust and living relatively comfortably, if modestly, growing vegetables and flowers in the large gardens surrounding their homes.

When fighting intensified in Slavyansk, Semonyovka, at a strategic position between the city and a major supply route from Russia, became a rebel checkpoint. For weeks hundreds of separatists held out against the Ukrainian army, but eventually the onslaught of shells and fighting defeated them, and Semonyovka was left broken and alone.

The homes that are still standing are open to the elements like dolls' houses. The remainder are splintered piles of timber, tiles and shattered lives, open for the world to see.

Bullet holes and shell craters have made a new landscape. A corrugated iron fence is riddled with bullet holes. Armchairs sit on mounds of rubble, a broken television lies upside down in a fireplace. A tattered rag that had until recently been a shirt clings to a tree and broken crockery glints white – shattered bones in a carpet of wild flowers which have outlasted the battle. The dark recesses of the storage cellars in the ground have been blasted open and their shelves, where once jars of pickles and preserves would have sat to ferment, are burned and soaked in vinegar.

The gardens of each home are now messy, disturbed by battle and neglected by their absent owners. Trees are stripped and charred, flower beds buried beneath bricks, raspberry frames flattened by broken windows. Bindweed has been left to run amok.

The storm of war has passed, at least for the moment. But the population is returning to piece the rubble back together. As we approach, there are sounds of tinkering and hammering. The latest pop song blares out from a radio, and what few roofs remain are dotted with shirtless men shifting sheets of corrugated iron to make their homes liveable. A few children forage in the debris for toys and books, and in the gardens people are trying their best to harvest what little is left.

Victor and Lupfof are staring at the broken skeleton of their roof. A satellite dish is hanging from one of its steel rafters like a tiddlywink. They were lucky; some of the walls at least still stand. But that is all.

However it isn't the material loss of house and home they mind, it is the destruction of their garden which extends beyond the rubble of their walls and into a twenty-metre-long field. As people of the land who usually subsist from what they grow, usually at this time of year they would be harvesting their vegetables and preserving for the winter.

Lupfof picks her way gingerly over broken glass in lurid green sandals to show me their garden.

It is a crop graveyard. The trees at its border are already dropping fermented, rotting fruits, useless to anyone or anything apart from wasps. The vine which had crawled so eagerly through its pergola frame has dried to a crisp brown. The ground beneath it crunches with its dead leaves. The ranks of small white metal frames for bush and climbing fruits and vegetables stand shoulder to shoulder – empty, null and void. There is only one feeble shout of colour: two red peppers – half living, half dead – their necks drooping, waiting to die.

Victor and Lupfof are usually able to sustain themselves from their garden, which this year would have yielded strawberries, potatoes, grapes and red peppers. What they didn't eat they would sell to the local restaurant or at the side of the road to passing motorists. 'We were just beginning to harvest the strawberries when the fighting started,' Lupfof says, scratching her head.

Victor bends down to pick the dried peppers. 'As soon as they had established a major checkpoint, the shelling and fighting intensified. There was a lot of shooting and we hid in the basement. The first four hours were the most terrifying; there is no natural light down there and you just don't know how long it's going to last or have any concept of time.'

Lying in the dark, counting heartbeats, counting shells. Hidden and trapped, suspended in time. It is a chilling thought.

Victor sent Lupfof and their son to safety with his mother, but he remained for six weeks, living off last year's pickles and preserves. 'Why didn't I leave? It is *my* house.' He looks up at me. 'I was born here. I had to defend it, stop looters, protect our land. This,' he picks up a handful of dried stalks, 'is everything we have worked for together.'

We walk to the end of his garden, the burned soil crumbling beneath our feet. He explains that eventually it became impossible to stay, and when he emerged from the cellar not a single house on the street still had its roof.

'We came back after the village had been liberated and it was like walking through a nightmare in slow motion. My mother in law had a heart attack when she saw how much had been destroyed,' Lupfof says, sadly.

We are standing at the far end of the empty garden by an apple tree. Beneath it is a broken glass storage jar that Victor pokes with his feet.

Lupfof tuts. The jar is fresh evidence of pilfering.

I ask them what their biggest loss has been.

'I think it is easier to say we lost everything,' she says. 'Now we just need to focus on repairs, regrowth and protecting our land from looters. Not that there is anything left to loot. I do not really know if I can say I'm angry with anyone. I do not know yet.'

'The only thing we have left are these peppers. Just two peppers,' Victor says, holding them out.

I stand outside the front of their house surveying the destruction again, trying to imagine what I would do if I had lost everything I had ever worked for.

I feel someone watching me and turn to see an elderly woman wearing a white bandana, perfectly framed by a glassless window in a red brick wall. A scrap of curtain covered in blue roses flickers across her face in the wind, but she doesn't move and I realise she is not staring *at* me, but *through* me.

I teeter through the rubble in front of her house. Her garden is open to the road – the fence having been razed – but there is still a gate and I knock. She looks up, nods and disappears from the window to meet me at her door-less porch. Her clothes are stained and smutted, and on her feet are green Croc shoes.

'I'm already famous,' she proclaims wildly with a mad cackle as Artem translates. 'Look me up. Alexandra from Semonyovka! A foreign radio station interviewed me, so you are too late.' As she laughs I notice that behind her thick glass lenses, her eyes are flat and unsmiling. She is not laughing at all: she is half-crazed. But she wants to talk.

We sit on her porch and she describes the weeks of darkness in her storage cellar.

'My neighbours are Jehovah's Witnesses and often we would hide together, but the shelling became too much for them and they left.' Having nowhere else to go, she stayed below ground for a month, emerging only to take the eggs from her hens and to pick the strawberries she had been growing.

When the hens died she began to sell or barter the strawberries to rebel soldiers in exchange for bread.

'I thought I would die in that cellar. It was like a tomb. I was alone, not even God came to visit. I tried to have conversations with him all the time and recited the *Otche Nash* (Lord's Prayer) all day long. How else can you get used to the noise of the bombing?'

She still hears the bombardments in her head and is crippled by insomnia.

'Do any of your neighbours have camomile daisies?' I ask.

'No idea. Ask them,' she replies belligerently.

'Well if they do, why not dry them to make a tea. It could help you to sleep.'

She nods curtly. 'This time last year I was beginning to preserve and pickle everything I had grown for the winter. Now look...' We go inside to her kitchen, or rather, the ruins of her kitchen. The wallpaper depicts pink vine leaves and succulent grapes, but everything has been smashed and broken. The only things still standing, miraculously, are the glass storage jars that will remain empty this year. There are a few succulent pot plants she has rescued from the garden centre at the edge of the village and she bustles over them, wiping their leaves clean.

Her garden is nothing but loose earth and splinters of red bricks. The displaced soil from a shell crater is piled next to the house like a slag heap. A few wild flowers are beginning to sprout and there are a few rows of strawberries just visible. I take a few steps towards them.

'Stop!' she shouts. 'Stop!'

I turn to her and she shouts something at Artem who in turn shouts that there are still unexploded shells and ordnance lying beneath the earth's new surface.

Gingerly, I retrace my steps through the minefield. Panic over, we sit back down on the porch.

She looks around the wreckage of her garden and shrugs. Behind her glasses, her eyes are very small when she says, 'This is usually just a nice, quiet suburb of Slavyansk, and this is everything I have ever worked for, there's nothing left. Not even the vegetable preserves.'

A dog appears in the garden and trots towards her, wagging its tail. She becomes engrossed in petting him like a toddler, immediately oblivious of me, so I leave her sitting on the doorstep, surrounded by mines.

A small boy picks flowers in front of a bullet-laced corrugated fence. He clutches wild daisies, cow parsley and marigolds and seems lost in their careful collection. I stand at the door of the family's skeleton home and his mother appears wearing a pair of large gardening gloves, which she uses to push the frizzy hair out of her eyes and smear a streak of mud across her forehead. Her name is Olga and her son is Oleg.

Unlike Victor, Lupfof and Alexandra, Olga is upbeat and practical when she shows me what remains of their possessions. The carpet of glass splinters and walls of protruding nails and hooks do not faze her.

'This was our garden,' she says when we are standing in the rubble of a room which has been blown out and into the open with the force of a blast. 'It used to be very productive with fruits and vegetables but they've all gone now, isn't that right, Oleg?' She ruffles her son's hair.

Like her neighbours, they sheltered for two days straight but left as soon as they could for her parents' house 'in a village just beyond the lunatic asylum a few kilometres away. From over there, we watched the destruction but then we realised our whole house was hit. It took half a life to build what we had. Now we have nothing again.'

We move through the house and the rooms are interconnected and disjointed like a warren. A wallpapered corner of the adjacent room looms yellow against the open sky. A whisk and a toaster stand on a windowsill that once had an idyllic view out into another part of the garden. Time sped up in their prolonged absence; the ruins are overgrown with thistles and thorns. Cornflowers, poppies, tiny daisies and a single snapdragon colour the sombre undergrowth.

Her stoicism cracks when she stops to look at them. 'The only thing to have withstood the battle,' she sighs, tiptoeing over to them.

'What are those flowers called? The ones where you say, "he loves me, he loves me not"? Daisies! That's it. I love daisies.'

I asks Oleg what he remembers about the shelling. He squints up at me and squeezes the flowers in his fist. 'We lived like moles,' he says shyly, 'there was no light down there. It was . . . it was frightening.'

He clambers over the rubble to his mother with youthful ease and gives her the picked flowers. She runs her fingers through his hair again. At least, I think, they have each other. Alexandra at the other end of the street is not as lucky.

Artem is anxious for us to cross back over the front line and return to Donetsk before dark. We walk back to the car our driver has parked next to what had once been the garden centre.

But I notice a woman sitting on an upturned bucket under a tree. When Artem looks at his watch and nods, I approach her.

She is dressed in holey red leggings, a green T-shirt and a white sun hat, and feverishly shelling a small pile of half-dried-out beans into a wooden drawer from a chest which is nowhere to be seen.

Situated so close to the crossroads, her house is the worst hit. All that remains are two walls and a garden path. It is hard to tell where the house ended and the garden began. Everything else has been obliterated and turned inside out: three balls of colourful yarn sit next to a pile of smashed-up preserving jars; a spade sticks out of what was once a fireplace; a broken sink sticks out of the roots of a tree. Lines are blurred; her private worlds are now open for all to see.

'I cannot stop,' she says busily and without looking up. 'I am harvesting and I have to do this quickly before the other things dry up and die too. Do you mind if I carry on while you ask your questions?'

Of course I don't, and I sit cross-legged opposite her on the ground. Lupvov's garden was her *raison d'être*, she tells me.

'It was always full and neat with lots of flowers and vegetables. I have lived here for eighteen years, working in my garden every day. Can you not tell from my hands?' she says as she holds one up; it is bramble-scarred and muddy. 'It was a serene place. Yes, I used to feel as calm in the garden as if I was knitting socks by the fire – it always made me happy.'

Lupvov grew everything, from ornamental flowers to potatoes, beetroot, beans, peas, carrots and cabbage to sell at the crossroads in order to supplement her pension. In addition, she would make one hundred litres of wine a year to drink or give to family. With singular dedication, she would wake at four o' clock in the morning to work in the garden until it was too hot.

She barely draws breath and her hands flit rapidly over the beans. 'When the checkpoint was set up I didn't know who they were – rebels or army – and I still don't know who they were. Do *you* know?' she asks Artem, but answers her own question. 'I think they were rebels. They must have been rebels. I didn't realise life could be like this, Ukrainian fighting Ukrainian. Maybe in other countries, or by other countries wanting to invade us, but not brother against brother. My parents are from west Ukraine – so why are people calling us Muscovites and Russian? I am neither; I am Ukrainian. I worked hard all my life as a good Ukrainian. I garden like a Ukrainian.'

It was after a week of the bombardment that Lupvov withdrew to the preserving cellar. Her windows were blown out shortly afterwards but it was seeing her pear tree destroyed which forced her to leave for another village. 'I loved that dear tree,' she pauses, 'It was always so generous in the autumn. When it was destroyed I heard airplanes overhead, and now whenever I hear them I think it's going to happen again.

When she returned, her heart broke; her garden withered and died on account of the blistering oblast heat and the lack of water. 'The people at the checkpoint weren't interested in keeping my garden alive.' Her clothes had been scattered by the force of the explosions into a neighbour's garden. It was Oleg next door who brought her a jumper he found in a tree.

'There is not much of my life left to live. I have nothing to rebuild with – not even a needle or thread. Only these beans.'

The silence, when she stops talking, is deafening. Only the sound of the dried bean shells falling keep time. It is hard to leave her in the ruins of her home, and we ask where she is going to spend the night. Her daughter, she says, will come for her after work. Artem gives her his phone number. 'She reminds me of my mum,' he says quietly when we walk back to the car.

We begin the return to Donetsk, but the front line we had crossed that morning has moved again and war blocks the roads. Every road we try to take is either blocked with soldiers waiting to deploy south or jammed with lines of cars queuing to escape the inevitable fight.

We stop the car to ask someone for directions or for another route. With the engine dead, the landscape is quiet and mellow. There is neither breeze, nor flutter of leaves, no whirring tractor or tank here. The stillness is broken only by a cooing wood pigeon. The ripe fields await the harvesters. In a week or so they will be baled into perfect rounds of straw. The late summer sun begins to decline into a long August dusk. A woodland copse on the other side of a field darkens. Only the silver 's' shape of a heron's neck is visible. A few fat spots of rain fall, inexplicably, from a purple sky. I yearn for home but realise I have lost a sense of what home is.

We drive through a village but turn back immediately when we

Alexi in his garden, Donetsk, August 2014. 'Tonight I will sleep in the shelter in the ground like my plants.'

Alexandra in her strawberry patch, Simonyovka, 2014. 'My son has told me not to garden because of the mines.'

Oleg picking flowers outside his home which has been levelled, Simonvka, Ukraine, 2014. '[During the shelling] we lived like moles in the shelter. There was no light down there.'

Igor in his garden, Donetsk, 2014. 'I can't leave, this is my family's home. Where else would I go?'

Bracha, Male Ifrahim, West Bank, 2016. 'They [cacti] are the plant of Israel; patient to take root with little water.'

Mohammed Hammud in his garden in Qalindiya refugee camp, April 2016. His house and garden were set for demolition as punitive action for his son's crimes against the IDF.

Sameer, founder of Amoro Mushrooms, in his empty mushroom farm, Jericho, April 2016. 'The Israeli musroom farmers are afraid of competition.'

Ayed in his garden in Boudrus, April 2016. He lead a non-violent resistance against the occupation and destruction of his village's ancient olive groves. 'It is land that our families have cultivated for thousands of years. Through our blood lines we are intrinsically connected to it.'

Hani Amer in his garden, which is separated from the rest of his village by the security barrier, April 2016.

Sylvia on her balcony in Beitar Illit settlement, West Bank, April 2016. 'I used to go walking in the hills below, where the Arabs live. But we're not exactly free to go there now.'

Fayez and Muna Taneeb in 'Muna's field' next to the separation barrier, Tulkaram, West Bank, April 2016.

Zleika on her balcony overlooking Al Shuhada street, Hebron, April 2016. The cage is to prevent Israeli settlers from throwing rocks at her, shadows of which are cast on the wall.

Ofer Gruneweld, a bonsai specialist at the Botanical gardens in Jerusalem, April 2016. 'I'd like to work with olive trees ripped up from the West Bank.'

Ramesh in his greenhouse in the old City, Kabul, November 2015. 'Children now are only interested in their phones and Facebook. That is their only hobby. Flowers freshen your mind, mobile phones destroy it!'

Kaka Khalil watering his garden in the old city, Kabul, May 2017. 'The situation is not good in Kabul now, security, unemployment, you know. And the city is so noisy and polluted these days, but at least flowers bring you peace.'

Hamidullah in his garden in Parwan, 2017. 'I had a friend in the army, an officer. He was like a brother to me. He was killed, fighting, about a year and a half ago. I was so sad. I … I couldn't sleep for grief. I tried to garden to forget him but in the end, I planted flowers to remember him and when one grew, it was like I had a new friend.'

see people running from their homes, carrying their most precious possessions. They are looking up at the clouds, dashing from an imminent storm. A little girl clings onto a cat and it mews loudly in protest.

We crisscross the back roads, doubling back on ourselves and having to start again. Either side of us Ukrainian Army tanks rumble into life and the horizon begins to smoulder with smoke seconds before we hear the thud of a landing shell. Artem and the driver are talking very quickly to each other and I have no idea what is happening. I am scared. I grip the sides of the seat. What am I doing here anyway? This is not my war.

By the time we reach an empty Donetsk it is dark and adrenalin has exhausted me. I sit in the Ramada restaurant listening to other journalists' stories from the day. Two photographers describe going to a mental hospital. 'It was really crazy, wasn't it?' one says earnestly to the other with no apparent sense of irony.

A television screen blinks with news from Afghanistan, Azerbaijan and Iraq. Nothing from Eastern Ukraine. The war here is not important today, I think sadly.

I think about home again. I think about Afghanistan again too, relayed across the screen with another attack by an Afghan soldier on a NATO counterpart.

I nod to by now familiar faces and try not to stare at the group of rebel soldiers who have arrived with a troupe of girls draped in military hot-pants and mini-skirts. An American journalist I had met a few evenings ago, seeing me alone, invites me to join his table. There are six others, an international and distinguished mixture of photographers and writers, and as we know some of the same people we exchange idle gossip. But I feel uncomfortable, an outsider. The names of rebel leaders, Ukrainian battalions and Cyrillicly unpronounceable towns trip off their tongues. Someone makes a joke, likening me to William Boot, Evelyn Waugh's hapless fictional nature journalist who finds himself covering war. It is a slight against me and I cannot be bothered to engage with the war talk any more. When the rebel commanders take control of the music system, I excuse myself.

Listless in my bedroom, I stand at the window looking out over the city sprawling nine floors below me. It twinkles and illuminates the black night. A supersonic boom reverberates and darkness falls like lead. A power line has been hit. The hotel lights, running on a generator, hum on, and I can see only my own reflection, standing, staring, looking down into the dark and empty city.

Except it is not empty. I imagine all the gardeners I have met scuttling to their shelters in the damp earth, living each minute as an hour, with only the tinned foods and blankets they thought to bring with them. Cowering below ground, frightened. Strangely close to the roots of their gardens and wondering if they will find comfort there.

When I dream that night I dream I am drowning.

In the morning, I decide to leave for Kiev on the next sleeper train. Artem has other work to do and, with no other fixers free, there is little I can do; I'm not going to wait around for Donetsk to fall and become a media playground.

The station is packed with people leaving and laden with as much as they can carry. Suitcases and plastic bags packed hurriedly explode onto the platform and children fight over toys. There are two people on makeshift hospital beds who are given a priority to board. As soon as they have, other passengers elbow their way into berths. I wait until the last moment; I cannot help feeling that they have more right to a comfortable departure from their homes than me, for when they return it could be to nothing.

I find my berth. This time my co-passengers are a mother and son, and we smile hello but are mutually happy to sit in silence. As the train pulls slowly out of the station and into the countryside to begin its 730 kilometre journey I lie on my front with my chin resting on my hands and watch the still wheat fields just as I had done on the journey here. The summer is fading fast, the sunflowers are over, their tragic, black faces hanging low and mournful.

The West Bank

April 2016

'I should see the garden far better,' said Alice to herself, 'if I could get to the top of that hill; and here's a path that leads straight to it – at least, no, it doesn't do that.'

Lewis Carroll, *Through the Looking-Glass*

1

A terrace on my right is dewy with cow parsley and beyond it rustle ears of barley in the first green flush of spring. A single, scarlet poppy is the only break in its expanse. A street sign points right to North America and left for Europe. I continue straight on the chalky path through Australia, fragrant with eucalyptus oil, and step past a child's sandy playpen. A miniature peace pagoda perches between two rocks, accessible only via a narrow rope bridge made out of wooden lollipop sticks and a pipe cleaner. Beyond it lies Asia.

The sun on my back is gentle and warms my bones from the inside, much needed after a particularly long, grey winter. I am unsure of where I should be going but I am not rushed or hassled. For April the blooms are a month or so more advanced than in northern Europe. Sweet pea and jasmine fill the air. It was the same smell which had hit me with the heat of an oven when the plane doors opened in Tel Aviv's Ben Gurion airport two days previously and had followed me through the night to Jerusalem. Early for my meeting with Dr Ori at the Botanical Gardens in Jerusalem, I am enjoying a meander through this version of the world devoid of maps and borders as we know them.

Abu Awad, the Gazan fisherman with nowhere to fish, had first planted the seed of the idea three years ago. When asked about his dreams he had said it was to build a home for his family and to travel to the West Bank, which he heard was 'the most beautiful place in the world'.

The creation of the state of Israel in 1948 in the aftermath of the Second World War was a bloody one and immediately resulted in conflict with its Arab neighbours. In 1967, after yet another short and bloody Six Day War, Israel took control of various Palestinian territories including the Golan Heights up north from Syria, Sinai and Gaza down south from Egypt and the West Bank from Jordan. Most Arabs fled to refugee camps in neighbouring countries but many stayed to protect their land from the Israelis who were rapidly expanding with military settlements. Increasingly harsh treatment of Palestinians by the Israelis throughout the latter half of the twentieth century fanned the flames of Palestinian nationalism and the two sides have been at loggerheads over land and ownership of religious sites ever since.

Until the late seventies there were only around thirty-six Jewish settlements – or military outposts – in the West Bank. In 1977, under the new government of Menachem Begin, that number steadily rose to over one hundred. They were mostly agricultural smallholdings built on abandoned land which they claimed not to belong to anyone. Abandoned or not, the Palestinians grumbled; the land was not there for the taking.

New settlers were given huge advantages by the government. They were provided with good roads, schools, tax breaks, subsidies, medical services and access to greater water supplies. Palestinians meanwhile were subjected to roadblocks, house searches and increased taxes, with a legal system weighted against them. Furthermore, the settlements attracted some of the most radical members of Israeli society who treated their Arab neighbours abysmally.

Anger and fury gathered in the skies and the ground trembled with war. In December 1987, the first intifada, or uprising, was born, and for six long years Israel and Palestine drowned in violence.

Peace talks began in 1993, but it wasn't until 1995 in snowy Oslo that Israel and the Palestinian Liberation Organisation brokered a deal and agreed to a disengagement. The West Bank was to be divided into three areas – A, B and C – and today the divisions remain. Area A contains most of the principal Palestinian cities and large towns and B the villages. Area C, the only contiguous territory in the West Bank and the one with the most land reserves, remained in Israeli control and contains all of the illegal Israeli settlements as well as numerous highways and new roads largely restricted to Israelis and secured by the army.

The planning and zoning restrictions put in place by the Israelis for the Palestinians in Area C is as restrictive as the physical blockade in Gaza and has resulted in a series of localised wars and skirmishes, (some worse than others) over the one thing both sides want: land. And, as I learned from Gaza and the kibbutzim, land in this part of the world is an existential issue.

But walking up a sharp incline in a botanical globe, war and unrest is the last thing on my mind. When I arrive at the garden nursery on the top terrace, Dr Ori is up to his arms in alliums and tulips. He removes his gloves and we walk past a class of young schoolchildren armed with plastic spades and buckets. Half of the 200,000 visitors he estimates to be children. 'There is a definite move to educate the youth, especially the Orthodox children who only learn about land from religious texts.'

The thirty-acre site of the gardens was originally created in partnership with Hebrew University and conceived in 1981. It split from the campus in 1994 and was divided into geographical zones designed to be universally attractive for Jews, Arabs and Christians alike. 'Here is one of the few places where people can relax and coexist,' he says.

We talk as we walk through the world towards the blossoming fruit trees of Central Asia. 'It's a huge geographical region,' he says, 'but the climate suits the plants here so we don't need to artificially irrigate.' We pass a bonsai collection, another miniature world worthy of Gulliver's Lilliputians and on to the softer colours of a Mediterranean corner of lavender and rosemary.

Working with the Israeli Seed Bank and the Society for the Protection of Nature in Israel, Ori and his team have been able to save plants on the verge of extinction in Israel and reintroduce them to the wild. The Botanical Gardens are home to over 6,000 species of flora and fauna – the largest in the Middle East. Three hundred of them are endangered and the collection is vital to their survival.

Ori's favourite plants are irises. 'They are sophisticated and structured like no other,' he says, but his speciality is in bulbs. 'Everything starts with a seed, it's just energy.' It was this universality of horticulture that first attracted him to botany. 'In this conflict, people are coping rather than solving. But at least gardening fosters an attitude of coexistence and integration.'

'It is our duty to act as a back-up for nature here – in case Armageddon happens,' he grins. 'There is a butterfly effect within horticulture. If we lose one species of plant in the world, the rest are all vulnerable.'

The Botanical Gardens are planned on the Jewish calendar, and last year observed *shmita*, the seventh and final year in the agricultural cycle laid out in the Torah. During *shmita*, nothing can be grown, planted, pruned or harvested, only maintained as fallow – a sort of garden sabbatical. 'A lot of the visitors are religious so it was important that we observed this,' he says.

We arrive at a small lake covered in water lilies. Two house martins dart and chase as fast as arrows overhead. Water boatmen pull hard across eddies and I imagine a family of frogs learning how to swim beneath the rocks.

The garden is glorious in the afternoon light. If this is what it looks like after a year of being fallow, then I can only imagine the colours due to bloom over the coming summer months.

In a café in upmarket Jerusalem selling mojitos and olive wood cheese boards, I meet Zara, an Israeli-Palestinian friend of a friend. She is fluent in both Arabic and Hebrew and I beg her to help me, offering to pay her more than I can afford but a lot less than she is used to, and in the end, she relents. We exchange a few ideas and contacts and the following day, after a shock of coffee with my hostess and old friend from Kabul, Ros, Zara picks me up outside Damascus Gate and we drive out through the suburbs of north Jerusalem, passing bland, identikit apartment blocks.

For millennia the landscape has been the principal character in the drama here. Historical importance hangs from every corner and cultural heritage settles over every town, but as we continue on our way over the asphalted road, an intangible, ancient wind blows across the plains of Samaria. It stirs the dust around Bedouin tents perched at the side of the road, it shivers in the mountain olive trees and when the skies expand it swirls the bruised clouds.

We pass a white limestone settlement. Its red roofs crowning the horizon are to become very familiar. We continue on to Jordan River Valley and the landscape becomes lunar and rocky. The hills ahead of us rise like knuckles; an inhospitable Mars and just as dry beneath a suddenly sulphurous sky.

We turn off to Ma'ale Efraim, perched on the crown of the knuckle. The road to its entrance winds us up and around, and it feels like we are approaching a deserted castle.

Zara unhooks the prayer beads from her rear-view mirror and stashes then in her glove compartment. 'These aren't the sort of people who want to see Arabs in their homes.' Her transition between the two sides and two identities is something to which I was to become accustomed.

Although the gates are heavily guarded she adopts her most coquettish, flirtatious Hebrew and the soldiers let us in. It immediately feels like we've entered another country.

Where the countryside was open and wild, now there are wide streets lined with modern white bungalows (red roofed) set back behind creosoted fences. There are driveways and acacia trees, lamp-posts and pavements, street signs and pedestrian crossings. It looks neither like Tel Aviv nor Jerusalem, but a flat-packed suburb ripped from the dreams of an eighties urban planner.

I cannot get over its modernity and stark contrast with the ancient hills outside the yellow gates. 'I know,' Zara says, 'It is weird.'

I choose a street at random and scan the front gardens for signs of life. It feels empty and abandoned, but at the end of a cul-de-sac there is a patch of green. There is no car in the drive, the shutters are closed and there is a sign saying 'Beware of the Dog' next to a picture of an Alsatian with bared, bloodied teeth.

The garden is full of curios: upended urns on their sides, old-fashioned sewing machines, traditional farming utensils, cow bells and an anchor amidst hundreds of cacti of every shape and size. Their uniform green is perforated with even thornier bright roses.

In the distance is the Jordan River Valley. It is so vivid it looks superimposed behind the settlement.

Zara has remained in the car, dubious that my door stepping tactic will work.

I knock, and immediately a dog inside barks, so I step back from the gate. I can hear someone placating it so I knock again and, when the front door opens, a squinting face as pale as the moon peers out the darkness.

'*Ken?*' she says in Hebrew. 'Yes?'

The face reappears at a garage door above a red velvet dress embroidered with daisies. The woman's name is Bracha, Zara tells me as she leads us around the back of the house.

'What do you want to know?' she asks, not without hostility.

Bracha, I learn, is sixty-seven and moved from Yotvata, a Nahal oasis-kibbutz in the southern Negev where she was brought up, in 1983. Ma'ale Efraim was founded as an urban hub for the neighbouring settlements. 'In the beginning, there was nothing. No houses, no plants, nothing. We were given some land and the first thing we did was plant a garden,' she explains.

'We wanted to hold green in our eyes so we laid down grass seeds, planted roses and tried to nurture them while we built the house. But they needed water, and that is something we don't have a lot of.'

They attempted to save the roses by planting them in pots but it was all in vain. Everything withered. 'It looked worse than when we first arrived.'

She did not give up on her desire to 'see green', however, so she set about saving up for succulents from the local nurseries. 'They aren't as soft as grass but they are just as green and easier to look after. The soil here is too poor. But if they grow too big, we just repot them. They're the plant of Israel – patient to take root with little water.'

I ask if she has a favourite. She points to the largest one and chuckles. 'It is called the mother-in-law.' Its other name is the golden barrel and it is also the favourite of Sabaar, the cactus man in Gaza and Esti on the other side of the border.

After a wave of violence spread during the second intifada of 2000, many Ma'ale Efraim settlers, aware of their vulnerability, left. The settlement began to empty. Enterprising students have recently taken up residence there but, for the most part, Ma'ale has become the equivalent of a depressed market town.

Why, then, I ask, does she not go somewhere else? 'We have nowhere else to go. The government has us here and is concentrating on expansion elsewhere.'

Splodges of rain hiss like fat on a flame but she waves away the idea of an impending shower and rolls her eyes. 'It never rains here, you can be sure.'

We have arrived in Mas'ha, a Palestinian village on the border of the West Bank and Israel about forty minutes away from Ma'ale Efraim, and have parked as close as possible to Hani Amer's garden. Zara hangs the prayer beads from the rear-view mirror. 'I don't want them to think we're settlers'.

We walk a little way over to the security fence. The secret door to Hani's garden is locked, and as he is late we spend half an hour sitting in the dirt by the fence, idly throwing stones at a large post and wondering if the security cameras are on.

Amer arrives, slightly breathless, with his white skullcap skew-whiff and crossed eyes looking flustered. He lets us into his garden and we sit on a small concrete veranda beneath a young vine.

When construction of the security wall began in 2000, Mas'ha residents found out later that it would cut through their quiet village and olive groves. Bulldozers arrived in 2003 to rip out the olives and destroy any dwellings in the way, most of which belonged to Amer. He was told to leave his home, his garden and pleaded with them but to no avail. 'A soldier said, "You are fighting with Israel, Israel is God. You can't fight God."' The wall sliced through his land and he was cut off from the rest of the village.

'I was not just a poor labourer,' Amer tells me proudly. 'I was a man with assets. I had a plant nursery and sold every kind of flower you could imagine and the tools to go with it. I had a chicken coop too and a restaurant, but they were both knocked down.

'They built the wall, destroyed my land and took away my income. We were locked inside here by that gate and surrounded by settlers who were screaming at us to get off their land. *Their* land! It is mine! They threw stones at me and then at my children so I picked them up and threw them back.'

He staggers over to an old tree in the middle of his runner beans and uses his walking stick to shake a branch full of fruit. 'Here, try this,' he says, handing me a handful of juicy sweet-and-sour long mulberry fruits. The burst of acid sugar is a jolt and my hands are quickly stained red and smear the pages of my notebook.

Amer's garden occupies a liminal place on the border but the disturbance is psychological. 'I am not angry about what they did to me, I am not even angry about them breaking into my home. I am angry that they treated nature so badly. When they uprooted the olive trees it was like they were uprooting me. The garden that remains makes life steadfast. Without it, I do not exist. When the settlers come to hassle me, I know that some of them take joy from seeing my garden, that they feel rooted there too.'

At night, things worsened. 'Twenty or thirty soldiers would come and stand in the garden, just by that mulberry tree, and point their weapons at the house demanding to search it. It was a psychological game they liked to play.'

It was a long game too, and the battle between Hani, the settlers and soldiers lasted for seven years before the international community stepped in. 'Now they leave me alone, more or less, but I am scared they will shoot one of my children playing out here and claim it was an accident.'

Through his back fence is one of the three settlements surrounding him and I feel we are being watched from the net-curtained windows. The garden suddenly feels incredibly vulnerable and eerie. Hani is resigned to prowling lions around him.

The shop is tiled white and the thick glass counter reflects the geometric sweets a thousand times over. Sugar within cheese within sugar: *knefeh*. The northern city of Nablus is famed for this Palestinian sweet. I am dubious about the combination and look instead at the more familiar layers of filo pastry and pistachio baklava, but when the maker gives me a sample, the savoury sweet is addictive and I buy five pieces.

We circumnavigate Nablus, a city sinking into the valley from the road. A bowl of bricks, satellite dishes, washing lines, power cables. Leaving it behind, the green grassed hills fade up. The landscape is quite different now and verdant beneath a blue mist.

The prayer beads are snatched quickly from the mirror and we follow the road up into Shavei Shomron.

With its proximity to Palestinian Nablus, the settlement is on one of the front lines of Jewish-Arab tensions. But today it is tranquil and, from its elevated position, the settlement has a glorious view over the countryside.

I remark on this to Zara, somewhat naively. 'Yeah,' she says, 'It is just a shame that no one else can see it.' And she explains that the roads around here are strictly off-limits for Palestinians.

The gardens surrounding the settler houses are larger than those of Ma'ale Efraim. Plastic butcher's grass catches my eye through a wire fence, not least because its edges look almost shampooed with nasturtiums, pansies, petunias and roses. There is a wooden Wendy house suspended above the grass from a tree where last year's winter leaves still stir on the breeze.

A man in a red lumberjack shirt and jeans answers the door. 'Oh,' he says, surprised to see two strangers. 'Come in.' His wife, Eta, shakes our hands graciously and smooths her flowery shirt flat as she apologises. 'We are having an early lunch but I do not think it will stretch to four. If I had known we were having guests . . . Would you like some dandelion tea?' It is warm and unexpected hospitality and, without waiting for a reply, she boils the kettle and rootles around for some raisins and nuts like a mother hen.

Theirs is a patriotic settler ideology born out of the horrors of the Second Wold War. Eta's father, she explains, 'came here after the Holocaust. His family were killed in Auschwitz and he arrived with just the clothes he stood up in. He devoted his life to building Israel and this is the idea I was brought up with.'

Schloma's parents were also pioneers in the foundation of Israel. 'We felt like we wanted to do something more meaningful with our lives and to help build the country.'

When Eta and Schloma first arrived to settle Shavei Shomron in 1978 there was nothing but white sand. 'We Jews got on with the

Arabs back then. We gave them jobs and an income.' Like a kibbutz, Shavei Shomron is a largely agricultural collective and, for a while, Schloma worked on the fields. 'We did not have a garden then – at least, not until we had built the house. But we are outdoorsy people so it didn't take long to get going.'

It was built in stages: first the grass, then the fir trees, then the trees, flowers and lastly, the vines.

In the corner of the room I see a flame-orange tropical flower. Compared to the modest interior of the house it is garish, exotic, the confluence of its petals meeting like the beak of a bird; it holds its leaves in an awkward, abstract dance pose like a crane.

'A bird of paradise,' Eta explains, 'and the only remnants of Schloma's hothouse business.'

'I used to export exotic flowers to a shop called Marks and Spencer in Europe but there was a rise in anti-Semitism and people stopped buying Israeli products from the West Bank. The business started to crumble and well . . .' He trails off for a moment. 'But anti-Semitism is an international problem so being angry doesn't help or solve anything.' Forced into redundancy he now works with wood.

Eta interrupts, desperately imploring. 'You don't understand. The land, the flowers, it was all he had. It was his oxygen and soul. Giving it up like that was unnatural.' She takes his hand across the table and he pushes his glasses up on the bridge of his nose. 'It is true. Land *was* everything to me. But my wife is also everything to me.' He winks at Eta.

We drain our cups dry and I am eager to see his garden.

'The grass,' Schloma begins when we are outside, 'is not the grass of a gardener. But it is for our grandchildren. There is no point having real grass when they are around.' He bends to remove the dead leaves. 'I grow seasonal vegetables and, well, everything you see here. Geraniums, clock vines, ferns, buddleia, roses.'

It is much larger than I had first realised, for around the back of the house there is a carefully clipped and manicured lawn. The beds continue with colourful pansies dotting the greens, and there is a small banana tree and a date palm. A pink climbing rose hauls itself up its trunk as if for a better view of the countryside.

It is a mature, well-established and organised garden, and I like these two gardeners. The settlement's dubious status does not appear to trouble them. There is a quiet, received dogma that to them is nothing more than a logical nationalism.

'If I did not garden, I think I would go mad. It is part of who I am, just like these.' He shows me his collection of old-fashioned tools which he explains had belonged to his father; the tools that had been used to carve Israel.

Zara and I discuss the couple in the car as she replaces the prayer beads and we re-enter Palestine. We agree that they are nice people but the settlement should not be here. The confiscated road, she explains, was intended as a barrier against the Palestinians who, guess what, were only fighting for the return of their ancestral land stolen by the settlement.

We ease into the journey south discussing patriotism and nationalism, and eventually she sighs. 'It's the West Bank; it's fucked up.'

Zara wants to introduce me to Sameer. 'He has got this mushroom thing . . . hold on a minute.' Her voice trails off as we reach Gush

Etzion junction, which had been the scene of recent unrest and requires her total concentration. In March, a Palestinian attempted to stab two soldiers and was shot dead. Since then Israeli soldiers have been shooting Palestinian civilians in dubious circumstances and tensions are high. 'People are a little jumpy,' Zara says, her nose pressed against the windscreen having whipped away the beads. The roundabout is full of soldiers and surly looks thrown between bystanders. Everyone seems to be waiting for a fight.

A change falls over the landscape as we keep driving south, sinking lower and lower as the land sinks to a valley and we enter a temporary empty wilderness, bare and brown. Cartographic contour lines of old terracing scar the dust – wood knots and whorls, fingerprints of Old Father Time.

Our ears pop as an emerald ink spot appears in the dust valley. Small at first, it expands through shimmering ribbons of heat as if seeping into the fibres of blotting paper. The emerald blurs into banana groves and date palms as we cross into another version of Palestine.

Watered by springs, the soil in Jericho is rich and fertile and has thus attracted continued habitation for somewhere between nine and eleven thousand years (archaeologists are still battling it out).

Recent history has not been too kind to Jericho, but it is still a magnet for religious and archaeological tourists. Business is booming. We can see buses of pallid Europeans decked out with sensible shoes, shorts almost entirely made out of pockets held up by money belts, and cameras slung over shoulders. Hawkers read out menus of falafel and kebabs, shops offer to change money and send postcards and idle, hopeful-looking drivers tout for extra work. I too begin to feel like I am on holiday.

But we drive out of the city, through a giant date palm grove and down a lane to an old Palestinian stone house with arched windows and tiled floors. Sameer, the mushroom man, is waiting for us outside with his wife.

He and Zara are old friends and, as they catch up on casual gossip, he leads us around the back of the house where there is a shipping container rigged up with ventilators, thermostats and enormous steel doors.

Bored of working in an office in Ramallah, the de facto Palestinian capital, Sameer yearned to be his own boss. He founded Amoro, Palestine's first official mushroom farm. The cultivation of fungi was an idea that grew slowly.

'Mushrooms aren't indigenous to our cuisine, but they were becoming more popular on the hipster restaurant scene in Ramallah, Bethlehem and here. There were no Palestinian farms and we were being supplied by Israeli producers who wanted to offload their rejected produce.'

With a background in computers, he had to learn about bacteria from scratch. 'Mushrooms need three things to survive: water, spores and compost. Water is always a problem so I rented land here where it is in abundance and the rent is cheaper. It's also outside Area C and there is better electricity too. No one produces compost so we imported that from Holland, the mushroom capital of the world.'

It was the speed at which mushrooms grow that attracted him too. Within three weeks, providing the conditions have been optimal, they could have a bumper harvest. And then start again on the next one almost immediately.

He built a state-of-the-art growing farm connected to the internet which he can control remotely from anywhere in the world. 'The micro-details of this kind of farming matter so it has to be monitored all the time. There is a fraction of a degree between nitrogen and oxygen. It's a precise and delicate art.'

I am eager to enter Sameer's wonderland when he opens the factory door but his enthusiasm has waned. 'Usually I would make you wear a contamination gown and face mask but there is no point.'

We are in a short corridor, off which are a few dark rooms. He switches on the lights and I am expecting to view a sea of soft white buttons steeped in black soil.

But no, the room is empty. There are no mushrooms, there is no wonderland. Only steel shelves, shining bare beneath the stark bulbs.

For Sameer, in all his enthusiasm for fungus growing and state-of-the-art techniques, did not bet on one thing: success.

Until he established Amoro, Israel dominated one hundred per cent of the local mushroom market. 'We took away a large share of their business, which means they could not offload their rejects to the Palestinians so easily.' His voice echoes in the empty room. Israeli producers tried an economic war and slashed their prices, massively undercutting Amoro, but the Palestinian producers already had a popular following and their mushrooms were in demand.

But then the next thing they knew, a container of compost from Holland was detained in Ashdod, one of the major ports, for 'security reasons'.

'Of course they have been charging us for storing the stuff as well, and now we have to pay a release fee for it but they have held on to it for over eighty-five days and the contents of the container will have rotted and be worthless. Compost is the essence of the work; without it, you can't grow mushrooms.' He leans on the empty metal shelves and sighs heavily. 'I can't win. If I pay for it, I lose because it's spoiled and not usable and takes all our savings. If I do not pay, my name is on a blacklist and I have no chance of being allowed to import again.'

If what he says is true, it is a crippling conundrum that puts an end to Amoro – and his dreams – just a few short months since launching.

'What will you do?' I ask.

'Carry on fighting the system,' he shrugs. 'We have always had an economy of production, and to continue to produce is to continue to fight. There is a saying I was brought up believing: "No good will come from a nation which eats what it does not produce and wears what it does not weave."'

In his office he shows me a time-lapse video of mushrooms growing. 'They are roads being built over a map. This is our map, our power,' he says.

As the car climbs out of Jericho the landscape empties again. April storm clouds gather to dull the sun. The black road ribbons us back to Jerusalem and the security barrier which appears on the horizon like the underbelly of a mushroom.

Zara unhooks the prayer beads from the rear-view mirror and re-enters her own world of betwixt and between. She drops me outside a row of shops by Damascus Gate next to a group of IDF soldiers. The evening lights are already twinkling above the shop awnings, illuminating the interior of each with crystal clarity. A tinker selling everything from buckets and padlocks to spades and pestles shouts a joke to the fishmonger next to him where women in tightly knotted headscarves queue for the catch of the day. Two old men on plastic chairs smoke in silence outside a fruit and vegetable shop. The boxes of mushrooms precariously balanced amongst the punnets of grapes and peaches are battered and bruised and ignored.

2

'Hey, would you mind if we stopped in Ramallah? I need to drop off some papers.' Zara asks. We are gridlocked in rush-hour traffic. 'I am going to see if this woman I know of is around too.'

A few kilometres from Jerusalem, another urban sprawl begins. It is just a few half-built buildings at first. Then the city appears. Modern white tower blocks appear on the crest of the hills. When we pass through Qalindia checkpoint, shopping malls, minarets, cypress trees and cranes emerge.

Home to under 60,000 people, Ramallah started life as a small Christian-Arab town. Today, construction is at an all-time high and the city is estimated to be growing by eight to ten per cent annually. While Jerusalem sprawls with tension and religious tourists, the temporary capital of the West Bank is affluent, liberal and (judging by the posters for art galleries and achingly cool coffee shops) a lot hipper.

And just like any growing city, its inhabitants are increasingly deprived of green spaces and urban escapes.

'The city encroaches daily,' Iman Batonya says, leaning her head against her roof terrace's fence just outside the city centre. 'It is hard to find peace and quiet anywhere.' The skyline from her apartment is of hoist ropes, levers, steel bars and skeletal half-buildings rising slowly to an orchestra of pneumatic drills and beeping forklift trucks. 'Early this morning it was so peaceful; all I could hear was birdsong. It reminded me of the old, traditional Palestine. The one my mother used to know.'

Iman turns back to the room and smiles. She is a mini-cactus collector and her balcony overflows with prickly plants. 'Cacti are strong and tough as well as patient, like us.'

I think of Bracha sitting on her upturned bucket in Ma'ale Efraim who had said the same thing. The cactus is a strong metaphor for Jews and Arabs sides and their struggle in the same arid land, the sovereignty of which they both claim to be theirs.

Iman grows her cacti out of abandoned objects she finds and which sit on a shelf at the end of the open balcony. Amongst the tin cans there is a shell, a teacup, a kettle and a child's shoe, all now redeployed as cactus pots. 'I like bringing old things back to life,' she smiles, handing me an old tin paint pot. It is not just home to a single plant but five or six miniatures and, together with a few stones, it looks like a garden suitable for a shrunken Alice in Wonderland.

Zara drops off her papers and we stop for iced coffee before driving north again to visit a walled garden.

Passing Ariel and Nablus we continue for another hour or so through a driving rainstorm, smearing the world outside. Eventually we turn off at a messy intersection of tarmac, wall, mud, soldiers, barriers and fanged razor wire.

We pull over at a mechanic's workshop in the middle of a trash-strewn track a hundred metres or so inside the wall. 'This is it.' Zara points to a sliver of land running along beneath it. We slip and slide our way through the mud and cross the road.

Fayez Taneeb is a very busy man. He shouts hello to us, finishes giving orders to a band of twenty-something-year-old boys and girls, checks through some papers handed to him and shouts a joke to another worker struggling beneath the weight of a barrow which makes Zara crease up with mirth. His own shoulders shake when he laughs, which he does often.

But Fayez *should* be a busy man; his garden farm is a work of permaculture resistance. Permaculture has become increasingly popular as a form of farming and psychological resistance in the West Bank in recent years. If the principles of raw nature are adhered to, the ecosystem within a permaculture can sustain itself without any chemical help. Fayez runs his farm with the precision and authority of a military commander.

Having jokingly lambasted me for being British (and therefore part of the root cause of all of the problems in the Middle East), we take refuge from the rain in an office next to his students' living quarters.

His land is surrounded on two sides by the security wall, but that is now the least of his problems. There is a chemical factory a few hundred metres away, its chimneys visible over the wall, belting out a thick, black smoke.

'The waste is pumped into the soil and was killing our land. I started planting things which produce nitrogen to try and re-energise the soil but it didn't work so I complained. When they ignored me I kept at them and they eventually agreed to dig their waste deeper into the soil, but it's a short-term solution. The waste will end up in the soil again and poison everything. They do it to poison us but they do not realise that my land sits on a water spring and if that dries up or gets polluted, they will suffer too.'

The ranks of greenhouses below the window look like army tents beneath the militarised razor wire and wall.

There is a break in the clouds and the rain stops. We scuttle down, jumping over puddles and sliding through muddy tracks, our feet quickly heavy with congealed mud. Inside the tents, it is stiflingly humid but very, very green. Fayez grows everything – from tomatoes, cucumbers and runner beans to strawberries, aubergines and peppers. Picking his way over to a box hanging from a supporting post he points proudly. Bees: his natural pollinators. 'If you follow the rules of nature, everything is available!' he claps excitedly.

Fayez walks to an olive grove on the other side of the tents beneath the wall where there are two sofas.

Ignoring the water swilling around on their surface he perches briefly on the arm of one. 'When the wall was constructed in 2002, sixty per cent of my land was confiscated,' he explains. To add insult to injury, the road leading to what remained his was blocked by soldiers and a wire fence was erected. 'They said that my land was part of their military zone and that civilians were forbidden from entering. We used to cut the fence with clippers every day until they had enough and let us farm.'

In the adjacent field of thyme at the foot of the security wall is a small woman who, for some reason, is wearing an apiarist's smock, net raised, and waterproof trousers tucked into rubber gloves and galoshes. She calls out to us.

'My wife,' he says and runs to her with a chuckle, arms outstretched and ready for a bear hug.

'This,' he tells us when we join him, 'used to be an olive grove, but now it is Muna's garden.'

As a vocal and active opponent of Israel, he was constantly monitored and arrested; to date, twenty-five times, mostly for 'unspecified reasons'. On one particularly fraught afternoon while they were fighting for the right to work their land, Fayez was buried up to his neck in the olive grove. 'They prepared to drive over me but Muna fought them. She climbed into a tractor and one of them relented. They let me go, but as a punishment they made her uproot the olive trees. She cried as if they were our children,' he says, squeezing her shoulders.

She takes us to the seed bank. Carefully labelled jars and plastic bottles line each shelf of a small shed. It is an almanac of horticulture. 'This is the answer to all the companies who are genetically modifying the seeds which make you sick. It is the answer to Armageddon! When it happens, we, at least, will have everything we need to start again.'

The garden is a well-oiled machine of defiance and, like Sameer, Fayez is part of an agricultural resistance. He calls a young volunteer to collect a bag of courgettes, aubergines, peppers and tomatoes, which he gives us. 'God created us from the soil, we eat from it and bury our dead in it. I can't describe the link between man and land more clearly than that.'

The water appears behind the hills. It is purple beneath a lurid haze and then blue, before shining silver. Then it sits filled with a strange light, peaceful, stationary. There is no sign of life, no birdsong or humdrum activity, no laughter. Only the paused, still water below and the damp dust cloying the road descending the 400 metres or so to its shore. Up close new colours reappear: turquoise, pink, sky and sand. A settlement emerges at the water's edge: quiet buildings and immovable date palms.

Kalia began life as a commercial kibbutz in the late 1920s to accommodate Jews and Arabs working in a potash plant. In the forties it was destroyed by the Jordanians, but after the Six Day War in 1967, it was rebuilt for the military. Today it has a small population of a few hundred who are largely dependent on agriculture and date palms, but the settlement also runs Kalia Beach, one of the most popular Dead Sea resorts on Trip Advisor, which boasts the 'lowest bar on earth'. I hope that it will boast the lowest garden too.

Through a gap in a bougainvillea-covered fence I can see a lawn and small herbaceous borders. When we walk up the stone stairs to a gate I turn to look at the Dead Sea. A thin wall of rain is coming in.

A young woman opens the door. Her timid eyes shine brightly. The ceiling is double heighted and the walls are scattered with pictures but the house feels melancholy and our voices bounce off the tiled floors. A toddler stands in a cot in the kitchen staring at us and the woman ruffles his hair with one hand while checking the baby monitor on the side. There is a third, she explains, at nursery.

The rain begins outside, heavy droplets spatter the window like forgotten constellations and reflect the garden upside down.

The woman, Hannah, pushes the bowl of bananas towards us and waves her hand to scatter a cluster of fruit flies. She moved to Kalia five years ago with her husband. They were worn down in Jerusalem and wanted a better quality of life for themselves and their children. Hankering after a bygone era familiar to their parents, they wanted above all else to contribute to Israel as kibbutznik.

But what Hannah and her family found was not a collectivised, semi-rural utopia but rather a corporate machine. The ideology of the kibbutz mentality has found itself more and more out-dated in modern Israel. Its rural origins sit at odds with the proliferation of the aggressive nation-building of urban settlements. Old settlements and kibbutzim like Kalia have had to diversify and commercialise to keep the pace.

'We came here as Zionists but the people who are here now don't value Zionism. They are more proud of their profits, the consumption of goods, and are obsessed with wealth. I see it in the children my eldest plays with. Most kibbutzim are about the earth and growing, but not this one.'

There is a break in the rain and we go out to her garden. 'I think I must be the only gardener here,' she says. 'You have to pay extra to be a part of the community, so it is like buying into a private members' club and therefore against the socialist principles of the kibbutz in the first place. They only call on us when they need municipal donations for security against the Palestinians.'

At the back of the house she shows us where they are hoping to build a conservatory. Her husband has picked away at a mosaic of paving stones in preparation for the work. There are a few citrus trees there but she is keeping them in large pots for the moment. 'They like the hot, dry climate but not the earth.'

For the earth, she explains, is troubling. Being a stone's throw from water nine times as saline as the sea, it was impossible to grow anything; not for nothing is the sea called 'dead'. 'We imported and laid down fresh soil but when the roots grow, they hit salt and the new earth weakens and things die. So I try to stick to plants with small roots for the flowers.'

She has a lawn and a young herbaceous border of pansies and geraniums. Next to a small shed lies a vegetable garden. Sage, rosemary, thyme, mint and a very small bay grow on one side; on another, tomatoes, lettuce and tired-looking rocket exploding with seed pods. In a corner is a cabbage, its leaves pockmarked and mangy, ravaged by snails. 'I don't know how to get rid of them,' Hannah says.

'We really wanted our children to relate to the land, to run free outside, but Kalia is not that kind of place. It is a consumer society and it has spoiled people,' she sighs. 'With wealth comes greed – we saw that in Jerusalem and Tel Aviv but we didn't imagine we would find it here.'

It is easy to identify with Hannah's frustrations. She is the mother of a young family in search of a rural, patriotic dream who just wants to live a decent life. Instead, she occupies a netherworld and, as she stares out of the window through her garden to the still, flat lake where nothing grows, I think of Persephone roaming the underworld.

'We thought we had found paradise when we arrived,' she says in a dazed monotone while peeling a banana for the toddler who has begun to simper.

*

The Dead Sea is dying. On average, its level has decreased by a metre a year since the sixties thanks to over-extraction of its minerals and damming. In a hundred years, I think, this will all be a flat desert valley. The shore as we drive past it is crystal white with drying salt. We pass beach-side settlements and advertisements for health spas and beauty-inducing mud. The café attached to a petrol station when we stop is patronised by road-trippers, similar to those we saw in Jericho. They are milling through the straw hats, the bottles of mud promising glowing skin and sea salts for aches and pains. Underworld tourists at the bottom of the earth.

Umm al-Khair village teeters on rocks. It is nothing more than a handful of shanty dwellings open to a north wind bringing a bleak, boreal chill. A frayed Palestinian flag flutters over a pile of corrugated-iron sheets and a handful of skinny goats. A ragged urchin draws lines in the dirt next to transport crates and rubble. Umm al-Khair looks more like a construction site than a place of habitation.

A chicken wire fence a few metres away is the boundary with the neighbouring Carmel settlement. Its red roofs glimmer between green trees. A man appears and waves us over to park near his tin shed home.

Moments later we are sitting in the shade of Yasir Hedelin's garden, or what is left of it. The only thing still living is a scrap of grass and a tall fig with anaemic leaves and undernourished buds of fruit. Two tiny kid goats bleat feebly as they feed on scraps from his hand, eyes still only half open to life.

It was not always so. Umm al-Khair was settled by Palestinian goat herders and farmers who purchased the land after expulsion from the Arad Desert in the early twentieth century. For decades it was home to a handful of families making a living from shepherding and farming on the green arable land around them, content to live as their forefathers had in tune with the circadian rhythms of life. 'My whole life is in this village,' he says with his hands on his hips. 'It is as important to me as my spine.'

The construction on their land of Carmel, a new Israeli settlement in 1980, quietly but surely condemned Umm al-Khair. Villagers were denied basic rights including continued access to the electricity grid. Then the water supply was cut off.

'Five years ago I planted fourteen different types of vegetable. I was so excited to see them grow and know that I could help feed my family. The settlers must have been watching us because one night they came and uprooted everything. They punctured the irrigation tanks and cut up all our hoses.'

The tin sheds erected in lieu of stone houses directly contravenes Israel's ban on building in Area C – despite the need for them in the wake of Israel's destruction of the village – and they are set for demolition. When the last of them are razed, Yasir and his family will be homeless and exiled. 'My blood and sweat is in this land. But what can I do? If they force me to go, where *can* I go? My family is here. Planting and growing physically roots you in the earth.'

The contrast with Carmel when we enter the settlement from the other side is immediately stark. While Umm al-Khair is a dried up patch of nothing, not even fit for livestock, Carmel is a suburban utopia with municipal flower beds and street lamps. Its gardens are peppered with acacias and geraniums. A bright yellow child's tricycle sits upended by a front door and a radio fizzes with pop music at an open window. There is even a state-of-the-art commercial poultry barn run by the settlement.

'This is the sort of settlement where crazies live,' Zara whispers when we knock at the door. 'Don't mention Umm al-Khair.'

A woman in a yellow turban holding a paintbrush appears and Zara deploys her most charming Hebrew.

The woman looks at her watch. 'We are doing some renovation, but why not? Coffee?'

Eva and Zara chat while we wait for the kettle to boil. I understand not a word but I nod and smile along like a dummy, aware that one false frown and she could send us packing as interlopers.

A large eucalyptus tree in the garden rustles its grey-green leaves heavily. The circle of butcher's grass surrounding a herbaceous border comprises most of the garden. Irrigation pipes run through the pansies, and the earth around them is freshly wet. A pair of china boots sits in one corner next to a rockery, and an ornamental wheelbarrow overflows with rockery plants. Like Iman in Ramallah, Eva grows things out of objects lost and found.

A girl, her daughter, brings us steaming mugs of Nescafé and I am self-conscious in my line of questioning, anxious not to antagonise. Eva skirts around her arrival in Carmel. Her rocking chair creaks on the veranda boards like a ticking clock.

'My family had previously lived in Jerusalem and Haifa but moved here in the early eighties. There was nothing here when we arrived.

No houses, just dirt. I knew we needed to put down a garden as soon as possible.'

Her love of gardening was inherited from her father, a teacher. They used to work in the soil together on Friday afternoons.

'We grew all manner of things, but his favourite flowers were sweet pea and roses. He could identify the variety blindfolded just by their smell.'

Gardening in Carmel, she explains, is a huge challenge: 'It is very dry and windy. We are on the edge of the Judean and Negev deserts so the temperature varies from night to day and you need double the amount of water than normal. In winter it is bitterly cold and it's unusually cold at night now.'

'You were right,' I say to Zara when we drive away.

'What?'

'The West Bank. It is fucked up.'

The sun drops from a thankless sky. Carmel appears in the last light behind us – a new constellation surrounded by a black darkness shunned even by the real stars.

3

The red roofs of Beitar Illit's monolithic apartment blocks dominate the skyline from the motorway. 'It is a massive, super-religious settlement,' Zara says when I ask, 'and I mean, massive. It just keeps growing. Shall we look?'

We have just met a dirt-poor farmer in Wadi Fukin, the Palestinian village beneath it. He had described the sewage and contaminated water flowing into his land from the settlement. And although we are supposed to be going to Hebron further south, we make a detour via Beitar Illit. The prayer beads come off, the gates open and once again we enter a suburbanite's dream. There is a municipal flower arrangement at a roundabout. The streets are wide, the buildings wider still; apartment blocks soar like cathedral spires above us. There are bus stops full of queuing people and a traffic jam honks on the other side of the road.

The inhabitants are all dressed in the Orthodox black hat and coat. Elegant, elongated shadows engrossed in religious texts. I am aware that I stand out in a comparatively bright and frayed denim jacket, faded black jeans and muddy white plimsolls, but Zara adopts an unapologetic stance and asks someone loudly in Hebrew for directions to a car park.

We stand below a street of apartment blocks overlooking Wadi Fukin and scan the apartment façade for urban gardens. Peach-coloured flowers drip over the white stone balcony five buildings along, three floors up, and we walk towards it, counting the doors and floors.

Inside the block, it reeks of stale rubbish and cooking. Even well-established settlements have their municipal problems, it seems. The plywood door of the apartment belonging to the garden echoes hollow when we knock, but a young woman answers. Zara explains what we're doing but she shakes her head, 'My husband wouldn't allow it.' She will not be persuaded or cajoled and closes the door on us firmly.

We return to our original standpoint at the foot of the road and try again: three along, basement. There is real turf, Etruscan urns and daisies. But when we knock, the same thing happens; the husband is not home and the woman who answers is not allowed to speak to strangers without permission.

The gender division and conservatism is remarkably familiar. 'It is like Afghanistan,' I say when we are back in the stairwell on the ground floor.

'I told you. They are super-, super-Orthodox,' Zara retorts as we climb the stairs.

A door behind us opens and a very small woman in her late seventies, wearing a pale blue velour beret, peers out. 'Who are you looking for?'

'Oh, well,' she says adjusting her jaunty hat, '*I* have a garden. Come in.'

'Here,' the small blue lady throws the tinted glass sliding doors open onto her balcony to reveal several window boxes of tired-looking geraniums, a rose and a spider plant whose tendrils spill messily over the wall. The balcony walls are at her shoulder height and the window boxes the same level as her head, hiding the view into Wadi Fukin below.

It is not the type of garden I had in mind but it *is* a conscious effort to cultivate an otherwise bland piece of urban architecture, and we sit at a cane table inside to interview her.

Having observed last year's *shmita* she couldn't maintain her plants. 'Now the geraniums are just getting going again. I hope we have good weather. But you should have seen my garden in Canada,' she sighs. 'It was huge. I had roses, vegetables and great tall fir trees. It used to make me feel so free.'

'Do you feel trapped now?' I ask her.

'No, of course not,' she says sharply. 'Why would I?'

Her parents moved to Israel after the war. 'The Germans didn't give them a very good time. They made a better life here from nothing. I met my husband and we emigrated to Canada.' When her daughter emigrated to Israel for *aliyah*[23], she followed her as a widow.

In her forty-year absence the country was changed beyond recognition. 'There are many more people now: Europeans, Russians, Americans.'

When she first moved to Beitar Illit, it was a small settlement of a few hundred people living out of caravans. 'I used to go walking in the hills below, where the Arabs live. But we are not exactly free to go there now. Some of them are OK; they sell us things cheaply, which is good, and they know that if they misbehave they will face the consequences. I had one work for me who was quite tame, but you never know with Arabs – they might stab you in the back.' I can hear a tractor in Wadi Fukin far, far below us as she prattles on.

'People say they are really poor. It is rubbish. I have seen them buying clothes in Zara shops in the malls in Tel Aviv. They live in luxury now and it is all thanks to the prosperity we brought them.'

I steer her back to her garden, her pots, but she wants to talk to Zara about the gold plating of her necklace. Her own has been causing her considerable annoyance.

Half an hour later, having extracted ourselves from Beitar Illit, we hurtle down the narrow road towards a city divided.

Looking out onto Al Shuhuda Street between the hanging baskets of succulents from Zleika's balcony is eerie. I press my head against the metal cage enclosing us and crane my neck to get a better view. Some awnings hang over boarded-up shop windows, faded and torn. There is a checkpoint a few hundred metres away, but apart from a handful of wild dogs, the street is completely devoid of people. Not a soul passes, just an empty plastic bag tumble-weeding a haphazard course and a Star of David flag flickering from a lamppost.

When I pull away, the wire cage has left an indentation on my head. 'It is protection,' Zleika tells me later, 'against the stone throwers and wall climbers.'

We are in Hebron, the capital of the conflict, and Zleika's balcony sits on the no man's land of its front line.

The religious sites of the ancient city are of equal significance for both Jews and Arabs; it is believed that the graves of the four most illustrious prophets are buried there with their wives and that Eden is somewhere nearby. In the late nineteenth century, Jews and Arabs happily coexisted, sharing shops, hospitals and indeed the holy sites.

A bloody history combined with the city's religious identity amplified Hebron's role as a protagonist in the conflict. After Israel's victory in the Six Day War in 1967, Rabbi Moshe Levinger, a Zionist activist, along with a group of followers masquerading as tourists, barricaded himself in the city's main hotel and refused to leave.

A settlement was born. Unfortunately for Hebron, the settlers it attracted were the most extreme and fanatical. They also retain disproportionate power and will attack soldiers if they deem them to be too lenient with the Palestinians.

Since then Hebron has witnessed some of the most unholy acts of inhumanity the world has seen, and violence from both sides continues to escalate. The city is divided into H1, governed by the Palestinians, and H2, governed by the Israelis.

When we met Zleika in a deserted car park she guided us through narrow streets and flat-stoned houses. The cobbled stones beneath my ragtag espadrilles were worn shiny smooth with the passage of millions of tourists that used to come here. I slipped over them like black ice. We passed empty bazaars, boarded-up houses and faded brown heritage signs. A side alley led directly onto Al Shuhuda Street, blocked by a thick metal gate and tresses of razor wire. The ancient stone walls were freshly graffitied with Palestinian flags and blue Stars of David crossed out with red X's.

For the last few months there have been so many clashes that even Zara was unsure about coming here.

All the restrictions and curfews around the narrow winding streets of the Old City remain, including the continued closure of Al Shuhada to non-Jews.[24] Even if, like Zleika, they live there.

With her front door welded shut we had turned into a narrow doorway and she led us out onto the rooftops and into a baking heat. We climbed up and over and through and around a warren of corridors and secret doors. 'I'm sorry,' she had said, 'it's the only way to get to my house.'

Born and bred here, she is a Hebronite through and through. When she is not working in the kindergarten, she works as a tour guide. Of course, tourism has dwindled in the last few months and, much like the factory workers in Eastern Ukraine with no job to go to, Zleika has been able to devote more of her time to her green roof garden of ferns, jasmine, carnations, marigolds and runner beans.

'Wherever I go I garden. It is good for the heart, the soul and the spirit. If you want to see art, look at the flowers; in them is manifested the beauty of the universe and the greatness of God. It is both meditation and inspiration.' Her own favourites are red carnations because 'they look like royalty', and violets which are 'sweet and rare'.

As a teacher, she takes it upon herself to pass on her love of gardening. 'I learned it from my own mother when I was only five, so I understand that when a child plants something, they feel it. Some of the children here have suffered huge amounts of violence and trauma, but when I watch them planting or playing with soil, I know that they feel it healing them.'

She adjusts the knot of her headscarf. It is covered in blue roses and butterflies.

'If you talk about Hebron forty years ago, you are talking about a safe, open place. But in the seventies, everything changed. There were no social occasions, no weddings. Life stopped. I had to have a permit to be here, in my own house! And I was not allowed visitors.'

Of the official division of the city in two she says in English, 'They made pieces, not peace.'

We step onto her balcony again. Plastic pots of yellowing dill, a cactus and a citrus fruit in one corner, a geranium and a creeper of some sort along the back and small pots of succulents tied to the outer edge of the cage. It is a modest collection on a precipice.

As she plumps up the leaves and waters the small pots, she talks gently of a peaceful coexistence.

Above us on the cage-roof are rocks, one as large as a fist. 'They used to climb up the walls and try to break into our houses or shoot at us. Now they can only throw rocks.' Sticks and stones, I think, really can hurt you in Hebron.

She navigates us through the other roof garden to the maze of ancient alleyways and back to the car park. The roof garden is such a peaceful, contemplative place that I wonder then why she bothers with her balcony garden.

'The things I grow, they are an existence. It shows we aren't beaten,' she says without hesitation.

Kiryat Arbar is a suburb of H2, the Israeli-administered part of the city. As the crow flies, it would be a short walk from Zleika's house, but we navigate the checkpoints on a circuitous route to get there. It is almost identical to Beitar Illit from the outside: red tiled, white teeth, gnawing at land.

We make for the municipal building. The situation here is too fraught to allow doorstepping. Outside there are a few sandbags, and a couple of soldiers smoke next to a concertina of barbed wire.

Inside, Zara prattles away to the administrator, asking if she knows of any gardeners, and I peruse the public information posters which are full of visual instructions on keeping yourself safe against intruders. I think of Zleika and her balcony caged in protection.

'We are in luck. There is a lady here we can speak to,' Zara says, clutching a scrap of paper with a telephone number. 'And she is from the good old US of A,' she grins.

All the houses are raised from street level and accessed via narrow steps to private, enclosed front gardens. It is hard to gauge how well tended they are behind the fences. One gate is slightly ajar, and through the gap are terracotta pots, a trowel and scattered fresh earth. On approach, we can hear someone humming.

The gardener, Milly, is hard at work when we approach. Not at all the image I had in mind of a hardliner spoiling for a fight. Dressed in a mid-length denim skirt and shirt with a blue bandana, she reminds me of a fifties housewife – the kind of woman who would bake cookies and cakes for a motley crew of scuff-kneed children or knit scarves on a porch overlooking a prairie, and who almost always smelled of soap.

She steps lightly, carefully, through her garden.

She *was* an American, she explains, her voice as soft as a cobweb, but has been an Israeli for fifteen years.

We are sitting in a shady corner of her garden surrounded by dark evergreens and a fig. 'I did not want to come at first. I was happy in Chicago teaching English in a local high school, but my husband persuaded me. It's a lot easier to be a Jew here, you know? The food, the holidays, the practices. Back home, you always had to compromise. Now I would not leave for anything. It would be hard to leave this garden too. When we first moved, there was nothing here at all.'

The semi-overgrown ivy clinging to her house makes me feel like we are in an outdoor room. The earth at my feet is damp – a soft velvet carpet. The beds facing us are colourfully dense with red begonias and lobelias as blue as the star in the national flag at the entrance. There is a single shyly flowering red cordyline and a small rockery in amongst the geraniums, almost as hidden from us as we are from the road and her neighbours. It is an enveloping garden, but I cannot shake the feeling that it has faded somehow.

'When we moved here, it was the first thing I started doing with the kids. I do not understand people who do not garden, it is the most relaxing thing in the world, but maybe it is in my blood.' Both her mother and grandmother were avid gardeners back home.

Milly now spends at least two hours a day weeding and watering but it is not her ideal garden. 'There is not enough sun on this side of the road and the trees block out the light. Everything is struggling a little with the *shmita* last year but I am using a fertiliser which seems to be helping things along.'

The extreme temperature variation around Hebron is also a challenge. 'It is peaceful when the weather cooperates,' Milly says, looking up at the sky, 'but it gets down to below two in the winter and in the high thirties in the summer, with strong winds from the south. To be honest, I miss the warm rains and the size of the forests back home. But gardening is very meditative, you know.'

Zara asks her to translate a few plant species we had not been clear on from interviews in other settlements while I photograph the garden, wishing the light was less blinding. We stand to leave and she leads us back through to the entrance gate but stops suddenly in the path and turns to face me.

'I guess I should tell you, if you are writing about gardens . . .' She searches for the words, picking at a leaf like an embarrassed child, the Star of David flickering behind her. 'This garden became really important to me after I lost my son.'

One sunny afternoon a few years ago her son had been driving along a road not too far away when some angry Palestinians started throwing stones at his car. 'One went clean through the windshield and killed him instantly. He veered off the road and crashed in a ditch. When the ambulance came, they also pulled the body of my grandson out of the wreckage.'

My stomach lurches with the revelation. Gone is the benign 1950s housewife, for Milly is a mother shrouded in deep, deep loss. Her garden is too. The dark corners, the small path which intersects the dried grass; it isn't *shmita* which has caused it to fade, but grief.

'Losing a child, it is the hardest thing in the world.' She pulls a tissue from her pocket and wipes her eyes clean, trying to smile, trying to hold it together.

'So that is why I garden. It helps me grieve, and when I am here, I am filled with sunshine. I mean, even if it is dark. Anyway,' she trails off and stares at the ground, 'I hope it is helpful for you. For your project. To understand.' She dabs her eyes again.

The crossing is unusually busy. Lines and lines of cars, queues of people waiting to be searched. Idle soldiers take their time. A couple flirt, the girl tosses her enviably glossy plait over her shoulder and laughs. The security wall zig-zags the horizon and it feels like we are at the gateway to a maximum security prison. I am just not sure if we are leaving or entering it. The sun ekes higher and brighter in the sky and its heat makes me sweat.

We are waved through and turn off the main road into Qalindia refugee camp.

There is a flat-tyred yellow taxi on the other side of the road when we pull over. It is being used as a climbing frame by two small boys. Another appears at a window with a plastic gun. 'Pah, pah, pah.' He giggles loudly, before disappearing. Wires intersect the sky above; some hang loose and dangle out of buildings. I can hear sirens and engines roar from the checkpoint and I feel a little dizzy in the morning's glare and chaotic heat.

Moments later, we are sitting beneath a tree on a paved veranda surrounded by dark green ferns, peppered with buckshaw blue and tiny white trillium. The noises and furore outside are muffled to obscurity behind the garden's high walls, and a sense of calm descends.

The garden belongs to Mohammed Hammud, who lives in one of around a thousand permanent homes in a Red Cross-built camp. It was first established as a temporary measure for exiled Palestinians in 1949 but is now a permanent fixture at the border.

Hammud appears at the top of the steps, tucking his black polo neck into black trousers. When he sits next to the dark green flower bed, he becomes part of their shadows and lights a cigarette.

A young boy brings out a tray of tar-black coffee. The glass cups rattle unsteadily on the metal when he sets it down with intense concentration and pours.

Mohammed and Zara discuss his son. She offers sympathy and he wells up instantly. 'I would never have let him do it. He made his decision without asking me because he believed he had learned what to do from me.' His hand shakes as he fumbles for a white-tipped cigarette. 'And now he is dead and this house and garden will be demolished.'

On 23 December 2015, Mohammed's son, Anan Abu Habsa and his friend, Issa Assaf, stabbed three Israelis outside Jerusalem's Old City Jaffa Gate. In the four months leading up to the incident there had been a rise in Palestinian attacks against Israeli civilians and security personnel. Anan and Issa were shot and killed on the spot.

Their act of terrorism is to be collectively punished: their families' homes – and gardens – are to be demolished.

The declared rationale of punitive home demolitions, despite being illegal under international law, is deterrence. The authorities argue that the destruction of properties of families of Palestinians carrying out attacks against Israelis or who are suspected of involvement in terrorism will deter others. From 2005 punitive house demolitions were unilaterally halted, but in 2014 the measure was brought back after three students were kidnapped and murdered by Arabs. The irony is, of course, that the demolitions not only involve innocent parties, they usually incite more anger and acts against the state.

As a political activist, Mohammed is no stranger to the Israeli justice system. He has been imprisoned on and off for fifteen years, eight of which were spent under house arrest. 'I think I can safely say I've seen the inside of every prison in Israel,' he says, exhaling a ribbon of blue smoke.

He has also been on hunger strike and been sentenced to death, but solitary confinement was by far the worst experience. 'No paper, no pen, no coffee, no cigarettes,' he sighs. 'Just a small window covered with thick netting I could not see out of. When you don't speak for six months your tongue stops working, so I used to recite prayers and poetry I had learned at school and count the ants as they climbed up the wall. I wondered where they were going.'

When he was placed under house arrest, things were brighter. 'They would come and check on me five times a day, but during the first intifada they lost interest, so I would work out of the garden. I managed to buy a load of chickens, build them a coop, and I kept two cows over there.' He points to a lawn on a lower terrace which has gone to meadow. In a magnanimous act of social responsibility he gave a third of the produce to the poor, a third to his family and the remaining third went back into buying fodder.

'It was all part of the struggle, and in those days, I had a real sense of joy being outside. Although I wasn't allowed to go anywhere, I did not feel confined. People would come and speak to me here and I would see that all the time I had spent counting the ants in solitary had been worth it.'

For him, the conflict is simple: land. 'We know we are from this land. We have seen the trauma our parents have borne, their expulsion. I have Ottoman empire papers proving what land I own, but they [the Israelis] are greedy and want it all for themselves. I am tied to this house as both my prison and my escape, but my heart and soul still beat inside my family's land.'

He lights another white-tipped cigarette. 'What would you do if I took your shoes, right now? You would push me away, right?'

I look at my grimy espadrilles and for a moment wonder if I really would, but I understand the point.

'Where will you go?' I ask, 'when your house is destroyed. Will you miss your garden?'

He is silent as Zara translates the question and he looks down at the overgrown leaves and the parched pots. It is colourless, there is no light-hearted bumblebee staggering through the air, laden with pollen, nor are there cheery marigolds or geraniums, no charm. The dark green ferns I had originally thought so calming feel heavy and oppressive now and I already know the answer.

'This place will be gone soon. So what is the point? It used to give me joy, but now my son is dead.'

4

'Do you mind if I film this?' Caleb asks suddenly.

'By all means.' I am calm but my heart thuds.

'Dude,' Zara whispers when he is out of the room, 'WTF? He's going to *film* us.'

'Play it cool. We are not doing anything wrong,' I say.

'You are right.' She fans herself with her hands.

He returns and sets up a hand-held camera. 'So what was I saying?' he says, sitting opposite us on an armchair, legs crossed and relaxed.

'Your new garden,' I prompt, leaning forward, pen poised. 'You were talking about style.'

'That's right,' he re-finds his stride. 'Everyone has his or her own garden style. We did not want to make ours too formal or perfect. Just nice and simple, and a reflection of who we are.'

So far, so normal, if you discount the filming. But we are in Yitzhar settlement, just south of Nablus. In 1983 it grew from an outpost into a community of around fifteen hundred strictly religious settlers. They soon became known for hate crimes against Palestinians which to date include arson, murder, attacking school buses filled with children, stabbings, plus regular vandalism and rock throwing.

Of course there is retaliation on the part of the Palestinians but Yitzhar settlers are as ruthless and fanatical as Hebron settlers. Even the Israeli security forces tend to give the settlers here a wide berth.

And that is why I had wanted to come here. After two weeks flitting between the two sides of the conflict and existing in a half world of both and neither, I am still baffled by it.

The drive up to the summit of the lonely hill had been in silence. I expected to encounter armed and surly-looking louts, but instead we found a group of labourers working on a garden who directed us to Caleb. He was moving rocks lining a pathway to his front door when we pulled over. The rockery beds either side were sparsely planted with small daisies, rosemary, a red ivy leaf geranium, French lavender, mint and aloe vera, 'a healing plant', which his wife uses to make organic beauty products.

He invited us inside for an interview. But now that we are being filmed, it is uncertain who is interviewing whom exactly.

'Do you smoke?'

'Reformed,' I sigh, with a mock-tragic face, which raises a smile.

'In the morning I go out to the veranda to smoke with my coffee and I thank God for the view.'

Through the window behind me there is a makeshift gym – a pull up bar upon which a crow is perched and a set of heavy dumb-bells – but the landscape beyond is an epic one. The undulating green plains roll out beneath loaded clouds, ready to explode. The tracks and roads scar the ridges with yellow chalk-like fingerprint whorls. A break in the billowing mass shines a fast-moving shaft of gold on another outpost a few hills over.

'A person who believes in God believes he has something of God in him,' Caleb is saying. 'A garden helps to affirm this. It makes your heart grow, it heals. It makes you think you just want to spread your roots and grow, don't you think?'

I nod thoughtfully while writing, acutely aware of the camera recording my every move.

He had come to religion late and, until thirteen years ago, had never so much as crossed the armistice line in Jerusalem, living a faster, hedonistic and more materialistic life. A friend's rabbi uncle, sensing a disillusioned urbanite, encouraged him to become acquainted with the 'virgin land'. 'It was at a time when I wanted to run away from the silly city to somewhere where the air was clean and to start again.'

He moved into an outpost. 'You really cannot imagine how beautiful it was as an urban refugee. It is as if you are living in a virgin forest and when you open the doors in the morning . . . Trees don't self-promote. Spirituality up here is clean and enables you to receive new things.'

He uncrosses his legs and leans into my personal space. 'Israel is just a small piece of land filled with the Jewish dream. So many prayers have been said on and about this land of ours, so many people have come here to fulfil the dream over the centuries. In agriculture every plant, every seed has its rightful place, right? That's how I look at the diaspora of the Jews. When we had to leave, we left behind our roots. If you put us where the soil is weak we won't grow.'

Roots, I think. It is always about roots. They connect us to something intangible – our ego and identity – and they connect us to our home.

'Man's relation to land is almost erotic, don't you think?' I look up and stutter, embarrassed, borderline prudish and British. 'When the Jews were exiled, the land grew thorns so that no one was allowed to or able to grow anything out of her. When we came back, we were able to de-thorn her and made her conceive again.'

'Gosh, that is so beautiful,' I lie quickly. His words *are* poetic, if overly anthropomorphic, but to think that the land's only purpose is to bear fruit for man is taking the metaphor just a little bit too far. It renders it a teleological argument and vastly inflates man's position in nature. To me, at least.

We move away from doctrine and philosophy and back to the physical garden. 'The only real problem up here,' he says, 'is the wind. It is lovely and cool in the summer but blows harshly in the winter.

'Are you worried about security?' I ask.

'The world thinks we are a problem and we are hated up here,' he sighs with injured bitterness, 'so I always sleep with a gun under my pillow. Arabs are always trying to attack the Jews and my daughter is scared. The other day when we were driving I wound down the window and shouted, "We are not scared of you, Arabs."'

'But if your children are scared, is it really worth it?' I ask, 'I mean surely their safety is more important.'

'The fact that we are here makes it worth it. You have to keep faith that it will continue to be worth it in the bigger picture.'

We have been there too long and it is time to leave. 'Thank you,' I say brightly in my best 'jolly' voice. 'I will just take a few snaps if that is all right and then I think it is on to the next appointment.' I take him outside to compose a portrait. Two swings hang from a pergola – for his daughters, I presume. A dog chained up beneath them begins to howl in the wind and the bruised storm clouds gather with the same intensity as the heavy lavender heads at his feet. The soil, his land, is freshly turned and ochre. He surveys the hills of Samaria, hands tucked into his belt loop. 'Our promised land. Isn't it magnificent?'

Aside from owning a gun there is nothing he said which was remotely threatening, but his dogma and obdurate conviction is uncomfortable. Only when we are at the bottom of the hill am I tempted to pinch one of Zara's cigarettes, but instead we turn on the radio and listen to mindless pop music.

The security wall grows as we approach the edge of the West Bank. The wooden prayer beads jangle as we roll over uneven ground and Zara mutes the radio. She leans forward onto the steering wheel, lost in memory.

For centuries Budrus was just a normal Palestinian village famed for its olive groves. The construction of the security barrier jeopardised its very existence, but villager Ayed Morrar was just not going to let it happen.

We pull over at Ayed's house at the end of the village. He is smartly dressed in suit trousers and a crisp white shirt, and he and Zara greet each other as long-lost friends.

His garden is dripping with that universally bewitching golden light of the end of a day. The wide beds are covered with ice plants, the pink flowers, growing in irregular patches. Musky-smelling hybrid tea roses grow in healthy clusters and ivy geraniums crawl greedily at their feet. Yellow poppy-like flowers scatter gold coins beneath a date palm.

We sit on a raised platform away from the house beneath a young vine, and Ayed's daughter brings out a tray of tea and Coca-Cola and hugs Zara hello shyly.

'Budrus was built on olive oil,' Ayed begins. 'Our grandparents used to say, "If you uproot an olive tree, you will be damned twenty times over." Their point was that with wheat and oil, you can build a family. It is land that our families had cultivated for thousands of years. Through our bloodlines we are intrinsically connected to it.'

When the plans for the security wall were made common knowledge, he began to protest. 'They were going to build across our land and uproot the olives and our livelihoods.' Having seen what happened in Mas'ha, he realised that writing was not enough. Instead, he mobilised the entire village, including women and children, to act. 'We protested with non-violent resistance. Our aim was to protect our ancestors' land. No bullets, no stones, no Molotov cocktails. Just peaceful protests.'

It was an extraordinarily peaceful and courageous act in the face of violence. I have found the continuation of conflict between Israel and Palestine so troubling because of its absurdity; it should be amenable to reason, but it turns out to be beyond the limits of rationality. Ayed's peaceful, non-violent reconciliation proves resolution is not only possible but tangible.

'I am not against Jews or Israelis, we can live together – we *should* live together. But I *am* against the settlers and the soldiers. They are faces of the occupation,' he says, 'the worst kind of people.'

'My garden is part of the story of resistance,' he continues. 'It needs a lot of work, but I know it better than anyone. I built it with my own hands, just like my ancestors built their lives with olives.'

Ayed planted different types of flowers which bloom throughout the year, 'it is important to have colour and what better colour than Mother Nature?'

Like a proud and expectant father, if he suspects a flower is about to open he waits for it. He is so in tune with his trees that he knows when each is due to be in fruit almost to the day, and the family celebrates accordingly. 'The children love it – they post pictures on Facebook, but they don't yet understand what it is to grow.'

For Ayed, growing is living and living is control. 'It is a horrible feeling knowing that you are not really in control of your own life. It affects your mind. People outside – in your country, the UK, Europe – they do not understand the meaning of freedom because they *are* free. What does beauty mean if it surrounds you, what does love mean if it is all you know?'

It is an existentialist's argument. If the world around you defined within the parameters of your immediate surroundings then where does it stand when compared to others?

'Here, soldiers have a right to stop and search you, interrogate you, arrest you on your own land. Freedom tastes sweeter than an almond, because here we are not masters of our freedom. Only after freedom can there be peace.'

When we drive back to Jerusalem, skirting the separation barrier, I am mentally still in Budrus. Ayed's peaceful garden as an opposite of the absurd war is remarkable, but I cannot help thinking that if freedom doesn't exist here, what does it even mean?

The Botanical Gardens smell fresh and familiar as I approach. The lake's surface is covered in water lilies and there is something quite mesmerising in watching them; I think of Monet.

A century after he had begun work on his canvases of blues and greens his water lilies are still considered to be some of the most sublime depictions of a garden that the world has ever seen.

When he started work on them, however, gunfire was shattering the peace of his garden from a front line of the First World War just fifty kilometres or so away. When everyone else fled Giverny, he stayed to paint. It was his patriotic war effort.

Looking at the serene surface of the lake before me now I cannot hear gunfire, but I feel rather drained from the never-ending situation here.

'Hey, Lally?' It is Ofer calling me from the upper terrace. 'I'm up here, do you want me to . . .' His voice is lost in a willow.

Moments later he appears in an electric golf cart and we drive up to the top terrace, where I had first met Ori some weeks ago. Ori had introduced me to Ofer in passing and I have returned to talk about bonsais.

We step inside a large hangar to look at his collection. There are numerous specimens, ranging from a two-foot tree to one half a foot high. Bonsai figs, ferns, pines and olive. 'You can bonsai out of anything if you know how,' Ofer says.

I perch on an upturned log while he describes the techniques he used to bring the original bonsai collection he inherited back to life. 'They were in poor condition when I got them and it was a challenge to build composition into something that is essentially just a stick.' He holds up a pine tree bonsai as example. Its young green fronds are feather soft.

'I got into it by accident but I think that maybe the intention was always there. I was brought up with my hands in the soil.' Instead of going to summer camp in the US, Ofer and his siblings were sent to work in kibbutzim as farm hands.

'Which one?' I ask.

'Oh, one in the south. Nir Am. Know it?'

I smile. 'Yes, it's on the Gazan border.'

'Back home in Philadelphia, my parents used to take us to the public gardens at Longwood, Pennsylvania. I pestered them to get me this bonsai book in the gift shop and eventually they relented. Of course, like most kids, I flicked through it once and immediately forgot about it. But then sixteen years later, when I was twenty-three, I found it again and it sparked my curiosity. The basic materials for a beginner seemed easy to get hold of here and so I started playing around.'

By that time he was living in Israel full time, running a successful translation business. He joined the Israeli Bonsai Club as an amateur. One summer an Italian bonsai artist, Marco Invernizzi, was visiting for a workshop.

'That was the crunch. Italian art is based on a technical foundation from which expression flows easily. Working with him opened my creative door.'

In need of a change Ofer sold ninety per cent of his translation business to focus one hundred per cent on Bonsai.

He found work at the Botanical Gardens, where there was already a collection donated by the two founding fathers of Israeli bonsai, Haim Shir and Refael Shemi. 'It is old school bonsai,' he says. The trees were in a pretty poor condition when he arrived. 'They had been kept in the southern coastal region, but we are 800 metres above sea level here and it is colder. It was a challenge to get them into good shape.'

It wasn't long before he wanted to modernise the collection but, facing a mountain of import bureaucracy, he started to think laterally.

'I began salvaging roots of olive trees that had been displaced by construction and torn up by settlers. There is value in the old trees but there are chunks of roots left over which are usually used for firewood. Some of them are two to three thousand years old and I started to work with those. It only takes around two weeks for them to grow new shoots if done properly.'

He picks up a gnarled specimen he estimates to be around fifteen hundred years old. It is covered with contour lines like a map, its knots swirl like the chalky pathways connecting and dissecting the West Bank.

He turns it over in his hand carefully, as if it were porcelain. 'Bonsai is an art without a product. In so many other art forms the artists are the ego; they force themselves on the medium and take from it. When you work with a living organism you can't do that; you have to let go of your ego and work *with* the tree, not against it. The trees outlive us. They outlive our children, our grandchildren and so on. So long as they are looked after.'

As an artist living and working in a place so hotly contested by three major religions of the world, Ofer is always trying to find links between them. 'There are elements of the practice which already correlate in Islamic art. If you look at the forms on their own they look like Arabic calligraphy.'

Beyond the physical similarities, bonsais tell their individual histories, according to Ofer. 'Each tree swallows itself whole once a year and there's something in that perpetuity, like an echo. When you look at the rings of a tree it is like going back in time; they are trying to tell you their story. Sometimes you might find a charred layer from three or four hundred years ago and you think, "what happened then? Why was the tree on fire?" It is a beautiful mystery.'

'Each one,' he says, 'is unique, and there's a randomness in working within a static process. You never know how it's going to end up. It lends perspective, forces you to focus on the here and now, but makes you feel mortal at the same time; it helps you to retreat and respect the beauty of life.'

One day he hopes to help salvage and rehabilitate olive trees destroyed by settlers in the West Bank. 'The trees there,' he says placing the root down carefully, 'are as old as time.'

Kabul

2017

I will arise and go now, and go to Innisfree,
And a small cabin build there, of clay and wattles made;
Nine bean-rows will I have there, a hive for the honey-bee,
And live alone in the bee-loud glade.

And I shall have some peace there, for peace comes dropping slow,
Dropping from the veils of the morning to where the cricket sings;
There midnight's all a glimmer, and noon a purple glow,
And evening full of the linnet's wings.

I will arise and go now, for always night and day
I hear lake water lapping with low sounds by the shore;
While I stand on the roadway, or on the pavements grey,
I hear it in the deep heart's core.

WB Yeats, 'The Lake Isle of Innisfree'

1

The bright sun warms the miserly mountain air over the city below which is traced into the ground in regular squares and straight lines; lives lined up behind wattle walls built from the earth, fragments of a jigsaw puzzle beginning to cohere. A fort crumbles behind me; vague, crenellated ghosts turning slowly to dust with every cold breath of wind. It is wild and bitter, and when it bites I shiver into insubstantial layers more befitting the English winter I had left behind than the cold landscape around me. My hands are red raw and I blow on them to little effect. I look down at my boots as I stamp them. Where once they were clean and unmarked new rubber and leather, they are now a messy canvas of scars from this blood-soaked land.

I am standing on the edge of Kolola Pushta, a small hill in the middle of Kabul, and using its elevation to capture GVs – general views – at the end of a cold winter. It is March 2017 and I have returned, somewhat reluctantly, to Kabul to make a documentary about gardens for the BBC. At the same time, I can begin a final goodbye to Kabul. I move the tripod a few inches to the left, reframe, refocus and press record. My hands stick to the metal of the camera body.

I turn the camera and tripod again, lifting it precariously in the wind, and scan for a gleam of blue in the sludgy beige neighbourhoods, but new high-rise buildings muddle the horizon I used to know so well. There is a billboard advertising over-caffeinated energy drinks promising to make the drinker as strong as a bull blocking my view. The poster peels away from the backing and flaps. The leafless trees blur and confuse my sense of direction. I turn the tripod head again and zoom in.

The blue mosque dome blurs into focus in the middle-foreground. Triumphant, I count the streets beyond it and land on Street Seven, Qala-e-Fatullah. There are too many trees in the way but I point the camera into the obstructive branches and press record anyway, for beyond those is my old garden.

When we landed that morning, the armoured car had hurtled away from the airport and down the main thoroughfare of Taimeni. I caught a glimpse of the dogleg kink in the road beyond which the garden lies. It has been two years since I was there, but I still think of that garden as mine – my own world within a world.

I remembered then the halcyon mornings arriving after the same journey seven years ago. I would sit on the veranda sipping nuclear-strong coffee out of a chipped mug with my housemates. On bamboo garden furniture we would watch the sun climb, making jokes and swapping news. The mornings then would always smell of woody geranium leaves, cut grass and mineral earth.

But Kabul today is a different place, and I know I will never be able to return to that house. After ten years as a haven for expatriates, in 2016 the Old Flower Street Café, as the house was first known, was handed back to the landlord next door. Both it and the garden, our haven from the war, would by now have been concreted over to make room for cars.

I should pack up my camera. The light is fading fast and a crowd of curious children is beginning to gather. My throat is parched dry with the altitude of Kabul and its fine dust particles, my eyes streaming. Later, I know, I will have a nosebleed; I always do whenever I come back here.

But standing on the edge of a lonely hill, defying a savage wind, looking out over a wilderness of history at the scraggly branches – the limbs full of life – is the closest I will ever come to revisiting our old garden.

2

In the far distance, the palace roof grazes the underbelly of an overcast sky. A shaft of pale yellow light sears the morning and the wet mud tracks either side of the road glitter beneath its luminescence.

The palace looks squatter, more solid than before and, as we approach, I realise it is encased in a complex frame of scaffolding poles and green mesh construction fencing – the type used to stop debris from falling onto passers-by, but here it looks like it is trying to hide the palace away from prying eyes. At its foundations is a barrier of three-metre-high blast walls and a large military checkpoint.

Darulaman Palace is being rebuilt.

I want to meet Mohammed Kabir, the 105-year-old gardener who started his own flower garden in the palace courtyard, whom I had first met five years ago. The armoured 4 x 4 I am in pulls over next to the checkpoint, but we are ordered to move away by suspicious Afghan soldiers. Above them, a new flag flutters.

Zia, my friend and fixer, telephones to find us and, within moments, is at my window. I almost do not recognise him. His thin, wiry frame has filled out, he is trying out a new Inspector Clouseau-style moustache and has brushed his hair forward with thick hair gel. Gone is his *shalwar kameez*; instead he wears beige technical trousers and a fleece, a uniform usually favoured by military contractors and 'men on the move'. He looks older too; the lines around his eyes are more pronounced when he lifts his wraparound sunglasses.

But it is still the same old Zia when he smiles, and we both express a reserved excitement to see each other after so long. If we were not in Kabul, we would have hugged a hello. I have a parcel for him from Leslie Knott, a Canadian film-maker and former Kabul resident (and one of my closest friends). It is a basic metal detector; Zia is convinced that his fortune lies in prospecting in the mountains and has been desperately trying to get hold of a detector for nearly two years. He turns it over in his hands, wide-eyed and grinning – for once speechless.

The exchange and reunion is so absorbing that through the half-open car window I almost miss the small figure behind him. He is leaning on a bicycle which looks far too large for him, watching the cars circumnavigate the palace, and is dressed exactly as I remember. The sleeves of his suit jacket are longer than his arms and his brown trousers have been cut short above his ankles and hitched up high over his waist. His dark grey turban is solid, his beard is white and wispy. On his feet he wears two pairs of socks and a pair of mud-splattered, rubber penny loafers. It is Kabir.

The photograph I took of him in the palace garden in 2012 has been published widely. I have written about him countless times, given talks about him in London and MIT, and stared in minute detail at the lines on his face and the veins on his hands when retouching his photograph for prints or commercial publication. He is a celebrity of my own imagination, and re-meeting him in the flesh makes me feel almost star-struck.

I wave at him and, smiling, expect to see him mirror my elation, but he looks back blankly. Zia beckons him over and I get out of the car to salute him with my right arm held across my chest – an appropriate greeting between unrelated genders.

He scratches his beard and it is clear he has no idea who I am. While Zia explains, his confusion grows.

'You want to buy plants?' he asks. He has absolutely no recollection of me, and it is the anti-climax of anti-climaxes.

Zia tries to explain again and he glances over at me, uncertainty written across his face. 'The lady came to photograph you and the garden a few years ago, Uncle.' Zia is talking loudly and simply. 'Do you remember? She came to photograph your garden in the palace!'

'My garden?' he looks at me with a glimmer of recognition. 'I can't work there any more. My garden was destroyed when they started to rebuild.' Zia translates. 'No one can go there any more.'

Having failed to make the connection between reconstruction and necessary destruction, I am floored. His garden is gone.

'Hey, I know you,' Kabir says eventually, grinning through his few remaining teeth. 'You came with your camera.' He turns to Zia to impart his new understanding of the situation. 'She came with her camera!'

Zia rolls his eyes but says patiently, 'Yes, Uncle.'

Kabir explains that the reconstruction of the palace began late last year and that he lost his job and his garden. He still has his own greenhouse, out of which he grows and trades flowers, however. He might have officially retired but, with no pension system in place, Kabir and others like him will continue to work until their dying day.

He leaves his bicycle with a policeman he somehow knows and, in Zia's car, leads us out around the back of the palace through quiet backstreets and an unfamiliar neighbourhood on the road to Logar province.

There are few people around when we stop. Beneath a windless, sheet-white sky, the sporadically planted trees are static. We follow Kabir – who never stops talking at Zia – through the narrow alleyways and side streets. There are remnants of winter snow flurries on the ground. Mounds of dirty white, imprinted with shoe soles and freckled with mulch debris. It is beginning to rain and the cold bites painfully at my fingers. Someone somewhere is burning plastic, an acrid yet nostalgic smell that reminds me of military embeds in the south and which, oddly, I have come to love.

He rummages in his suit pocket for a key and rattles it in a flimsy tin door. It opens onto a large walled courtyard of bamboo- and brick-framed tents the size of agricultural polytunnels. The plastic sheeting which covers it is smeared and splattered with mud.

I am directly behind Kabir, filming him as we teeter along a foot-high mud wall next to a greenhouse. He is still muttering but I concentrate on keeping my footing. He stops abruptly at an opening covered by a heavy carpet which hangs instead of a door.

Pulling it back, he beckons me to follow. While the world outside is smudged-muddy, ill lit and vulnerable to the cruel elements, the world here is an oasis of over a thousand fragrant plants, keeping warm for the winter. A few light bulbs have been rigged up and, beneath them, a multi-hued green palette emerges. There are regiments of geraniums and pelargoniums – ivy leafed, lemon scented and trailing. There are a dozen or so yellow angel trumpets in larger pots halfway down the greenhouse and fragrant citrus trees further beyond.

A line of small cyclamen, flowering a fragile white, and rows of gingham-blue and white hibiscus. There is a verbena which will flower white in the spring. At the back of the enclosure are literally hundreds and hundreds of spiky euphorbia millis – or crown of thorns. Hardy, I think – like Kabir – and a jolly, warm red in defiance of the cold.

Kabir walks between each line, pointing, and stops at each new variety like a teacher picking out the best students. He seems to gain energy as he walks through the plants, his frailty dissolving with every step. By the time we get him to sit still on an upturned bucket for his interview, he has all the fidgety restlessness of an excited child.

'Eat, eat!' he says, pulling some lumps of dried salted yogurt from his waistcoat pocket and ordering a pot of tea from a young man who has appeared at the greenhouse's entrance. 'This, plus gardening, is why I never get old!' he mumbles through a mouthful.

During the course of the interview he describes his life at Darulaman Palace as a teenager with his father, and recalling with misty-eyed nostalgia the beauty of the plants there.

'*Patooni* flowers, *falakes* flowers, *kafishan* flowers,' Zia lists, unable to find the translations even on an iPhone app, '*barbina, antari* and *jiriband*. Apple, pear, *qaisi* and *amiri* apricot, cherry, sweet cherry, green cherry, *kharmoosa* cherry.' Kabir goes on describing the flora

318

and fauna of yesteryear he had described five years ago. Seemingly now hard of hearing, he shouts his answers.

In an aside he informs us that in addition to working as a royal gardener he spent some time as a chef and airborne soldier – with no fewer than thirty-two parachute jumps. 'Gardening keeps me young,' he shouts again. 'If you use your shovel in the field or the garden, you will not age. The spade and the flower, they stretch your bones and will keep you younger more than football and all those other things.'

From where I am sitting, the greenhouse is now even bigger still – there is a whole section of terracotta pots, which had previously been hidden, given over to cuttings. The sheer number at my feet is itself testimony, I think, to the Afghan passion for gardening. And this is just one of three of Kabir's greenhouses. He is clearly confident of his market.

'Gardening used to be a normal profession,' he says. 'It used to be something the young would consider an honourable job. Now people just want to be drivers. People don't think about gardens. I know everything about plants' – he holds his finger up – 'and people know they can come to me!'

He may have had his job taken away from him, and selling what he propagates might keep him fed and watered in old age, but I sense there is something more altruistic driving Kabir to keep gardening: a desire to keep the fraternity of gardening alive. The palace garden he had nurtured was a metaphorical nod to a hopeful future amidst the physical ruins of the past. The sea of flowers and succulents at my feet *are* the future - they will be sold to other gardeners in about a month's time.

The plastic sheeting overhead ripples in the wind and the light is falling as fast as the slate clouds gather for a downpour. But inside it is spring, and it always will be, I realise. Perhaps that too is what keeps Kabir young: living away from the world outside and in the season of hope and promise.

Watching Kabul through the back window of the 4 x 4 I feel removed from it, disconnected, and yet every corner, vegetable cart, every glimpse of mountains, every flock of pigeons and donkey-swerving taxi, every bakery, beauty salon, is as familiar as home.

The 4 x 4 pulls off the tarmac road and rumbles through a police checkpoint and into the courtyard of a securely guarded guest house run by an ex-soldier. It is a dreary place, decorated for functionality by 'blokes' and lit by halogen strip lights. I would have preferred to stay with the few remaining friends I know here in the diplomatic quarter of the Green Zone, but the BBC has its own security rules and, as a temporary employee, I must comply. My room, at least, has an electric heater and it warms quickly.

I charge up the camera batteries, transfer the footage of Kabir to a hard drive and, after telephoning my boyfriend, spend the remainder of the evening logging the rushes: indexing each clip and its contents – a tedious but vital process in film-making.

I can hear the television at the other end of the corridor, but when I hear the muezzin call for the faithful at a local mosque, I go to my window. It opens onto a security wall but I stare up into a patch of starless black sky.

*

It has been five years since I last met Engineer Khoistani and, unlike the city, he hasn't aged. If anything he looks younger and, in his brown corduroy suit and matching flat cap, more dapper than ever.

He leads us through the caravanserai entrance of Babur's gardens and out to the foot of the central water channel. The vista stretches up and out before me, eleven hectares of the garden waiting for spring. There are few visitors today; not only is it still cold and dank, it is also the middle of the week. Khoistani walks with us, explaining the garden's history. We walk up the steep incline to the furthest terrace beneath the Queen's Palace, passing a number of labourers who are hard at work.

We ask them about gardening and Babur's gardens. Startled by the camera, their answers are not particularly enlightening, and while Ali, a radio producer, engages in a protracted conversation I turn away to film two men digging a hole. A cold-looking rose, recently extracted from the covered nursery, stands next to them, roots encased in a makeshift flowerpot fashioned out of a cooking oil tin. They are preparing the gardens for *Nowruz*, the Persian New Year, which also indicates the start of spring and falls in a few days.

We reach the upper terrace and I sit Khoistani down on a chair, precariously balanced on a wall. The information he relays is an almost verbatim replica of the garden's history he had described to me five years ago. But he bemoans the lack of building regulations, the impact increased pollution is having on the trees and the need for more public gardens for the benefit of the people.

'Planting in Islam,' Khoistani tells us, 'has a specific word: "khair" – "goodness" or "peace".' But for Khoistani, it is not the act of planting and peace which unifies Afghanis, however; it is the garden itself which transcends all divisions. 'You see it here all the time; it doesn't matter which ethnicity people come from. They leave their divisions at the gates and come here to sit beneath the trees in the summer, united in their enjoyment of the shade.'

Afghanistan is just outside the guesthouse compound walls, but security is restrictive and I may as well be on another planet. Determined to be part of the city, at least, I scamper up to the roof. Flat and spacious, it is usually the domain of the guest house maids; they will wash and hang laundry here tomorrow and chatter together, away from the prying ears of the male guards. There is a small wooden container accessed like a gypsy caravan via a step ladder. It is the 'live feed' box from where other visiting broadcasters can report live. A nest of cables, wires, telephone plugs, satellite links to invisible frequencies will transmit the news and the views halfway round the world within seconds.

But the box is empty now; there is no important news to send to the world outside today. I stand on the roof's wall, using the fencing to hold me up and look out at the city, inhaling the burning cedar from the thousands of *bukharis* – wood-burning stoves – dotted around the city. Yellow headlamps and red taillights smudge through the darkness of the backstreets, the tall fir trees from the UN compound next door whisper, single bulbs shine from a few of the shadowy houses on the hills rigged up to the power lines.

I cannot see much else up there. I realise I have not slept properly since leaving London, and my mind races with fatigue and caffeine.

I sit on the steps of the live box, hug my knees into my chest and look up to follow the passage of two Blackhawks buzzing beneath a familiar pattern of stars. I am jealous of their view; they can see the city proper, not just the vague shapes and colours – informed mostly by memory – that I can.

Small ribbons of black smoke spiral into the sky from the neighbours' *bukharis* over the back wall and, in the middle distance of the morning, the city reverberates with construction noises, traffic and bicycle bells.

The bird settles in the palm of my hand. As it grows cold its eyes begin to close. There is a drop of dried blood at the base of my thumb and its tiny heart is slowing. It will die soon, I think, and I stroke the downy head as softly as I can and will my hand warm for it.

I had discovered it flapping with a scurry of wings and feathers in the skeletal cherry tree at the end of the couple's garden. Early spring sparrows, I had thought, larking around in the feeble morning light; the only life in an otherwise dormant garden. When I realised it was just one bird and it had trapped its leg improbably between two twigs I scampered up a ladder to free it as gently as possible. I immediately set about soothing it back to life while maintaining a modicum of professionalism, conducting and filming an interview with the gardeners, Mr and Mrs Roami.

They are a sweet couple. When we first arrived, I had asked if they could potter around the garden for the purposes of the film. They needed little encouragement. He wears a golfer's jumper and woollen trousers against the cold, and she a grey scarf over her head and a thick purple cardigan.

They wait patiently for me to set up the camera (one-handed) asking them to move incremental centimetres to the right and left. Mr Roami's eyes water with age and cold but he does not complain.

'Before I retired, I was a science professor at the university,' he says in broken English before lapsing into Dari for Ali, a radio producer, to translate.

'My darling wife was a nurse, but it is down to her that the house is so comfortable. When we first moved here twenty years ago it was horrible. Very . . .' Ali searches for the English word. 'Slimy. No, wait. It was very unloved, run-down.'

The bird shifts its weight, the professor continues and Ali translates. 'When we made the house habitable we turned our attention immediately to the garden. We planted the lawn, installed the fountain and set about with roses and flowers.'

Mrs Roami shivers into her clothes and adds, 'We helped each other out as equals in the garden. We discussed where things should be planted, how things should look. I was always right,' she chuckles.

The garden behind them is a neat, oblong lawn surrounded on all sides by generously deep flower beds. There is a wire coop in a recess along the back wall, home to three indignant peacocks resembling captive princes. One splays its feathers; the opulent, regal, greeny blue plumage greens sit at odds with the pallid winter. In the middle of the lawn is a circular marble fountain surrounded by thorny rose bushes waiting for the season to change. It soon will, and when it does a new world will emerge.

'If you come back in the summer you will see how green and colourful this garden is,' she adds wistfully, 'but you should have seen the last one.'

'War destroys everything,' Mr Roami sighs, and he describes the life they had before the country fell to war.

The Kabul they knew was very different to today's.

'It was a very beautiful city back in the day. Clean, lively, full of parks and gardens. We lived freely and peacefully.' Mrs Roami adjusts her glasses. 'There was a women's garden too, full of colour. It exists today, but in name only; its trees have withered and died.'

I do not know if she intends it, but it is a powerful metaphor to describe the lot for Afghan women now. She goes on to describe the gardens and parks of Paghman, a town just outside Kabul renowned for its greenery and fruit trees.

In the early twentieth century Paghman was favoured by the Afghan upper classes and aristocracy, most of whom had weekend chalets there. Black and white photographs from those days show charming but curious scenes reminiscent of an E.M. Forster novel. Afghans dressed in Western-style Edwardian regalia, dining out beneath the dark woodland canopy on large mahogany tables decked in silver, military men doffing caps to ladies from their horses, tea parties amidst rose bushes.

There are more recent colour photographs from the 1960s and '70s. Two miniskirted young women, one posing while the other holds a camera at the end of a water canal. In another scene, a triumphal arch rises out of a woodland just on the verge of turning towards autumn; the yellowing leaves fringe the sky like flames.

Mr Roami raises his finger and continues to reminisce. 'This city was heaven. They used to say that the Kabul River was full of musk.' The idea of the Stygian waters of that river smelling like anything other than putrefied rubbish and dead animals is beyond me. The garden of their old house was, he says, a masterpiece of vines, roses and fruit trees, and a stream running along the other side of the road ensured that it was always well watered.

The bird in my hand is growing cold so I excuse myself for a moment to wrap it up in a scarf and to leave it balanced on a flowerpot in the sun. I ask the security manager, Mike, an affable American and former special forces officer, to watch out for cats. 'Just don't let it die,' I say, and return to the couple.

The violence of the civil war in the late eighties obliviated any peace, but the Roamis refused to flee for as long as they could, trying to live as normal a life as possible. They had no choice but to send their children away to safety in Europe.

The war escalated beyond all reason and they tried to rebuild a life in Karte Parwan, an area of the city that until then had been considered safe. Soon the skies again rained rockets and, much like the residents of Eastern Ukraine in 2014, they took to the ground and hid from the war in the cellar.

Tragically, Mr and Mrs Roami lost the telephone number of where their children were living. Understandably, this was one of the hardest things for them to bear. But they found comfort in the natural world. 'When we weren't being rocketed,' Mrs Roami continues, 'we planted trees and flowers. It gave us a form of hope.'

'How?' I ask. 'How did it give you hope?'

She sighs heavily. 'We named the flowers after our children. Nurturing them kept us alive during those days.' She is still smiling and fixed with dignity but I have zoomed the camera in and her eyes fill the frame. 'The flowers became my children. I raised them like my children, spoke to them like my children. It gave us the belief that one day our children would come home. If anyone picked my flowers or tore off a leaf, I would feel the pain of losing them all over again.'

Through the camera's viewfinder her eyes come into sharp focus and brim with tears otherwise imperceptible behind her glasses. I understand in that single moment that she has never quite recovered from the choice they had to make.

The rockets and shells continued to explode the sky, burning nerves and breaking lives, but the Roamis were focused on keeping their garden alive.

'Once,' Mrs Roami recalls, 'we were besieged on all four sides by different factions fighting each other. Everyone else had left the neighbourhood. The garden still needed watering but it was increasingly dangerous to cross the road to get to the stream. The garden began to die. "Let's dig a well," I said to my husband.' She squeezes his arm.

'After five hours we could pull water from the ground and immediately we fed it to the vines and flowers. I will never forget how happy we were,' she smiles. 'Neither the rockets nor the fighting could stop us. I think that is the true story of flowers and war, don't you?'

Inevitably, the unrest in the city once again destroyed the life they had built but, determined not to be defeated, the Roamis found another house to rebuild with another garden to create – the one we are now sitting in – and have remained here ever since, enduring five years of Taliban government.

'We designed it together,' Mr Roami says practically, matter-of-factly. 'There used not to be any shade so we created the pergola for the vine to crawl through and then planted the bulbs and flowers according to where the sun fell. But,' he says, pointing up, 'you see all the new tower blocks? They are blocking out the sun.'

Mrs Roami adds, 'There are no building regulations. People just do what they like. We are desperately worried about our flowers.' It is a common gardener's complaint, but I wonder if a part of Mrs Roami still anthropomorphises the flowers, seeing them as the children she could keep.

'What is your favourite flower?' I ask them.

He smiles. 'Easy! My wife. She is the best flower of all.'

Although the garden is a winter palace of earth and thorns and drained of most colour, the blossom buds barely showing pink behind tiny acid-green leaves, they break the monotonous cold. There are freshly planted bulbs in those muddy flower beds too, I notice; layers of life held within a swollen heart, ready to enter the garden's stage. I look up at the mountains, now just visible over the wall; snow-capped, their summits disappear into the pale sky. A cat prowls along the back wall beneath rolls of razor wire, oblivious to the jagged jaw of steel teeth, eyes fixed on the two sparrows preening themselves ahead of it.

Alarmed, I look around for the injured bird, convalescing in my scarf. I hear a twitter and rush over, reaching out a hand to pick it up again, anxious it should not be easy prey for the cat. The bird looks up and takes flight, disappearing into the cold bright morning and the mountains beyond. The blood I had seen on my hand, I realise, was my own. I had caught it on the rose climbing through the cherry tree during the bird's rescue.

3

The day arrives with a demented flurry of snow and an outrageous cold. Beneath the white blanket, the land is muffled and the modern world vanishes. It slips back a century to the old country. It is replaced by details of the terrain that appear in isolation against the snow: shadowed gradients and irrigation ditches, bushes and trees all feathered and re-feathered with each unique flake.

The road inclines as we approach Qargha Lake, the man-made reservoir on the outskirts of Kabul. Surrounded on all sides by white, the water today appears a deserted, glacial blue.

We pass the junction leading off to the house of Dr Mojadidi, the former mayor of Kabul whose American-Afghan garden had been his escape from semi-house arrest. I wonder if he is still there; perhaps he is standing on his veranda with a cup of coffee, also watching the oversized flakes. But we continue on around the lake and follow the road into the next valley.

I want to film the trees scurried by snow and we stop at a fruit orchard we see from the road. The flakes swim through the air, independent of one another, frenzied and eager to conceal the orchard. The sky has fallen around me and is so low now that when the larger flakes settle on my headscarf I may as well be one of its clouds of frozen water. Slowly, I become white and a part of the preposterous cold. But I am happily isolated in that snowstorm, hidden by both snow and the witchlike orchard branches in a secret world where the only sound is a distant and muffled engine chugging somewhere in the distance.

But we have to continue to meet the next gardener and Mike, the American security manager, is twitchy; the road is known for bandits. Back in the car the world is viewed through a watery window of smashed-up snowflakes, screaming over the glass.

Buildings emerge at the roadside as we approach Paghman, the town formerly favoured by Kabul's upper classes for its gardens and green spaces. Little of that era still exists now, but there is still life. There are a number of shops beneath flimsy, snow-soaked awnings; the carcass of half a cow hanging frozen at a butcher's door, headless and tailless, the fissures of white fat indistinguishable from the ice. Piles of wood seem to shiver, passers-by hold their jackets close around them, and an elderly man wrapped in a *patoo* shovels a snowdrift away from a ditch. His efforts are in vain. The snow falls faster than his weary limbs can clear it.

We lurch off the road and into a blanketed white field as yet undisturbed. Zia, having driven on ahead, is waiting for us and appears from a shed door with a young man dressed in skinny jeans and a leather jacket. His hair is a trendy undercut currently popular among young men the world over. He is Hamidullah, an eighteen-year-old pharmacology student and, Zia has promised, a passionate gardener. I look at his hairstyle and am doubtful.

'So this is the garden,' he says nervously, standing on the edge of the snowfield. A walkway covered in a frozen vine leads to another more intimate area in front of a single-storey house. We are so enveloped in this sudden winter it is hard to gauge what it looks like in the summer – I struggle to imagine it as anything but frozen flat and pressed white beneath the heavy load of the sky.

'And this is the greenhouse,' Hamidullah says as we pick our way past a cow tethered to an outbuilding and a couple of hardy white chickens pecking hopefully at the solid ground, their combs sketching red in the snow. He opens the door of a plastic-covered brick lean-to and lets me in.

In an instant, the blank world outside evaporates. Every inch of the walls are covered in shelves upon which are crammed terracotta flowerpots of creeping geraniums, pansies, variegated ivy, primulas, pelargonium and black-eyed Susan.

My seven layers of clothing make me feel soporific in the cosy, scented warmth of the greenhouse. There is a chair in one corner and I eye it longingly; it would be the perfect place to curl up with a good book and a mug of sweet, milky tea.

But we have an interview to do so instead I ask Hamidullah to sit there, and I set about opening out the tripod and trying not to swear when the heavy clips nip my frozen fingers. Hamidullah waits patiently, politely and nervously.

He is still nervous when we begin but he tells his story with gentle eloquence. He is part of the millennial generation of Afghans brought up outside Afghanistan and happily exposed to the modern life of Kabul city. He and thousands like him spend hours on Facebook, they listen to Iranian, Indian and Pakistani – and sometimes even American – pop-music. They watch the latest film releases (pirated), are glued to the Afghan version of *Pop Idol*, cricket and Indian soaps, and follow all the latest trends in clothes and hair. Gardening is rarely on the extracurricular agenda. But it is for Hamidullah, for whenever he is at home he is in the garden or the greenhouse. 'I even do my homework in here,' he grins.

Hamidullah learned how to garden from his father when he and his family returned to Afghanistan after nine years spent as refugees in Tehran.

'Iran is a good country. It is peaceful and safe, but if you live as an outsider you will always be a stranger to the city. No country could ever comfort you more than your own.' Living in basic and highly urban conditions there was no space to garden, but as soon as they returned to their homeland, things changed.

'The first thing I remember seeing when we crossed the country was its greenness. There were flowers, gardens, trees, valleys. We didn't get that in Iran. I remember seeing my dad gardening in one of the meadows behind the house. In Tehran he was a mason and I had never seen him work like that. I asked him what he was doing and he explained what it is to garden. Then he gave me a seed and told me to plant it too. It was a wallflower, and it was the first time I had seen anything growing properly. When you plant something it teaches you patience.'

His academic ambitions are high. 'Obviously the situation here is uncertain and the war worries everyone, but I want to serve my people and my country,' he says. 'So many of my friends, guys my age, they have left to become refugees, may God save them. They have gone to Germany to start new lives. I want to stay and help. I wish I could serve society through my flowers,' he smiles, 'but instead I will work hard and become a successful doctor.'

'Will you still garden?' I ask, imagining an older version of Hamidullah dressed in a white coat with a stethoscope around his neck, striding down the wards of a modern hospital checking clipboards and ordering nurses around.

'Of course,' he says, almost affronted at my question. 'I will use all the money I earn to expand the greenhouse and continue to grow the best flowers in the whole of Paghman. Everyone has a responsibility to their homeland; planting flowers and gardening is part of that responsibility.'

'Sometimes,' he admits, slowly, 'sometimes if I am lonely I talk to the flowers. They are really good at keeping secrets.'

'What kind of secrets?'

He remains tight-lipped and blushes pale crimson.

'And you really don't want to leave for Europe?' we ask. He might feel tied to his motherland, but the country is visibly crumbling at the seams, with suicide attacks happening almost daily throughout the country.

'No,' he says confidently. 'My homeland is more important to me than anything else. Here I can study and I can garden. I don't ask or wish for anything else in life.'

I think about eighteen-year-olds in England. Would they say the same thing if we lived in a semi-permanent state of war and the glimmer of a better life was offered?

'Gardening gives you independence,' he adds, his voice without a tremor of uncertainty. 'No one asks you to do it; it is something you *want* to do, it comes from inside you and it makes you feel calm and enables you to forget the world.'

When I film him working on the pots, pulling out whispers of weeds and dead leaves, his eyes and mouth soften with a contented smile. He is totally absorbed in the work, part of the garden's world now, oblivious to the cold underworld outside.

Zia pokes his head around the door nervously. 'Lali-Lali? We have to go. The neighbour thinks there are people watching us in the hills. It is not safe here any more.'

A chill shivers down my spine as I pack up. It seems so improbable to be observed filming something so benign. Half of me thinks that maybe Zia is bored, hungry and cold, and, knowing my tendency to lose track of time, is trying to chivvy me along. But he and I are old friends and he is one of the few people in this world I trust with my life.

As we hoist ourselves back into the car, Hamidullah and his brothers start a snowball fight and the danger outside is, for a brief few moments, arbitrary and suspended. Even Zia retaliates when a ball crumples at his back, hurling a compacted fistful of ice crystals back at Hamidullah, who ducks and laughs. I look up at the hills and search for movement in the ragged trees propping up the sky.

We arrive at Murad Khani in a pearl-lit morning. The snow has been quick to melt and fast becomes a slurry of brackish mud. This part of Kabul is known as the Old City (although undoubtedly there are quarters buried beneath a modern veneer which are older still) and the buildings glimpsed through doors left ajar or over high walls allude to a different era entirely.

Most of the structures in Murad Khani were intended to house members of the Qizalbash tribe, descendants of the troops of Nader Shah – the Persian shah who marauded through Central Asia in the eighteenth century. The Qizalbash's regal associations secured their place in high-ranking levels of government and society. The Old City – or Murad Khani –was then a network of small streets (intentionally too narrow for a horse-drawn cart), caravanserai, ornate double storey buildings, a bazaar full of silversmiths, fortune tellers and a number of Shia shrines and religious structures.

History has not been kind to Murad Khani however, and a combination of Soviet modernisation in the 1970s, neglect and civil war and the general unavoidable decay thereafter led to the area's rapid decline. By 2006 it had become one of the poorest areas of Kabul and deemed to be one of the world's most endangered historical sites. It was also the city's rubbish tip; so much garbage had accumulated that the street level in some places was two metres higher than it should be.

The then Afghan president, Hamid Karzai, with the help of the Prince of Wales, a prominent supporter of heritage-led regeneration, founded Turquoise Mountain, a non-profit, non-governmental organisation whose aim was to regenerate the Old City and revive traditional Afghan crafts.

Today the charity is still going strong, and to date has restored much of the Old City and its decrepit and buried buildings, expanded an institute for Afghan arts and architecture and partnered with some of the best designers and master craftsmen in the world. It is one of the happiest places to work in Kabul. I should know, for I filmed much of their work in granular detail over six months for an exhibition at the Smithsonian Museum in Washington, DC. Before that, I had made a film about the children of the Old City and kite flying for the Victoria and Albert Museum of Childhood. My overriding memory of both projects is of happy laughter.

Returning to the Old City today fills me with delight, and I am eager to be enveloped in its labyrinthine alleyways, hidden corners and cosy familiarity. The man making shoes and buckets out of rubber tyres is still there. And so is the popcorn man, sitting cross-legged next to an enormous brazier of popping puffs, stirring every few moments with a spade and adjusting his chemistry-experiment-style goggles. The vegetable sellers cry out their bargains; carrots and potatoes today, and in a month or so their carts will be laden with scarlet tomatoes and bulbous cauliflowers.

When I walk past the row of blacksmiths battering red-hot slabs of metal into spades they look up to wave hello. 'You are back?' one asks, waving his hammer and smiling and a little bit of me feels like a celebrity.

This is Kabul at its purest; normal people just getting on with their normal lives and hoping to be left alone by the world. It is a corner of the city that I hope will never change.

But I am not here to ruminate among the blacksmiths; I am here to film the garden of Kaka Khalil, a descendent of the original Qizalbash tribe whose family has lived in Murad Khani for hundreds of years.

I lead the radio crew and Mike the American to his house, passing the fortune tellers rolling out dice to women in burkhas, trying to find answers to impossible questions, and through an intricate maze of narrow alleys.

Footsteps approach on the other side of the heavy door and it opens. It is Waheed, Kaka Khalil's son, and one of the three 'stars' of the kite-running film. I am taken aback to find that he has grown about six inches into adolescence. His grin has not changed, however, and he calls out to his father along the corridor behind him, 'Dad, the woman is here.'

'What?' the reply is muffled.

'The one to take pictures. Lili the foreigner.'

Kaka Khalil appears at the end of the corridor holding a length of hosepipe. Behind him is the garden – empty, apart from frozen clods of mud and a tired box hedge.

Nevertheless, he is hard at work. 'There is much to do before *Nowruz,* the ground needs waking up!' His eyes twinkle. 'And so do the plants!'

He takes us back out into the Old City streets and to the greenhouse where he is keeping the flowers warm. It is high enough for Khalil to stand in but I still hit my head on the crossbeam. There is a radio and a television set perched on one chair and an old newspaper yellowing on the one opposite. The greenhouse is Khalil's man cave, I realise happily, an escape from his six children and responsibilities as a community elder.

Back in his garden, I film Khalil 'waking up' the soil; he hoes and rakes, picks out large rocks and potters around his pots, sussing the best place to put them.

Adiba, his daughter, appears at my side. Her milk teeth are small and gappy when she grins cheekily. Unlike her brother, she has not grown. I ruffle her hair and, still as rambunctious as ever, she tries to ruffle mine.

When we return two months later at the end of May, the Old City is just as beguiling as when we left it. Tomatoes and melons are hauled on wooden carts. Early yellow mangoes are piled high on a tarpaulin on the ground. The popcorn man is nowhere to be seen, however; it is Ramadan, and during the month of fasting the market for street snacks is slim to none. The rubber-smiths and blacksmiths are still in situ, however, and wave, as does the one-legged man who guards the ceramic school at Turquoise Mountain just around the corner.

Repeating the journey to Kaka Khalil's house, we knock on the door and Waheed is there within moments, ushering us inside and skipping down the dark corridor, calling for his father.

Khaka Khalil and his family might be of modest means, but the garden, now awake after the winter, is a jewel. The central square of grass is emerald green and seemingly held in place by four large roundel flower beds of bright pink, lilac and yellow petunias, snapdragon and catmint. Fragrant white jasmine trundles over an arch and a pale yellow dog rose chases it. A riotous assembly of scarlet and pink geraniums sit on a set of stairs leading up towards his house.

The house, he tells us, was originally built for King Ammanullah Khan's secretary in the 1920s. Khalil's father was the tailor to the royal family and moved his family there when Khalil was still a boy.

'There used to be another building on that side, but we demolished it to make the garden bigger. At that time we had apples, cherries, pears and pomegranates, but we never picked them. My father used to tell us to leave the fruits there to make the house more beautiful.'

During the civil war, Murad Khani was one of the front lines and the Khalil family moved away for safety. 'Only my brother stayed to protect our belongings from looters. But we missed this place; it was our home.'

'Did you garden then?' I ask.

'Absolutely not,' he replies, 'there was no water here! All the wells had dried up here. Everything died. It was heartbreaking.'

Under the Taliban, life had not been much better for Kaka Khalil. 'People were stressed out and tired. If you didn't have a long enough beard, they beat you. If your hair was too long, they beat you. They beat me for both crimes. Women were lashed for not being covered like this' – he pulls his scarf over his head to cover his face, the effect of which makes us laugh despite the ghastliness. 'People who had money left for Pakistan, but we stayed.'

'And then?' I ask, 'Did you garden?'

'No, no,' he says, 'there was no gardening, everything had dried up, people were sad and there were no jobs, no money. The Taliban were only interested in lashing people. But when they left . . . that is when we could start gardening again.'

He and his brother started with the grass and, little by little, they sourced flowers and plants from wherever they could.

'The flowers,' he tells me very earnestly, 'they reminded me of my childhood.' Having grown up in a netherworld of war, Khalil's desire to garden is nostalgic. It stems from a desire to wipe clean the past and revert to a better era – to those delicious days when the trees were heavy with fruits and the air sweetened with blossom.

'The situation is not good in Kabul now: security, unemployment, you know. And the city is so noisy and polluted these days, but at least flowers freshen your mind and bring you peace. It is a joy!'

Before we leave the Old City I want to meet Ramesh, the gardener who owns nothing.

I first stumbled across Ramesh's small garden years ago. It was the comparatively new wall that piqued my interest. I couldn't believe it when I stepped into a garden about two metres wide and five long. There was a vine, roses and geraniums plus a metal and glass shed on a raised platform at the back full of pot plants and canaries.

I learned from Hajji Engineer, a splendid man always sharply dressed in a waistcoat and jacket and one of the community officers of Turquoise Mountain, that the garden was on stolen land.

'Ramesh built the wall without asking,' Hajji Engineer had explained in heavily accented English, and rubbing his prayer beads together as was his habit. 'He is a . . .' – he searches for the translation – 'bad man.' He spits the words.

I am surprised; the man I met in the garden that morning appeared to be nothing but convivial.

Tommy, a friend who had introduced me to Jolyon Leslie all those years ago and who went on to run Turquoise Mountain, was on hand to elucidate the local politics. 'He is a bit of a troublemaker and built his garden to grow cannabis in the greenhouse,' he explained. 'People were annoyed that he built it on land that wasn't his. But Kaka Khalil, Hajji Engineer and the other elders figured it would be better to have him indebted to them rather than to enrage him so they let the garden stay put.'

When I met him again a few days later with a translator, Ramesh's greenhouse was full of yellow canaries in cages stacked floor to ceiling. Their twittering was deafening when he approached to feed them. I looked for signs of marijuana plants but there was nothing.

He told me that the land belonged to his father-in-law. I may be gullible, but I believed him simply because he just didn't *look* like he was lying.

Today, two years later, Ramesh is waiting for us outside the gate to his garden and holds out his arm to shake hands. He stoops a little more now, and his hair is greying fast, but when he smiles it is with bashful and boyish jollity. A small marijuana plant is growing in a flower bed by the entrance, almost hidden by a young geranium. Inside his garden, the flowers are feeble and rather sparsely planted.

'I have had problems with the salinity of the soil this year,' he says. 'I put some compost down but it was poor quality and I don't think it worked.'

Kaka Khalil appears and the two men chatter amicably enough.

Ali tells me they are talking about fertiliser and, even though I know that this is for the benefit of the camera, I film them anyway. Khalil suggests to Ramesh that he weed a little. It is a helpful enough suggestion, but it is also a nuanced affirmation that Khalil is higher in the pecking order here; he is the one who commands. But Ramesh is happy to oblige and squats down on his haunches to cut away at the weeds with a mini-sickle – freshly smelted by the blacksmith in the bazaar. It is such a simple garden tool, nothing more than a rough piece of wood and a metal claw hook around six inches long. But Ramesh is deft and, within moments, has hacked away at the weeds.

His youth was happier than his present, he tells us when we interview him later. His father was head of an agricultural bank and the family were well off. 'We had a huge house with an enormous garden. My father loved flowers and gardening and I learned his passion after school, helping him to weed and water.'

His family's story is one of riches to rags during the build-up to the civil war, and in its aftermath. 'My father was a good Muslim and never took bribes. But when he died the security situation worsened and my brother, who was working in the ministry of finance, left the country.' Shortly afterwards, the remaining sisters and brother left too. Ramesh stayed put, determined to see out the war and live once again in their family home.

He had a chequered career as a conscripted soldier, a security guard and a gardener, so he says. But his dream of returning home was shattered by the Taliban, who demolished the family house to make way for a road. Ramesh was alone in Kabul.

After the fall of the Taliban he found a job as a gardener for a cultural organisation, the name of which he has forgotten, but he was made to retire six years ago. 'As soon as I lost my job, I built this garden. I wanted to build one where we used to live but, well, it is just a road now,' he says. 'My father-in-law owns this land, but I built the walls and everything you see here now.' I want to ask him about his domestic arrangements but I am with too many men. If Ali was to ask about his wife, it could be taken as crude curiosity, even though the question is innocent and comes from me. 'It took me about a year. I started with the roses and then I added a peach and berry trees. Oh, and the grapes. It is a really good hobby and a way to spend the day. I really like just sitting and thinking and sometimes my friends join me.'

The trees he planted have outgrown the garden, however, and the whole area is completely in the shade, apart from the vine which climbs up to the light.

'Would you like to work as a gardener again?' I ask.

'Of course,' he says, 'I would love to work in Babur's gardens. If I had a chance, I would take all my favourite flowers there.'

I ask if his children like gardening.

'No,' he snorts, raising a finger. 'Children now are only interested in their phones and Facebook. That is their only hobby. Flowers freshen your mind, mobile phones destroy it!'

I know the interview has only scratched the surface of his life. I want to know about his father-in-law and the whereabouts of his siblings – how did they do so well in life when he faded so quickly? The inconsistencies are also typical in a country where storytelling is rarely linear and often muddled, and where so many memories are sad and need replacing with happier – albeit fabricated – ones.

The issue of land ownership has yet to be resolved too, and the supposed drug propagation – although the marijuana plant does shed some light here. But I begin to suspect that the garden and its walls are at the heart of a land squabble between old families, each preserving their claim on the Old City. If I am right, Ramesh is just a pawn in this game, but a happy one in a place which lets him retreat to a time when he was happy too. To yearn and look for a more innocent past is part of the human condition, and our escapism.

I imagine a younger version of Ramesh desperately looking for his childhood home where he will rebuild his father's garden. But try as he might, he cannot find it. He looks everywhere, but the world is different now. A lorry whooshes past him and eventually he understands that the house has been buried beneath asphalt and tar.

I start packing up the camera equipment as he sits on a plastic chair beneath the vine. The space is too narrow and he angles it towards the greenhouse, crosses his legs and looks up vaguely at the dappling leaves. This garden of his is, I realise, his *world in a lost world . . . a little perfect world.*

The wind is ferocious. Young fruit in the orchard trees hold steady, determined in a storm of flurried leaves, but gradually the sky thickens orange. The wind pitches and scatters mountain dust. Fine particles of earth coat everything and flatten the light. But I do the best I can in Babur's gardens, filming the length and breadth of the cosmos terraces, the rose-lined paths and the quiet corners of buddleia. One gust of wind is so strong even the heavy tripod wobbles.

It is the 'Parwan wind' Emperor Babur describes in his *Baburnama*. 'It does not fail Kabul in the summer,' he writes. Having rushed 'through the Parwan Pass of the Hindu Kush . . . it lowers the temperature in the windowed houses'. When he was writing, the wind was a cool blessing in a torrid heat.

Over 500 years later, the wind, although cooling, arrives every day at precisely the same time as the light is soft enough to film. I do not really have the luxury of time, so film snatches views whenever and wherever I can. The dust clings to my sweat, and dries my already parched mouth. The fine particles irritate my eyes and, unsteadied by the wind, I nip my fingers in a tripod clip.

But standing on the upper terrace and looking south-west over the city, the sky and land are indistinguishable. I set the camera on the ground, let the Parwan wind pull off my headscarf, and ignoring the dust, I gaze into the formless distance.

'You came back? You weren't scared!' Hamidullah is grinning from ear to ear. He is wearing a snow-white and freshly pressed *shalwar kameez*, a gleaming beacon against the wall of the greenhouse lean-to by the road.

My tongue is sticking to the roof of my mouth. I am so hot and thirsty, I am about to faint, but it is Ramadan – no food or drink in public. I muster a smile and try to mimic his enthusiasm as we park. Out of sight, I take a swig of water from a bottle and hope that its relief will last until we leave.

In the eight weeks since we were last there, the garden has revealed itself remarkably. Where we had shivered through a field of thick, untouched snow and tried to un-muddle tree branches from layers of ice, a country garden now sits. The house, freshly painted pale yellow and lilac, sits as happy as a wild primrose in a wayside of thick grass – the sort of grass that makes you want to lie down in it. Neat rose bushes, heavy and headily scented in varying hues of pink, fringe the grasses.

The front of the house is decked with the pot plants he had maintained in the greenhouse: geraniums, pansies and succulents. A wallflower, his favourite, sits next to the front door, which is framed by a clambering passion flower.

I set up the interview in the shade of a mulberry tree. We already know what he is going to say, but just need a few more sound bites for the camera. Afterwards, I will film him gardening.

He is more confident when he talks and expands on his family's journey back from Iran after the fall of the Taliban. 'It took us three days and my parents were so happy and excited. They kept saying "This is our home, this is our land."'

We ask him about his patriotic desire not to become a refugee in Europe but he looks at the ground and shakes his head.

'I wanted to stay,' he begins, earnestly. 'I wanted to serve my country, but security here is really bad now. All my friends are going and I'm really lonely. My best friend left for Germany two years ago and is now studying there. He says he is really happy. I've seen on social media that people are being deported but my friends haven't been.'

'Do you not feel safe now?' we ask.

'When I get up in the morning and go to university I am scared. More attacks are happening in the city, and every day I think it must be my last.' He is just a regular teenager trying to find a path through life, I think. Yet he is not regular; he is Afghan, and with that comes a lottery of indiscriminate violence, fear and grief.

'But I am relaxed when I garden,' he says, then stops, as if remembering something. Taking a deep breath he continues, 'I had a friend in the army, an officer. He was like a brother to me. He was killed, fighting, about a year and a half ago. I was so sad,' he pauses. 'I . . . I could not sleep for grief. I tried to garden to forget him, but in the end, I planted flowers to remember him and when one grew, it was like I had a new friend.'

He feigns a laugh to shrug off the memory, but in the viewfinder his eyes water.

'So what can I say? My flowers are good friends to me.'

'Will you go to Germany?' I ask.

He shrugs his shoulders. 'Maybe, if I can get the money.'

'And your garden?'

'Of course, if I go I will miss it but . . . I don't know.'

'Show me your garden,' I say, detaching the camera from the tripod in order to follow him around the patch of grass and pots in front of the house. But instead he heads off down a sheer slope I had not noticed and turns to beckon me.

We walk down to a crystal-clear water channel, a diverted tributary off the River Paghman and along a stone wall to a large fruit orchard sitting in a meadow. I had assumed that the grass and flowers around the house were his garden. But my assumption is wrong. Silly me; Hamidullah's garden is ancestral land – the land of the past his parents had yearned for as refugees and the land to which they returned to as a family.

'These are the fruit trees,' he is saying as we walk, 'walnut and sour cherry, and that is a willow. Those are the apricot trees and, beyond, the almonds.' It is simply charming. I feel like I am walking through a dream, far, far away in the land Babur knew so well,[25] where 'pome-

347

granates, apricots, apples, quinces, pears, peaches and plums, jujubes, walnut grow well in abundance.'

On the other side of the orchard we arrive at a kitchen vegetable garden, neat and established. Hamidullah reels off a list of produce: 'potatoes, carrots, parsnips, cabbages, lettuces and spinach here. Pumpkin, rhubarb, courgette, cauliflower there.'

We walk through yet another meadow of sweet clover and butter cups, at the bottom of which the still-melting snow from the mountains flows. There are poplar trees shaking their leaves on the other side of the stream, butterflies and bumblebees eat their fill from sweet clovers, mustard-yellow yarrows light the way to wild angelica heads as big as a dinner plate, and a wild purple creeper gently clings to dandelions. A weeping pear leans over the path in front of me. It is a remarkable and wild garden. Babur had written about stopping-off points in meadows 'suitable for horses', but I little thought that I would see them today. I am overwhelmed by the beauty and tranquility and I stutter and stammer whispered exclamations of stupefied surprise.

We approach a second greenhouse and Hamidullah turns around, grinning proudly. 'This is where I work.' Bereft of plants, this greenhouse is empty apart from a small table pressed against a wall, and a chair. On the table is a pile of files and books and four neatly lined-up pens. It is Hamidullah's private study. There is a single pot of pink begonias on the table. I don't ask because I am sure he will be embarrassed, but I am certain that this is what he planted when his friend was killed.

'Don't' go,' I say to Hamidullah when we reach the car.

'What?'

'Your friends might be happy but I think things are different now in Europe for refugees. I don't think you will find it easy. They are not letting people in like they did before.'

Zia translates.

'I don't know,' says Hamidullah looking at the ground forlornly.

It is a difficult, multilayered issue. Of course he wants to better his life, but as a young adult with no English or German, no vocational education and no money, at best Hamidullah might find himself on the waiting list of a government-run pseudo-educational programme somewhere in provincial Germany. At worst, he could end up sleeping rough or living in terrible conditions, shining shoes for belligerent passers-by in a downtrodden corner of Europe. In either case, he would be far from anything he had ever known, culturally alienated and in a permanent limbo. But I don't tell him these details. It is too complicated to describe, and anyway it is easy for me to think these things from the privileged position of being able to come and go as I like.

Instead I say, 'Don't go. You will never find a garden as beautiful as this in Europe.' And I mean it when I say it.

Iftar, the evening break in the day's fast for practising Muslims, is nearly upon us when we drive back to Kabul and the roads are empty. I rest my head against the car window and look at the mountains sinking into the purple night. I have an overwhelming desire to get out of the car and walk and walk and walk into their wilderness.

*

The alarm assaults the dawn. I have been asleep for less than four hours and feel heavy and slow, but I crank my legs over the side of the bed and pull on yesterday's clothes: a once-white man's shirt my boyfriend had been throwing away which comes down to my knees and a pair of wide-legged trousers which are too short for me. When I clip my lens belt around my waist and fix my headscarf, I catch a glimpse of my reflection in the window panes. A very peculiar-looking Robin Hood stares back at me. Everything is appropriately baggy, but no Afghan woman would ever wear such an absurd ensemble.

This morning is my last in Kabul and I will spend it in Kaka Khalil's garden. When I arrive, the rest of the world is still asleep, but he is sitting on his steps, surrounded by geraniums and rubbing the sleep out of his eyes. There is a pile of plates and cups by the front door, remnants from *sahari* – the pre-dawn meal of the day which will last him through a day of fasting until sunset.

I set up the camera and begin filming macro close-ups of petals, leaves, dew, an ant busying over a blade of grass, a beetle pottering up a rose stem. Kaka Khalil begins to water the grass and round flower beds, letting them flood. Like his morning meal, the water will nourish the plants all day. I film him meditatively watching the spray hit the geranium and snapdragon leaves.

His plants are neither splendid nor remarkable; indeed, in one corner, they verge on the gaudy. The varieties grow anywhere from the Middle East to Eastern Ukraine and further afield, and they are ubiquitous because they are hardy and resolute, easy to acquire and easy to maintain. What *is* remarkable is the effort that goes into nurturing them. I remember what Hamidullah had said in March:

'No one asks you to do it; it is something you *want* to do, it comes from inside you.'

Outside the garden walls the Old City comes to life; bicycle bells tinkle, shop awnings unroll, doors slam, a mother shouts for her children who huff in return, chattering starts. But in the garden everything is still and balmy and I am easily distracted by curious corners of old-world charm. Khalil's bicycle leaning against the stone wall, a box of onions next to it. A rake made of nails and a pitchfork ready for action next to a bundle of sickles and scythes, and gadflies dancing with butterflies.

We say goodbye. Kaka Khalil thanks me. I thank him and I tell him his garden is my favourite, which is true – although Hamidullah's is a close second.

He tells me that I will always be welcome, and to come back anytime, that the garden will miss me.

I thank him again. We are both unsure of what else to say, suddenly awkward and bashful. I turn to walk back through the Old City, retracing my steps for the final time.

The streets are already clogged with rush hour traffic when the car pulls out onto the main road and the pace of the morning slows to a crawl. I am uneasy. Many of the recent suicide attacks have taken place during the busiest hours and the targets have been high profile and included ministries, government worker buses, military convoys, expat restaurants, expat guest houses and supermarkets.

It doesn't take much for the calm to be destroyed. When we drive past the ministry of defence I hold my breath. As three trucks transporting prisoners roll past, furtive eyes peeking out of the metal grills, I grip the seat. An American convoy pushes through a roundabout a little way off ahead and my heart races.

A large orange sewage tanker rumbles past in the opposite direction, but the car circumnavigates the Green Zone and soon we are on the other side of it. We turn off onto the quieter road and then the dirt track leading back to the guest house.

In my room I begin sorting out my equipment for the last time. I fumble around for my telephone and search for a podcast to accompany the packing process.

It is my bones that feel it first, and a second later waves of shattered sound barriers clamour with debris and detritus from a supersonic boom that breaks over the city. The windows thunder with its audacity and my ears pop. Every single blast I have known immediately comes into sharp focus. My stomach tightens, my shoulders tense, I freeze for a second.

But then I run to the door and up to the roof, hauling myself onto the wall next to the 'live box' using the corrugated iron fence. The foreground is black, with a building's width of billowing, scalloped-shaped clouds. The sirens start wailing near and far.

I call Zia. Typically, he had slept through it. But at least he is safe.

I text Jess, a reporter for the *Wall Street Journal*, one of the only international friends I still have here.

'U ok?'

'Yeah. Was in the shower. Lucky. My room is a bit of a mess.' She sends me a photograph of her blown-out window.

Over the course of the morning and early afternoon the information and rumours start trickling in through social media platforms and text messages. It was a vehicle-borne IED, I hear. The target was the presidential palace. No, it was the ministry of finance. No, it was the German embassy. It was a truck bomb. No, it was a sewage tanker. An orange sewage tanker.

The tanker is confirmed. It was laden with fifteen hundred kilos of explosives, the largest in the capital since hostilities began in 2001, and one which left a crater nine metres deep. Casualty figures start mounting. Fifty, sixty, eighty, ninety. Almost all of them are civilians. I sit on the end of my bed, lost and incapacitated to do anything at all. I think about Hamidullah and wonder if he was on his way to university, I think about Kaka Khalil and Ramesh, who live only a kilometre from where it had happened, and I hope their old houses withstood the reverberations. It is all such a lottery, I think, such an unfair, bastard of a lottery. And I bury my face in my hands and sob, silently.

But I pull myself together quickly; no point moping. Time to act. Downstairs, the guest house manager, making a living out of insecurity, is almost rubbing his hands at the prospect of the international news crews flying in to cover the aftermath. My journalistic instinct is to go to the blast, of course, but for what? To report a mass casualty of an endless war? To gawp at the carnage, commit it to digital and visual memory? No. The hospitals need blood, I hear, so I arrange to go to a local one with Jess. We are both universal donors and, for heaven's sake, it is the very least we can do.

Inevitably we are too late and they are too overwhelmed to take more blood. We return to the *Wall Street Journal* house in the so-called Green Zone where the windows are jagged open mouths, fractured and splintered. Their glass is at our feet, shimmering an irregular geometry over the stone.

The house inside is worse: glass on the beds, stairs, sofas. Glass on the kitchen worktops and in the crevices of the gas hob. Glass in the shower and on the balcony.

While Jess works on a news update I step down into the grass and walk barefoot, dodging glass splinters. The garden has been recently watered by the guard and my feet are cooled by the earth. The fragrant hybrid tea roses, impervious to the disorder of the day, are potent. Above are the tall plane trees, immovable and solid. They flake the dimming light dappled and I feel very small.

I look back at the house with its gaping, wounded windows blasted into the garden. Slivers of glass cling to the furry geranium leaves, a marigold narrowly missed decapitation via a shard, and a portion of a book now lies akimbo in a window box.

It is nearly midnight. I have finished packing and am on the roof wall again, looking out at the ghost of the explosion. Above me are the stars. Perhaps they are gathering the souls from today, I think morbidly. I try to wipe the morning away and look up at the cluttered sky.

I think of the original garden at Eden and man's fall from grace after stealing from the tree of knowledge. I think of Monet, painting his garden at Giverny while the shells thudded fifty kilometres away. I think of Vita Sackville-West's dignified garden against the 'horrid wilderness' of war. I think of *The Secret Garden* and the way it brought two characters back to life, and of Alice, wandering through her Wonderland gardens in her many ludicrous shapes and sizes.

To garden in a time of crisis and conflict is to escape to 'a world within a lost world'. It is to rise above the 'horrid wilderness' – to treat war as an inconvenience. It is a refusal to accept a world defined by violence and destruction but instead create life.

Gardening in the midst of war simply turns the other cheek and looks for an escape to a 'little perfect world'. All these wars won't go away, not any time soon – so perhaps we are still falling from Eden. Reyhana, the hermaphrodite burned by her/his own mother in Herat all those years ago, Sorayah in the shelter and the satyr boy in Sangin. Perhaps they all knew this. Maybe the worst is yet to come before we can return to innocence or to Milton's 'delicious paradise'.

But no. That's not it. It can't be. The gardeners I have met here and in the south, in eastern Ukraine and in the Middle East, they don't think so. Perhaps gardening is not just an escape, it is a *collective* nostalgia – a way of returning to an innocent world we all knew in some way before we fell. And perhaps the gardeners all know this.

When I stayed in the garden of the Old Flower Street Café, far from home all those years ago, alone and inconsolable in the twilight of a foreign land, the moths were hurling themselves at the night lights. I was hoping to find familiarity in the constellations. Rootless in the wilderness, I had always looked up at them for comfort, but that night none were familiar and I knew I was beginning to unravel. I had remained there until the stars were so abundant that some slowly disappeared to make room for others.

In the end it was the gardens that saved me; here, in Donetsk, in Gaza, it was always the gardens that reminded me of innocence and the gardens that transported me home. I know that now, looking up at a gathering of a million baffling lights, a million galaxies, a million worlds: jewels in the darkness. Are any of *those* worlds perfect, I wonder.

And I am overwhelmed by nostalgia, but not for this city and the life I lived here, nor for the wars near and far. I am nostalgic for a home I don't yet have and for the garden I will make there.

And I shall have some peace there, for peace comes dropping slow,
Dropping from the veils of the morning to where the cricket sings;
There midnight's all a glimmer, and noon a purple glow,
And evening full of the linnet's wings.

I will arise and go now, for always night and day
I hear lake water lapping with low sounds by the shore;
While I stand on the roadway, or on the pavements grey,
I hear it in the deep heart's core.[26]

I will arise and go now.

Notes

Kabul 2012

1   Maria Bashir was listed as one of *Time* magazine's one hundred most influential people in 2011 thanks to her work as a defender of women's rights. The legitimacy of this was called into question in *The Times* newspaper after leaked figures showed that Ms Bashir prosecuted more than half of the 172 women who were jailed for so-called moral crimes. (Source: Jeremy Kelly, *The Times*, 22 October 2012.)

2   *Kaftar bazi* is a game that requires two trained flocks of pigeons which, when set free to the skies by their (rival) owners (who control their flight with a stick and whistles), follow their one female lead bird. The opposing flocks fly into each other and begin to mingle before separating again. This is repeated countless times until one or two of their number becomes tired or confused and when they are called home by their owner, accidentally follow the wrong flock and fly home to a victorious new owner. A ransom is then paid by the original owner to secure its release.

3   The Northern Alliance is a multi-ethnic opposition group who fought the (predominantly Pashtun) Taliban and was largely backed by the United States.

Gaza, May 2013

4   The Palestinian Exploration Fund was founded by a group of academics and clergymen in 1865. The original mission of the PEF was to promote research in the customs, culture, geography and geology of biblical Palestine and the Levant.

Israel Kibbutzim, May 2013

5   The First Intifada was the first Palestinian uprising against the Israeli occupation of the West Bank and Gaza, lasting from 1987 until 1991.

6   Nir Am was largely founded by Bessarabian immigrants of the Gordonia, a Jewish youth movement whose doctrines were based on salvation through manual labour.

7   Palestinian prime minister from 1994 to 2004 credited with brokering peace but also derided by Israelis as a terrorist.

War Machine, Afghanistan 2013–14

8   The war in Afghanistan was in some respect found by com-
    mittee with each member nation receiving its turn to assume
    command. Initially Command of the international coalition passed
    in merry-go-round fashion between NATO allies, with the rotation
    first spinning at six month intervals. This was cosmetic at best and
    for the most part the British and American troops did the heavy
    lifting. As the war became a more serious it turned into a year-long
    tour.

9   The purpose of the Provisional Reconstruction Team (PRT) was
    to improve stability and development in parallel to ISAF's opera-
    tional engagement. It is comprised of a team of both civilian and
    military staff, and Helmand's PRT was originally one of the largest
    in Afghanistan.

10 As part of the military's information war contractual agreement
    existed between journalists and ISAF – of whom the FCO are part
    here – stating that the embedded journalist has to turn over all
    material gathered from the military battlefield to be checked for
    operational security. Over the years, as the unlikely relationship
    between the military and media was forced to continue in Afghan-
    istan and Iraq, and as popularity for the wars decreased, the level
    of scrutiny morphed into outright story censorship and narrative
    manipulation, with every line of every story being sanitized into
    acceptability.

Helmand, April 2014

11   Detainees and suspected Talibs had samples of DNA taken via mouth swabs and the results kept for future reference.

12   Sexual repression in a country where the genders are strictly divided and women considered to be at the absolute bottom of the pile results in rampant paedophilia. Mujahedeen warlords regularly engaged in acts of paedophilia keeping one or more boys for servitude and sexual pleasure. The practice was outlawed by the Taliban.

13   'Truly Unprecedented: How the Helmand Food Zone supported an increase in the province's capacity to produce opium', David Mansfield, Afghan Research and Evaluation Unit, October 2017.

14   The Afghan currency is Afghani but in the south, the Pakistani rupee is widely accepted.

15   As a means of buying the loyalty of Helmandis, ISAF became involved in development projects similar to development-led 'Alternative Livelihoods'.

16   Al-Qaeda and the Taliban are two very different things. When two planes crashed into the Twin Towers on 11 September 2001, it is very unlikely that most rural and illiterate Afghans, Talibs or otherwise, would have heard of al-Qaeda, an Islamist group lead by a thin and wiry Saudi Arabian, Osama bin Laden.

17   *Pashtunwali* is the ancient code of living by which most rural Afghans live.

18   The Ghaznavids were a dynasty that ruled large parts of Iran,

Afghanistan and the northwestern part of the Indian Subcontinent from 977–1186

19 *Bodana jangi* – or quail fighting – is a popular Afghan pastime similar to cockfighting, and said to be thousands of years old. As a form of gambling, it was banned by the Taliban and enjoyed a resurgence of popularity after their fall.

Ukraine, August 2014

20 In 1970, 180 varieties of rose could be found in Donetsk at any one time. It is said that along with trees and shrubs, one was planted for each member of the population. For a long time Donetsk remained the cleanest industrial city of the world and was recognised accordingly by UNESCO.

21 Welsh engineer John Hughes founded Donetsk in the 1870s at the request of the Russian empire.

22 Dachas were originally small countryside second homes primarily used as weekend retreats. The failure of centrally administered Soviet agriculture to supply enough fresh food led to an increase of private, amateur farming for subsistence.

The West Bank, April 2016

23 Aliyah is the immigration of Jews from the diaspora back to the Land of Israel and is one of the basic tenets of Zionism.

24   In early 1994 Baruch Goldstein opened fire on Muslim worship-
     pers, killing 29 and injuring 125. Riots ensued and the Israeli
     Defence Forces, fearing more retaliation, closed Al Shuhada Street,
     the main thoroughfare of the city, to Palestinians. After the Oslo
     accords, the city was divided. H1, comprising 80 per cent of the
     city, is home to 120,000 Palestinians, governed by the Palestinian
     Authority and off limits to Jews. H2, meanwhile, is governed by the
     Israelis and is home to around 700 settlers and 30,000 Palestinians.
     It comprises of only 20 per cent of the city, but the inclusion of the
     majority of the prominent religious sites of Hebron has rendered
     it the hot zone of the West Bank.

Kabul, 2017

25   Kabul city at that time was a small walled citadel in Khorosan,
     Afghanistan being a land of the Afghan tribes living south of the
     Kabul–Peshawar road. In the *Baburnama* the domain of Kabul
     stretches from Peshawar (now in Pakistan) to the mountains of
     Ghor – an almost impossible to reach part of Afghanistan around
     400 kilometres from today's capital.

26   WB Yeats, Lake Isle of Innisfree which he wrote in London while
     he was homesick for Ireland.

Acknowledgements

Thanks to:

My parents: Jonathan Snow with helping to identify so many plants and again to my mother for filling in the gaps.

Mins, Bobby, Lily, Ellie and Rose Vedral for reminding me about Tom's Midnight Garden and letting me take over the Coach House.

Jon Rider, for taking the slack almost every day during writing, for all the books and for endlessly listening and reading and re-reading and listening.

To my agent, Roger Field, for encouraging me to write *War Gardens* in the first place, for persevering and for asking so many annoying questions. And to my editor at Quercus, Richard Milner, for listening to him but for letting me ignore them.

Thanks to the gardeners of Afghanistan, Gaza, Israel, the West Bank, Ukraine.

And in alphabetical order a huge thank you to everyone who has supported, advised, introduced, inspired, humoured, leant books and maps, translated, housed, fed, watered and wined me.

Miles Amoore	Paul Joyce
Roslyn Boatman	Jeremy Kelly
Jonathan Boone	Dr Mohammed Kharoti
Travis Burke	Leslie Knott
Alice Burt	Christina Lamb
Tom Coghlan	Edmund Le Brun
Marina de Coatgoureden	Jolyon Leslie
Owen Davis	David Loym
Jessica Donati	Irene Nasser
Mikhail Elimi	Clementine Malpas
Anthony Fitzherbert	James McLeod-Hatch
George Fitzherbert-Brockholes	Roland Oliphant
David Gill	Diana O'Laughlin
Emma Graham Harrison	Alastair Orr-Ewing
Lianne Gutcher	Sir Richard and Sarah Jane Shireff
Zia Ahmed Haidary	Nicki Smith
Camille Hennion	Jerome Starkey
Nathan Hodge	Flore de Taisne
Ghada Issa	John Wendle
Ashley Jackson	Tommy Wide
Harry Johnstone	Kelly Wilson

Index

365